# FERRIES
## of the Brit...
## & Northern Europe

ISBN 1 871947 36 7
Published by

FERRY
Publications

12 Millfields Close, Kilgetty, Pembrokeshire SA68 0SA
Tel: 01834 813991 Fax: 01834 814484

# CONTENTS

© *Ferry Publications 1996*

*Isle of Innisfree (FotoFlite)*

# INTRODUCTION

This is the ninth edition of this book, first published in 1983 and once more renamed. This year we are pleased to be sponsored by Sally Ferries, a subsidiary of Silja Oy Ab. It is perhaps fitting that sponsorship from this company, established by the Finnish company Rederi AB Sally in 1981, should coincide with the extension of the scope of the book to cover other major Northern European operators – international, Great Belt, Bornholm and Gotland. At the other end of the scale, coverage of the chain, cable and float ferries in the British Isles has been improved. One other change is the merging of the conventional and fast ferry sections to reflect the growing integration of both types of vessels in operators' fleets. As well as Miles Cowsill and John Hendy's review of 1995, we are pleased to include a brief history of Sally Ferries by Geoffrey Breeze and an article taking forward the HSS story from last year.

1995 was something of a 'wait and see' year as operators took stock of the impact of the Channel Tunnel. 1996 should prove a more eventful year with the introduction of Stena HSSs on the Irish Sea and an unprecedented level of service on the Dover – Calais route. In Scandinavia, Sweden – Finland business continues in the doldrums but there has been substantial growth in business between Finland and Estonia as well as many new fast ferry services on shorter routes.

The book lists each ferry operator alphabetically in sections – international and Northern Ireland routes, domestic services, freight only operations, chain, cable and float ferries, passenger only ferries, and other North European passenger operators. After details relating to each company's management, address, telephone numbers and services follows a fleet list with technical data and then a potted history of each vessel with previous names and dates. For the first time this year we have included a 'Stop Press' section at the end of the book where news of changes has been received prior to publication but it would not be practical to amend the text in the book.

Whilst every effort has been made to ensure that the facts contained here are correct, neither the publishers nor the writer can accept any responsibility for errors contained herein. We would, however, appreciate comments from readers, which we will endeavour to incorporate in the next edition which will be published in spring 1997.

The writer would like to thank all those in the various ferry companies who have helped in the preparation of this book and also others who have contributed – in particular Anders Alherup, Barry Mitchell, Jack Phelan, Mike Louagie, FotoFlite, Lawerence MacDuff, Mike Drewery and Pat Somner, Miles Cowsill & John Hendy of Ferry Publications.

March 1996
Whitstable, Kent

Nick Widdows

# FOREWORD

Once again I have the privilege to introduce this fine publication depicting a variety of vessels in an industry that is changing more rapidly every year. Certain changes in fleet disposition, illustrated well within these pages, have been brought about by the competitive effects of the Channel Tunnel, whilst others reflect the ongoing challenge for market share supremacy, speed of crossing and economical operation.

There will be more changes to come. Many routes have adopted the strategy of splitting their passenger and freight carryings thus enabling fast catamaran or monohull technology to replace less efficient conventional tonnage. There is much evidence to suggest that this trend will grow as new safety legislation for existing conventional ferries pushes costs up with a corresponding loss of operational flexibility.

Fast ferry technology has reached a premature zenith with the arrival into service on the Irish Sea of Stena's giant HSS, with two more in the series to follow for their Stranraer and Harwich routes. Competitors will watch with interest, scepticism and a degree of private, but nonetheless serious, concern. Like the Channel Tunnel it will frustrate what would normally be growth in the routes and tonnage around it, as others adopt a 'wait and see' policy.

As a lover of the sea and ships these vessels will never compete with the grace and splendour of their predecessors. They are hardly attractive vessels, and will need to prove themselves in difficult market and sea conditions before they are truly accepted by us all.

Silja Line, Sally Lines's parent company in the Baltic, who have the highest standards of any cruise ferry service world-wide, operate the only true, tried and tested, fast ferry. Their Finnjet, which at 19 years of age still attains 33 knots for its 1790 passengers.

Despite all this, the knocks that the ferry industry has suffered, and the fiercely competitive forces that it must contend with in the future, it is still a fundamental part of our lives and arguably the only remnant of our seafaring tradition. We must look after it.

On behalf of all readers, our thanks to Nick Widdows, Miles Cowsill and John Hendy for yet another superior Ferry Publications production.

**Bill Moses, Group Chief Executive, Sally Uk Ltd**

# SALLY FERRIES: HISTORY

In the early morning of 15th June 1981 The Viking commenced her inaugural sailing from Dunkerque to Ramsgate as the flagship of the then newly created Sally Line. The ship arrived in a virtually unsheltered English port in the true traditions of her ancestors, whose name she proudly displayed on her bows. The first season was a fairly short one and the initial difficulties associated with the open aspect of the port gave an early indication of some of the future problems that had to be overcome in order to maintain a regular ferry service with the minimum of disruption and cancellations. The Viking traditions came to the fore and the fact that Ramsgate is now a virtual all-weather port is a tribute to those traditions which are so characteristic of the company.

An unsuccessful attempt to run a car ferry service between Ramsgate and Dunkerque had been made in the summer of 1980. Dunkerque-Ramsgate Ferries encountered many problems and were finally forced to abandon the service amidst debts and the arrest of their ferry, the Nuits St Georges.

Early in 1981 the Finnish ferry company Rederi AB Sally, who were looking for expansion abroad with Britain being the main target, announced that they were interested in re-opening the Ramsgate-Dunkerque route with an investment of £5 million to develop the new service.

The vessel for the new service was obtained from the parent company's fleet in Finland, and this was the Viking 5 which had been in service across the Baltic Sea for about five years and was now considered too small for their needs due to expansion of their services. The ship was renamed The Viking for English Channel work. Operations were marketed under the name "Sally the Viking Line" and although there was initial reluctance on the part of the travelling public, trade soon picked up and by July the 10.00

*The Viking* (FotoFlite)

sailing regularly carried 600-700 passengers. All went well until 21st August when The Viking suffered severe mechanical problems and she had to be withdrawn and replaced by the chartered Safe Christina (now the Lion Prince), the vessel remaining in service until the close of the season on 25th October.

The engine damage to The Viking was subsequently found to be much more severe than originally thought and it was decided to replace both of her engines with ones of more modern design She therefore remained out of service until 20th May the following year which again proved to be very successful for Sally Line.

A two ship service was planned to run from mid-July for the1983 summer season and the company acquired the Danish ferry Kalle III of 4,371 gross tons. Having had problems of ships being re allocated by the parent company in Finland, and with the view of operating an all year round service, Sally took the vessel on a long term bareboat charter with an option to purchase. She had a service speed of 21 knots and following a major refit by her builders, in Bremerhaven, including the fitting of stabilisers. Essentially a short sea vessel, she was well suited to the Ramsgate service She was destined to become a much favoured ship in the eyes of the travelling public, being an excellent sea boat with her fine bows which gave a smooth and comfortable passage through the sea. Continuing the tradition of operating the route as The Viking, she commenced her duties on the route on 17th July as the company flagship and remained in service with Sally Line until the end of the 1988 season.

The open aspect of Ramsgate brought its share of problems for Sally Line in that the autumn gales created havoc with the schedules, 25% of scheduled sailings being lost and it became obvious that some form of port protection with breakwaters was required. Following tests and investigations at the Technical Research Centre at Helsinki University, a scheme was eventually devised to be implemented in three stages:-

1983:        An arm of the breakwater to be built from the existing land area.
1984:        Two island breakwaters to be constructed.
1985/86:     A full wrap-round breakwater to be completed.

This was a very expensive scheme and in order to reduce the financial burden it was decided to explore the possibility of developing Ramsgate as port for other operators. This resulted in the UK company being reorganised into a holding company to be called Sally UK Holding Plc with two operating subsidiaries,

(1)   Sally Line Limited, to operate the ferry services and
(2)   Port Ramsgate Limited, to develop and operate the port.

Since the reorganisation, the companies have continued to follow a policy of separate development.

In October 1983, following an agreement with Charles Schiaffino, a new cargo service commenced from Ramsgate to Ostend with one daily trip by Schiaffino Line. The arrival of this second operator enabled the development plans for Ramsgate Harbour to proceed at a greater pace than previously expected. Following the completion of a second berth in February 1984, Schiaffino transferred their entire operation from Dover to Ramsgate, thus bringing two additional ships to the expanding port. Schiaffino were eventually completely taken over by Sally Ferries in 1990.

# THE FREQUENCY FACTOR

For frequency and choice of cross-channel freight services, Port Ramsgate now has the 3rd largest number of vessel movements in the UK.

Consider the advantages of Port Ramsgate:

- 6 daily sailings to Dunkirk and 10 sailings to Ostend - To give you more sailings and more choice.
- At Port Ramsgate you're assured of space in advance whenever **you** want to go.
- Crossing the channel via Port Ramsgate costs less than the competition.
- You can ship most goods through Port Ramsgate including "hazardous" ones.
- Port Ramsgate's driver facilities are unequalled with a Driver's restaurant and an enormous "Park and Rest" area.
- You can enjoy the crossing and superb food on our ships with time for you to rest and relax.
- Trans-shipment and Tri-backing service for empty trailers to travel stacked at just one price.
- Fork lift services for containers.
- High quality level of service throughout the Port to make your journey quicker and smoother.

### Port Ramsgate.
**For freighting in Europe, we have the frequency and choice.**

For more information contact Reg Cooper, M.D.
Port Ramsgate, Ramsgate Harbour, Ramsgate, Kent, CT11 8RP
Telephone: 01843 587661  Fax: 01843 851170

**Take The Ramsgate Way**

# PORT RAMSGATE
**The Superfast Gateway to Europe**

*Viking 3* (FotoFlite)

Passenger figures for 1984 were impressive showing that the company had exceeded 600,000 passengers and 85,000 cars and with aims to increase these figures the following year, the company set higher targets and continued in their efforts to for a 10% share of the cross Channel market.

By the end of 1984 cargo traffic carried by Sally Line had increased to such an extent that the company became interested in obtaining a cargo only vessel. However, instead, an agreement was reached with the French company, Compagnie General Maritime for a joint service to commence on 20th November using the French company's ship Le Mans, 4153 gross tons (built in 1978) and capable of carrying 74 freight units. The new company, Sally/CGM Freight Service, operated a daily service from Sundays to Fridays. The joint venture was looked upon as a major advance in establishing Ramsgate as a key Channel gateway. Ramsgate was now becoming extremely busy with the three operators, Sally Line, Sally/CGM and Shiaffino now using the port facilities.

With the completion of the first phase of Port Ramsgate's development (the construction of the second berth together with reclamation of 25,000 square metres of land), thoughts quickly turned to the second phase – the long awaited provision of two breakwaters with a total length of 430 metres some 500 metres offshore. The operation, carried out by John Howard and Company Plc was entirely marine based so as to ensure minimum disruption. Transport of rock, from Sweden, was undertaken by barge. Four round trips were necessary to transport the required 80,000 tons of rock and these were carried out over a twelve week period. The whole operation was meticulously engineered and planned with each slab of rock being positioned to a high degree of accuracy. The

# CRUISE WITH
# SALLY FERRIES
# VIA DUNKIRK

EQUILIBRE TRANSVERSALES · Tél · 20.11.18.18 · RC 92 B 36

*The **Viking*** and ***Viking 6*** (FotoFlite)

work was completed by November 1984 and although the two breakwaters were not connected together at this stage, there was much improvement in protection of the harbour from the wave height that previously caused problems. With the completion of these breakwaters , the reliability of service was assured, but expansion of the port was to continue much more.

It was clear that a third linkspan would be needed and in early 1985 a further contract was signed with John Howard & Company for further land reclamation, strengthening and widening of the existing breakwater together with the joining and widening of the two sections, plus the construction of an extra section of breakwater from the end of the eastern arm of the Royal Harbour and extending in a south-easterly direction, thus narrowing the port entrance. This phase of the development would cost £5 million. The third linkspan was supplied by the Mattsson Group of Sweden at a cost of £700,000 and was ready for use by May 1985.

Early 1985 saw the first change of name for the company in that the words "the Viking" were dropped from its trading name. Previously marketed as "Sally the Viking Line", it simply became "Sally Line". This was in line with a change of image to a more formal advertising campaign which up to then had been of an amusing and frivolous nature, a common practice with many companies at that time.

Passenger and freight figures continued to expand by about 25% from April 1986 when Sally Line introduced a much larger ferry to replace their then Viking 6, which by then was considered too small, lacking in height on the car deck which made her unsuitable for the larger freight vehicles that where being used in increasing numbers.

The new ship was the Gedser of 5,300 gross tons, the company chartering her for a period of 5 years from her owners GT Ruten of Denmark, thus solving the one remaining problem i.e the lack of a permanent second vessel, this still being subject to changes by the parent company in Finland. Renamed the Viking 2 she became the seventh ship on the route to serve Sally Line on the Ramsgate- Dunkerque route and she remains in service to this day. It was also decided that she would sail with a complete French crew including catering and reception staff.

In Dunkerque the Port Authority spent Fr 8 million on a new side loading facility that gave direct access to the upper car deck of the Viking 2, enabling the ship to unload cars and lorries from both decks at the same time, thus improving discharge times and benefitting the travelling public.

Port facilities were progressing well on both sides of the channel. The summer of 1986 saw the completion of the long awaited Ramsgate breakwater. Reclamation of land had also taken place to provide 26,000 sq. metres of hard standing for a car park, freight marshalling yards and other much needed facilities.

With the completion of the breakwaters, plans were made for further development to provide the port with all the facilities that a modern passenger and freight port requires to survive the competitive climate of the 1990's. Negotiations resulted in the lease of the port being extended from the original 90 to 125 years.

In Dunkerque, a new Terminal at Dunkerque Ouest was opened in July 1987. It had been a joint design by Sally Line and the Dunkerque Port Authority and enabled passengers to walk via enclosed "Skywalks" in comfort whatever the weather conditions.. Full port facilities were available including cafeteria, banks, escalators, children's playground and underground car parks. The two ships switched from the original Dunkerque berth used since 1981 to the new berth at the Quai de Ramsgate in Dunkerque

*Viking 6* (FotoFlite)

Ouest and the loading ramp erected the previous year was transferred to the new facility.

A reflection of the expanding service and Sally Line's confidences in the future was shown in 1988 when it was announced that a new jumbo ferry was to be introduced on the route at the end of the year as a replacement for the ever faithful The Viking. The new ship, the 9,210 gross tons Travemunde Link, was also chartered for a period of 5 years.

Following a takeover of the parent company in Finland by the Effjohn Group (now Silja Oy Ab) and the severing of the Viking Line connections plus a change in company image at Sally Line, several thoughts had been made over the company livery. Only the lower half of the hull would be painted red with the remainder being white. The funnel would also be white with two red bands near the top. The words "Sally Line" would be dropped and the single word "Sally" in red paint would be used on the white section of the hull. It was expected that the new ship would be given a "Viking" name , but as part of the new image and following a major refit it was announced that the vessel would be named the Sally Star and that the Viking 2 would be renamed the Sally Sky. The Sally Star entered service on 6th December 1988.

In order to match the capacity of the Sally Sky to that of the Sally Star, it was decided to increase her capacity by adding a 20.8 metre centre section to the ship in such a way as to ensure that her engine room and machinery spaces were not affected in any way. The work was done at the time of her next scheduled refit in January 1990 the work taking almost three months to complete.

A new era commenced when in September 1993 it was announced that the Belgium Government's 147 year old link from Ostend to Dover with RMT Ferries was to close. A new agreement with Sally Line was announced, based upon a 5 year 50-50 partnership and all of the Belgian vessels, including Jetfoil services, would transfer from Dover to

*Sally Sky* (FotoFlite)

Ramsgate and the trading name changed to Oostende Lines. The new service started on 1st January 1994 and ensured that Port Ramsgate would become one of the busiest ports on the South Coast, with seventeen passenger and ten freight sailings per day. Plans to for the further development of Port Ramsgate at a cost of £8.5 million were also announced. Top priority was a harbour access road to reach the quayside via a tunnel and causeway, thus avoiding the twisting and congested route through the town, something that Sally have been requesting since the mid 1980's. The Belgian Flagship Prins Filip, almost twice the size of the Sally Star, required deep dredging of Ramsgate Harbour in order to accommodate her. She made her first appearance at Ramsgate on 27th January following her winter refit. The arrival of these additional services was a feather in the cap both for Sally Line and Port Ramsgate.

However 1994 was not to be a happy one for either Sally Line or RMT Ferries. The deal with the Belgian State-owned RMT Ferries had been concluded with some haste at the behest of the Belgian Government, which left insufficient time to ensure that the essential works were carried out before the start date. Several problems occurred with the Belgian ships at times touching bottom in the harbour approaches and also were unable to access the No 3 linkspan at Ramsgate, but the efficiency of Sally Line and Port Ramsgate ensured that all these problems were soon solved.

Freight services continued to expand when in March 1984, following the closure of Olau Line services from Sheerness, a new service to Vlissingen was introduced. A second ship was added in the summer so that two sailing daily were made. This service later transferred to newly re-named Eurocity Port at Dartford to take advantage of the adjoining M25 London orbital links which reduce truck mileage and makes the new

# CA&PABILITY.

# CA&PACITY.

# A&PPROVAL.

# ADA&PTABILITY.

**A&P Tyne Ltd., Benton Way, Wallsend, Tyne & Wear NE28 6EY.**
Tel: +44 (0) 191 295 0777. Fax: +44 (0) 191 295 0888. Telex: 537759 APAREP G.

**A&P Falmouth Ltd., The Docks, Falmouth, Cornwall TR11 4NR.**
Tel: +44 (0) 1362 212100. Fax: +44 (0) 1326 319433. Telex: 45536 FALDOC G.

**A&P Southampton Ltd., Western Ave, Western Docks, Southampton SO15 0HH.**
Tel: +44 (0) 1703 704488. Fax: +44 (0) 1703 704735. Telex: 477273 DRYDOC G.

**A&P Chatham Ltd., Chatham Docks, Gillingham Gate, Chatham, Kent ME4 4SW.**
Tel: +44 (0) 1634 827369. Fax: +44 (0) 1634 826344. Telex: 21275 APAFUN G.

**A&P Offshore Ltd., Benton Way, Wallsend, Tyne & Wear NE28 6EY.**
Tel: +44 (0) 191 295 0777. Fax: +44 (0) 191 295 0444. Telex: 537759 APAREP G.

**A&P Holdings Ltd., Lypiatt Rd, Cheltenham, Gloucestershire, GL50 2QJ.**
Tel: +44 (0) 1242 252625. Fax: +44 (0) 1242 250898.

A&P Group

WORLD CLASS
SHIP REPAIR

location very attractive. In order to create a new look and to take the company into its new phase of growth, a further change of name was made at the end of 1995 when they were renamed Sally Ferries and a new livery was introduced. The amount of red colour has been reduced and the Sally logo itself was changed from red to a softer blue colour with the name "Sally" being in lower case lettering surmounting a blue line along the total length of the hull. The Silja seal is also featured in front of the company name and also on the funnel which is now totally white with a blue base. The Silja seal highlights the association with Silja Line, the present owners of the company and a key shipping operator in the Baltic. Sally Ferries experienced considerable growth during 1995, car figures showing an increase of 3.8% and 8.2% on Ramsgate-Dunkerque and Ramsgate – Ostende routes respectively over that of 1994.

January 1996 saw the loss making Dartford – Vlissingen services taken over by the newly formed Dart Line, thus allowing Sally Lines to concentrate on their core Ramsgate routes where passenger and freight carryings are now exceeding company expectations.

In order to dramatically improve sailing times, Sally Ferries are currently considering the introduction of fast ferries to the French and Belgian routes. These plans to expand their services and to develop the port facilities should ensure that Port Ramsgate remains the UK's third busiest port. A success story indeed.

Geoffrey Breeze

***Sally Star*** and ***Sally Sky*** (FotoFlite)

**Sally Star** *(FotoFlite)*

# FERRY TRANSPORT ENTERS THE JET AGE ON THE IRISH SEA

The ferry industry is due enter the jet age in the spring this year with the arrival of the world's first high-speed superferrry, the £65 million *Stena Explorer*. The giant twin hulled craft will be able sail at twice the speed of conventional ferries, cutting crossing times in half, on the Irish Sea between Holyhead and Dun Laoghaire. At 126 metres long and 40 metres wide – about the same size as a football pitch – she is the first fast ferry able to carry commercial vehicles and coaches as well as cars with space for up to 375 cars (or 120 cars and 50 lorries), together with up to 1,500 passengers, giving her a similar carrying capacity to a traditional ferry. In addition, her on board passenger facilities are situated over 4,000 square metre deck, and maybe the benchmark for the ferries of the future. From the gigantic panoramic window at the front of the ferry, similar to that of the *Stena Fantasia*, to the entertainment complex at the stern, passengers will find also spacious air-conditioned lounges, bars, McDonald's and Stena Line restaurants, duty-free and tax free shops, a video lounge and the latest in interactive computer games. For children, the Stena HSS offers a totally new concept called 'The Incredible Voyage', a modern adventure area where technology and machines combine to create a friendly and challenging environment for youngsters. Entrance to this 'mini theme park' is through a cat's mouth and once inside youngsters can try 11 different 'virtual rides'. In addition teenagers can enjoy themselves in the Video Warp arcades featuring the latest 3-D graphics video games such as car racing and in-seat entertainment systems.

No passenger will be able to miss the massive wall-of-vision, situated in the centre of the ferry. Consisting of 27 back-projected cubes, the latest state of the art in televisual technology, this video wall is almost certainly the largest afloat, measuring 2.5 by 7 metres.

The *Stena Explorer* will initially make four return crossings daily, increasing to five during the holiday periods and during the summer. The 55-mile crossing will be made in just 99 minutes on day time sailings. In Holyhead and Dun Laoghaire nearly £60 million has been invested in new state of the art port facilities. Both ports have new passenger terminals, new access roads and large parking areas – all designed to speed-up check-in and loading and unloading, for motorists, lorry drivers and foot passengers. Check-in times for motorists and foot passengers have been cut to 30 minutes.

## THE CONCEPT AND DESIGN

In the late autumn of 1989 Dan Sten Olsen, Chief Executive Officer of Stena AB and chairman of the Board of Stena Line, posed the question: "High-speed ferries – could they be of any use to Stena?"

"It was a simple question but very difficult to answer," recalls Stig Bystedt, technical director of Stena Rederi AB. "When we took stock of the multitude of different ship classes, we soon realised that catamarans were the only viable solution if we were going to get the vessels into service this side of the year 2000."

Catamarans had speed, but their loading capacity, seakeeping and above all, their comfort were moderate. Quite simply, passengers suffered from sea-sickness and a number of designs had been taken out of service for this very reason.

Two views of the *Stena Explorer* off Dover *(Stena Line)*

A long series of tests were initiated at the National Experimental Shipbuilding Tank facilities in Gothenburg, while Norske Veritas conducted various strength trials on a variety of models. The problem lay in finding a hull form which was as "kind" as possible, to both the vessel and its passengers.

The practical method proved to be designing the hull with concave sides so that they were extremely narrow at the water line, but then swelled out again into large pontoons below the water line. Meanwhile, the angle at which the bows meet the onrushing water were made as sharp as possible – the Stena HSS's stems are only a few centimetres wide.

Stig Bystedt, technical director of Stena Rederi AB, describes the results of the design development: "There were two main motions we wanted to eliminate. One is called "heave" and is the way the boat moves when it is pushed up and down by the turbulence of the surface water. The concave design means the HSS ferry is less affected by this force. The ship's buoyancy lies in the pontoons, several metres below the surface of the water, and the waves' effect does not reach that far down. The ship's surface area at the water line, which is where the waves are, is very small.

The second motion, which is particularly unpleasant for the passengers is "pitch" – when the bow is for example lifted by a wave at the same time as the stern sinks into the trough of a wave. A normal vessel's centre of motion is well aft and the fore sections, in particular, move in a way which generates rapid movement up and down – rapid changes of position which induce a sinking feeling in people's stomachs and hence a feeling of nausea.

The centre of motion of the Stena HSS ferry is, thanks to the ship's buoyant aft section and sharply angled bows, shifted well to the fore. Hence the stern moves up and down instead of the bow, which means overall, fewer vertical movements and consequently, a much more comfortable motion. The third motion which normally affects vessels – the rolling caused by beam seas – is aimed to be virtually non-existent on the 40 metre wide Stena HSS 1500."

The HSS has no bow doors, and the car deck located eight metres above the water line, which should offer stability several times greater than that of a conventional vessel. The craft has a new efficient evacuation system and the company claim that the HSS exceeds the stability requirements currently applicable, as well as those it is thought will apply in the future, to this type of vessel in northern European waters.

"Even if the bottoms of both the hulls of the Stena HSS were to be ripped open and filled with water, the vessel would still retain sufficient buoyancy to keep the car deck approximately two metres above the surface of the water," claims Stig Bystedt. "That is the same height above the surface of the water as the car deck of a conventional ferry. And even if one of the two hulls were to be ripped open beneath the water line and consequently leak along its entire length, the result would be a list of no more than 15 degrees."

The company claim that the Stena HSS 1500 would still be able to proceed using the other hull's two engines. Two auxiliary engines would also still be intact and the electricity supply (and power) on board would therefore be assured. Both of the Stena HSS 1500's hulls are divided into nine self-contained areas separated from one another by water-tight bulkheads. The five areas furthest forward are also divided horizontally by a water-tight stringer deck, as it is known, thereby forming fourteen, water-tight compartments. It is stated by Stena that if both of the hulls were to be filled with water, the risk of foundering is very small, thanks to the presence of a large, water-tight reserve

# Kvaerner Masa-Yards Inc. - the experienced builder of successful ships

Kvaerner Masa-Yards is a Finnish shipbuilding company with long traditions of producing successful high-quality ships.

The company, employing 4 700 people, is part of the international industrial group Kværner a.s.

Kvaerner Masa-Yards operates two newbuilding yards, Turku New Shipyard and Helsinki New Shipyard, and a factory for prefabricated cabin and bathroom modules, Piikkiö Works.

Kvaerner Masa-Azipod is responsible for the sales, design and construction of the Azipod propulsion system.

Kvaerner Masa-Yards Technology covers R&D, concept design and engineering services, shipyard and welding technology, and includes the Arctic Research Centre (MARC).

Kvaerner Masa Marine Inc. is a consulting engineering and marketing company in Vancouver B.C., Canada and Annapolis, MD, USA.

Kvaerner Masa-Yards build cruise liners and passenger ferries, gas carriers, icebreakers and ice-going tonnage as well as all types of special technology vessels, such as tankers, cable ships, research vessels, offshore vessels, dredgers and crane ships.

**Kvaerner Masa-Yards Inc.**

*Marketing and sales,* Helsinki, P.O.Box 132
FIN–00151 HELSINKI, Finland
Tel. +358-0-1941, Fax. +358-0-650 051
Tlx 121246 masah fi

*Marketing and sales,* Turku, P.O.Box 666
FIN–20101 TURKU, Finland
Tel. +358-21-2666 111, Fax. +358-21-2667 488
Tlx 62356 masat fi

*Piikkiö Works,* FIN–21500 PIIKKIÖ, Finland
Tel. +358-21-474 300, Fax. +358-21-472 6000

*Technology,* P.O.Box 666,
FIN–20101 TURKU, Finland
Tel. +358-21-2666 111, Fax. +358-21-2666 700
Tlx 62228 masat fi

*Kvaerner Masa-Azipod*
Munkkisaarenkatu 1
P.O.Box 132
FIN–00151 HELSINKI, Finland
Tel. +358-0-1941,
Fax. +358-0-194 2480

*Kvaerner Masa Marine Inc.,*
Suite 207-1525 West 8th Ave.,
VANCOUVER, B.C., V6J 1T5, Canada
Tel. +1-604-736 8711, Fax. +1-604-738 4410

*Kvaerner Masa Marine Inc.,*
Power Technology Center
201 Defence Highway, Suite 202
Annapolis, MD 21401, USA
Tel. +1-301-970 2226, Fax. +1-301-970 2230

# Kværner Masa-Yards

View from the bridge of the HSS *(Stena Line)*

area between the two hulls – under the car deck. The buoyancy generated by this area is more than sufficient to keep the HSS ferry afloat on an even keel, even when it is fully loaded.

The ferry is fitted throughout with fire detectors and TV-cameras. In an emergency, passengers will be given instructions by the ferry's loudspeaker system, TV monitors and crew and if necessary, a newly developed guidelight system will guide passengers to the exits. The Stena HSS 1500 ferry has a shipwide fire extinguishing system which, with the help of high pressure water mist, enables a rapid and effective fire-fighting response. The system comprises both sprinklers and fire hydrants in the accommodation areas, engine rooms and on the car deck.

The Stena HSS 1500 also has a recently-developed lifesaving system on board, known as MES, or Marine Evacuation System, which it is understood can evacuate everyone on board in under 18 minutes. The evacuation system is divided into four separate stations, two on each side of the passenger deck, directly linked to the public areas. In an emergency situation, doors open in the sides of the vessel and the evacuation stations can be reached via marked escape routes from all parts of the deck. When the MES is activated – it is handled from a control centre directly linked to the evacuation doors – an inflatable latticework beam, made of polyurethane treated webbing, is let down from the ferry. There are two chutes on each of the latticework beams, which the passengers use to slide down to two large covered life-rafts. Each life-raft has room for 135 people. They have broad openings facing the platform, which makes them easy to board. Two

FOR MIVAN MARINE
OUTFITTING SHIPS
IS PLAIN SAILING

M ivan Marine continues to outfit ship interiors with unbeatable performance. Meeting not only quality, technical and cost requirements but also providing project finance.

Operating throughout Europe, Scandinavia, USA and the Far East, Mivan Marine continues as the world's leading specialist ship outfitting contractor, to supply a complete turnkey service for both the newbuild and retrofit markets.

Combining the skills of a 1600 workforce, 10 000m² of custom built workshops and state of the art computer aided design and manufacturing technology, Mivan Marine provide the highest quality in construction of public spaces for cruise and ferry vessels.

In other words "**plain sailing**".

MARINE

**Mivan Marine Limited,**
Newpark, Greystone Road, Antrim, Co. Antrim, Northern Ireland, BT41 2QN. Telephone: +44 (01) 849 481000. Fax: +44 (01) 849 481010.

Lounge area on board the HSS *(Stena Line)*

more life-rafts can, if necessary be sent down from the passenger deck. The system also includes four lifeboats.

The new Stena HSS 1500 ferry, has a top speed of more than 40 knots, will be able to compete with airline traffic in terms of speed on many of its routes. This is, perhaps,why some of the crucial parts of the HSS 1500's engines are taken directly from the world of aviation.

The smaller of the two different types of gas turbines are used in the Swedish airforce's new fighter, attack and reconnaissance aircraft, the Saab Gripen, while the larger of the two types is used in the long-haul Boeing 747 aircraft.

There are several reasons why Stena's designers elected to use aircraft engine type gas turbines as the power source for the new Stena HSS 1500. They produce cleaner exhaust fumes than conventional diesel engines, require less space, weigh less, have a high level of operational reliability and are virtually vibration-free.

The General Electric manufactured gas turbines on the Stena HSS have been rebuilt for maritime use, with each of the two hulls containing two types, one large and one small. The larger develops approximately 30,000 horse power at 3,600 RPM, while the smaller develops approximately 20,000 horsepower at 6,500 RPM. The maritime versions of the gas turbines are powered by a light diesel oil with a very low sulphur content.

The gas turbines, including the power turbines, are completely encased in fire and sound-proof containers, known as turbine modules. Each of the two hulls contains two turbine modules – one large, one small.

In narrow waters the HSS 1500 can be powered by the two smaller engine packages,

(Above) Panoramic views looking foward (Below) Ben & Jerry's ice cream parlour *(Stena Line)*

giving a maximum speed of 25 knots. When the larger modules are in operation, the vessel has an approximate top speed of 32 knots, and when all four modules are operating at full power, the ferry's speed can exceed 40 knots.

Stena has chosen to use water jets from the Swedish firm KaMeWa, in Kristinehamn, for the ferry's forward propulsion, instead of conventional propellers. Not only are the water jet units efficient at high speeds, they also produce benefits in the form of improved manoeuvrability and a radical reduction in the vessel's draught.

The four water jets, two in each aft section of the vessel, draw in water through inlets in the ferry's bottom. The impeller (the propeller in a water jet) is located inside the units in a space sufficiently large for a fully grown man to stand upright.

Right at the back of the water jet units lie the massive steering and reversing drives. Each steering drive can be turned 30 degrees to starboard or port and thus steer the ferry in the desired direction. The HSS 1500 reverses by dropping massive scoops aft of the nozzles through which the water jets are angled diagonally downwards and forward.

Aircraft technology on the Stena HSS does not stop in the engine room – it's also an integral part of the bridge. Except the bridge usually to be found on a ship or ferry now closely resembles an aircraft cockpit.

Being on board a ferry the size of a football pitch, which travels at speeds of 40 knots, has changed the way people work at sea. This was recognised at an early stage in the HSS development programme by Stena Line's engineers, who looked to the civil aviation industry, rather than conventional shipping, to design the nerve centre of the new ferry.

On the Stena HSS the cockpit/control room is situated in the furthest forward, topmost section of the vessel and is manned by three officers – the captain, his co-pilot/navigator and the chief engineer.

The ferry's state of the art electronics system is the most sophisticated ever to be found on a merchant ship. It includes differential GPS navigation, electronic sea charts onto which radar information can be copied, and a conning display, where all information on the vessel's manoeuvres and speed, as well as wind and current conditions, is shown.

There are a number of other tools to ease navigation and monitoring, such as light-intensifying night binoculars and an internal television system with a large number of internally and externally positioned cameras. There is even a camera mounted between the hulls to enable the crew to monitor the wave height between them.

The captain and co-pilot can select the information they want to display on three huge computer screens positioned directly in front of them. They have constant access via these screens to the electronic sea charts of ECIDS (Electronic Chart Display Information System) – which for the first time has been developed specifically for the waters in which the ferry sails.

Usually a ferry's position at sea can be shown to within 100 metres but in using a differential GPS the accuracy is improved to plus or minus 10 metres. In the ports of Holyhead and Dun Laoghaire a more finely-tuned differential GPS network is used and it can calculate the ferry's position accurately to within a distance of as little as one metre.

The chief engineer has a separate control panel with four screens displaying all the essential data on the ship's technical operation – such as the turbine engine's status and water jet units' compressive force. The chief engineer is also responsible for monitoring and activating the safety systems on board, which means the captain and navigator can concentrate fully on manoeuvring the ferry.

The HSS 1500 cockpit electronics have – just as in an aviation context – triple-layer safety built in with three separate computers able at all times to handle and process the information retrieved from the ship's operational and navigational systems.

A new docking technique to speed loading and unloading, as well as a new system for storing supplies, are among other unique features of the Stena HSS. It means the ferry can be turned around, re-stored and re-fuelled in just 30 minutes and if required, this could be reduced to only 20 minutes.

The linkspan for the Stena HSS – the docking and drive-on ramp to which the ferry berths at the stern – is a completely new design, which also includes a quick coupling with fuel, fresh water and waste water pipes.

When the Stena HSS 1500 docks in Holyhead and Dun Laoghaire, she reverses in towards the linkspan. The reversing manoeuvre is made easier by the ferry being fitted with navigation equipment, which can determine the position of the ferry to within one metre, four TV cameras, a special docking radar mounted low in the ferry's stern, and bow propellers in each hull. This system guarantees safe docking.

Once the HSS ferry has made contact with the linkspan's fenders, the quick couplings are connected on either side of the ferry's stern, pulling it automatically into the correct position so that gangways, drive-on ramps and quick couplings fit. The ferry's massive beam and a specially constructed aft fender – which prevents the ship from moving sideways – mean no additional moorings, such as ropes, are required.

Once berthed, rapid loading and unloading is achieved by using the ferry's four stern doors (there are no bow doors). Thanks to the massive beam, cars, coaches and trucks turn around on board in a wide U-turn.

Three of the doors are used simultaneously during loading. Two of them lead into the ferry's main loading deck, while the third leads cars up to an extra pontoon deck situated above the main deck, via a ramp. Three doors are also used during unloading as vehicles drive through the 180 degree curve on-board.

Foot passengers go on-board and ashore along two parallel glazed passenger gangways, located on either side of the linkspan, so avoiding stairs and other barriers.

Helping to keep docking time to a minimum is a container system for supplying the on-board restaurants and duty-free shop. Two containers are loaded on to a traverser running on rails on the outer roof of the ferry. The restaurant container is lowered through an outlet in the bow roof, whilst the container with the duty-free articles has its place in the stern. Both of the containers stay on board until stocks need replenishing.

To date, Stena Rederi (a subsidiary of Stena AB) and Stena Line have ordered five HSS ferries – three large HSS 1500s and two smaller HSS 900s – for delivery in 1996 and 1997. The second Stena HSS 1500 will be introduced on the Stranraer-Belfast service in June 1996 and the third on the Harwich-Hook of Holland service in early 1997. The first Stena HSS 900, which will not carry freight, comes into service on the Gothenburg-Frederikshavn route this summer.

*Miles Cowsill*

## STENA HSS CONTRACTORS

Main Contractor:

| | |
|---|---|
| Hull, superstructure, decor, linkspan: | Finnyards, Finland |

Subcontractors:

| | |
|---|---|
| Main engine: | General Electric, USA |
| Turbine modules: | Kvaerner Energy, Norway |
| Reduction gearing: | MAAG, Switzerland |
| Water jet units: | KaMeWa, Sweden |
| Cockpit: | Kvaerner Ships Equipment, Norway |
| Auxilliary engines: | Cummins, UK |
| Generator: | Stamford, UK |
| Main section, painted boards: | ABB Paiko, Finland |
| Evacuation system: | ML Lifeguard, UK |
| Lifeboats: | Viking Lifesaving Equipment, Denmark |
| CCTV system: | Process TV, Sweden |
| Toilet system: | EVAC, Finland |
| Air-conditioning compressor: | ABB STAL Marine, Sweden |
| Ventilation: | GFMarine, Norway |
| Automation/steering system: | Lyngso Valmet Marine, Finland |

## STENA HSS 1500 FACTS

| | |
|---|---|
| Port of registry: | London |
| Length: | 126.6 m |
| Beam: | 40 m |
| Height: | 27.5 m |
| Draught: | 4.5 |
| Service speed: | 40 knots |
| Engine: | Gas turbines, 2 x GE LM 2500 and 2 x GELM 1600. Power: 68 MW (approx. 100,000 HP) |
| Auxiliary engine: | 4 x Cummins KTA 38 G 3 diesel generators. Power: 4 x 910 kW |
| Bow thrusters: | 2 x contra-rotating KaMeWa, diameter 1,110mm. Power: 2 x 600 kW. |
| Loading capacity: | 1,500 deadweight tonnage: 1500 passengers, 375 cars or 50 trucks plus 120 cars. |

Publishers Note: At the time of going to press the first HSS craft had not entered service.

# ROUND BRITAIN REVIEW

Color Line's acquisition of the Color Viking (ex. King of Scandinavia) on their Newcastle – Haugesund – Bergen service saw a 22% increase in passengers during the final quarter of 1994. Meanwhile the DFDS service from the Tyne to Hamburg prospered with Color's former Venus which was renamed King of Scandinavia and commenced sailings on 9th April. The group's freighters Tor Dania and Dana Maxima were duly stretched in Norway and Spain thereby increasing overall capacity while the veteran car ferry Winston Churchill took up a new seasonal service linking the Tyne with the Dutch port of Ijmuiden on 19th May.

During early March, North Sea Ferries commenced a new Middlesbrough – Europoort link with the chartered Swedish vessel Cupria, renamed Norcove. She was joined by the Norcliff (ex. Bravo) in April. In October, the regular NSF Zeebrugge service freighter Norking was sent to Sweden for stretching and re-engining after which the Norqueen followed while the 18 year old Ipswich – Europort service was closed as from 24th April. Resulting from this, the Norcape (ex. Tipperary) was switched to the Hull-Zeebrugge link while the P&O Pandoro-owned Norsky (ex. Ibex) was transferred to the Liverpool-Dublin crossing and resumed her original name.

A second service to cease was the Mannin Line's link between Great Yarmouth and Ijmuiden which closed on 6th May. During its short history the route had never been successful, a fact which was partly put down to the lack of reliability of the Belard which was promptly chartered back to the Irish Sea.

At the Hook of Holland, a new linkspan was floated into position on 12th June and the Stena Line freighter Rosebay commenced using it a week later. The first phase in the complete renovation of the Hook terminal was completed in late June. During mid-December it was announced that the

**Rosebay** *(Miles Cowsill)*

Prins Filip (FotoFlite)

third HSS 1500 will take up the traditional Harwich – Hook route as from summer 1997 when the *Koningin Beatrix* and the *Stena Europe* will be redeployed within the fleet.

Although restyled the Clipper Line in 1994, the P&O European Ferries link from Felixstowe to Zeebrugge failed to make the profits expected of it and the year's third North Sea closure duly occurred on 22nd October. The *Pride of Suffolk* and *Pride of Flanders* were switched to the Europoort freight link running in tandem with the *European Tideway* and *European Freeway* while the Portsmouth-based freighter, *Thomas Wehr* was transferred to the Suffolk port to offer a trailer service to Zeebrugge.

The in readiness for the reopening of a passenger service across the southern North Sea, the Ferrylink Freight operation linking Sheerness and Vlissingen was duly restructured and renamed Eurolink The company, a subsidiary of the Mersey Docks & Harbours Company, chartered the A K. Ventouris vessels *Agia Methodia* and *Attika* which were renamed *Euromantique* and *Euromagique* respectively. The latter vessel took up sailings on Easter Sunday (16th April) offering passenger accommodation for 350 while, after a spell operating in a freight mode, the former ship (550 passengers) started on 19th June.

The rival Vlissingen service, operated by Sally Line from Dartford, introduced the former Truckline freighter *Purbeck* in May to operate with the *Sally Euroway* (ex. *Argo*). Although good loads were carried, the link ran into financial problems and in the New Year 1996, it was transferred to the newly formed Dart Line (Jacobs plc) with their own chartered Romanian tonnage renamed, *Dart 2* and *Dart 5*.

The Belgian Government's service linking Ramsgate with Ostend had a disastrous first year's trading making a record loss of BFr 2 billion – twice as much as that from Dover in 1993. More operational problems beset the line giving the unrefurbished *Princesse Marie-Christine* lengthy

***SeaFrance Cezanne*** *(Mike Louagie)*

When you consider the options for crossing the Channel, Dover/Calais consistently comes out on top.

Over 17 million people chose the shortest crossing point in 1995. They know you simply can't beat the experience on this most popular route to France.

Let's review the key benefits.

Easy access to one of the most modern seaport passenger terminals – not just in the UK, but the world.

Streamlined fast-loading onto spacious ferries from top operators P&O, Stena Line and Sea France. Plus the quick Hoverspeed option.

PORT OF
DOVER

The security of pre-booked reservations or the certainty of a place sooner rather than later thanks to the unbeatable frequency – up to 86 tourist departures round the clock, each way, every day.

The opportunity to have a meal and to do some duty and tax free shopping on the way. Or simply take a stroll on deck, taking in sea views and sea air en route.

The choice is clear.

It really is a Strait Choice – Dover/Calais!

**YOU'RE MUCH BETTER OFF ON TOP**

periods in service. The ferry even spent two unsuccessful periods on charter to pool partner, Sally. After three years of inactivity, the sale-listed Prinses Maria-Esmeralda was sold to Cypriot owners in February. Renamed Wisteria, she finally left Ostend on 1st May.

In spite of concerns that the opening of the Channel Tunnel would cause doom and gloom to the ferry operations across the Dover Strait, the situation has been promising with trade only 6-7% down on 1994. The Chunnel has attracted large quantities of extra traffic into East Kent, often to the detriment of the lengthier Western Channel crossings. The situation has been further complicated by the split between Sealink Stena Line (now trading simply as Stena Line) and their French pool partners Sealink SNAT who, as from 1st January 1996, have traded as SeaFrance. There had been a degree of animosity between the two concerns for some time with Stena unhappy with on board standards and the level of complaints made against the French ships/crews while they, in turn, objected to the "we know best" approach of the Swedish company. One casualty of the Chunnel was the closure of the Dover – Dunkerque West train ferry service as from 22nd December. The SeaFrance Nord Pas-de-Calais was duly transferred to the Calais link where she is proving to be an excellent asset for her new operators.

The Stena Line brand name and image was launched rather earlier than anticipated after the Stena Challenger was blown aground off Calais during September. The ship was eventually sent to the Tyne and became the first vessel in the fleet to receive the full-blown Swedish livery.

A second company to adopt a new livery during the year was Hoverspeed, the operators of the seasonal routes between Dover and Calais and Folkestone and Boulogne. Their much-heralded SuperSeaCat France was eventually refused on the grounds that it failed to meet its contract speed and so remained at the Austal yard in Western Australia.

During the year, market leaders P&O European Ferries spent some £2 million further uprating

Pride of Kent (Mike Louagie)

# Cruise to Calais in comfort...

RELAX and just cruise across from Dover to Calais
- the shortest sea route to France.
Large, luxurious car ferries with shops, restaurants
and entertainment on board, plus hovercraft,
provide rapid, comfortable crossings with a departure every
thirty minutes. Fast on and off loading on both sides
of the Channel helps to speed your journey.
Instant motorway access from Calais port provides
an open door to the entire European motorway network.

## Calais
### ...begins with sea

Stena Invicta  (Mike Louagie)

the on board facilities of the Pride of Dover and Pride of Calais and later to the Pride of Kent. The three ship Dover – Zeebrugge freight service continued to make profits with unprecedented numbers of trailers being carried on the route.

The year 1995 saw the demise of Meridian Ferries, the operators of two freight vessels linking Folkestone and Boulogne. The Spirit of Boulogne (ex. Marine Evangeline) and the Spirit of Independence (ex. Innisfallen) were effectively 'sunk' in March by the actions of French trade unions in Boulogne after Meridian had contemplated operating their second ship in a passenger mode using cheap, Polish seamen.

After two successive years of continued growth on the Newhaven-Dieppe service, Stena Sealink Line were to see a drop in passenger traffic on this route during 1995. Following the success of their high-speed services on the Irish Sea, the company decided to introduce a fast-ferry service on this link. Finally, following two abortive announcements in 1995, the new operation was due to start in March 1996, with the brand new Stena Lynx IV, a high-speed catamaran, capable of carrying 148 cars and 600 passengers. With a top speed of 37 knots, she should cut the traditional four hour crossing time in half. On the introduction of the Stena Lynx IV, the Stena Londoner was withdrawn. Meanwhile, her old operating partner, the Stena Parisien, was maintained on the conventional passenger service with the Marine Evangeline in a freight role.

Stena Line were not the only ones to be affected by a drop in trade in 1995 on the Western Channel. Brittany Ferries were to see a drop of some 5% in passenger traffic on their routes to France. The service which was to see the most dramatic drop in trade was the Caen-Portsmouth link, served by the luxuriously appointed Normandie and Duc de Normandie. In stark contrast, the investment that P&O European Ferries made during 1994 for the charter of the former Olau twins on their rival Portsmouth-Le Havre service, was to see the company have a growth of some 14% on this link. P&O European Ferries were also to see growth on their Cherbourg link. Despite record figures from P&O European Ferries during 1995, the company's ticket revenue was to drop substantially in the fiercely competitive market place. Had not sales in the duty-free shops increased dramatically, P&O, with their rivals, would have been faced with even greater losses.

One bright light on the Western Channel is that both Brittany Ferries and P&O Ferries were to see continued growth on their Spanish services, with the Val de Loire and Pride of Bilbao respectively.

A new high-speed service eventually started in June between Brighton Marina and Fecamp, in Normandy, using the 315 seater San Pietro, chartered from a Norwegian company. The operation was to have a less than successful year.

In the light of reduced fares on the English Channel and the opening of Eurotunnel, the offshore islands of Britain continued a downward spiral with their holiday industry. The cost of travelling from mainland Britain to either Jersey, Guernsey or the Isle of Man still remained competitively high compared to that of ferry travel for a family crossing either the Dover Strait or the Western Channel.

Both Jersey and Guernsey were to see the introduction of new and faster tonnage from mainland Britain during 1995. Condor's new £22 million flagship Condor 11, became the largest fast ferry on the English Channel routes when she entered service between Weymouth and Guernsey/Jersey on 18th May. Built in Tasmania, the new craft was able to accommodate 674 passengers and 130 cars. She was replaced by another craft during early 1996, the Condor 12, prior to a further larger craft entering service in September on a long term basis to Condor.

Bretagne (Miles Cowsill)

Condor's parent company, Commodore Ferries, introduced the first of their two Dutch built freight ships on their Portsmouth-Channel Islands service in June last year. The Island Commodore, together with her sister vessel, later named Commodore Goodwill, will eventually replace the existing chartered vessels which the company have had since 1986. The new vessels can accommodate 12 drivers and have space for 94 x 12m trailers. Once both vessels are in service they will provide a twice daily service to and from the UK, with arrivals in both Guernsey and Jersey early morning and each evening.

Meanwhile, Emeraude Line ordered a new fast ferry to replace the Solidor 2 as from Easter of this year at a cost of some £13 million. The new ferry was ordered from a Norwegian yard and is being specially designed to operate at a service speed of 33 knots, with a capacity for 430 passengers and 52 cars.

The spring saw Sea Containers of Bermuda duly dispose of their Isle of Wight operation, Wightlink, to British owners CIN Ven Ltd. for something in the region of £107 million. Meanwhile Rival operators Red Funnel launched the third of their 'Raptor' class ferries, Red Eagle, into the Clyde on 23rd November. She is due to replace the Netley Castle.

During 1995, the local authorities in Cork and Kerry in Southern Ireland disposed of their interest in Swansea Cork Ferries. The authorities were to receive criticism from the tourist industry for the disposal of their interests as those involved in the industry feel that the company is not investing enough in the marketing of the route.

At the end of the year, Strintzis, the Greek owners, announced that they were considering a new vessel to replace the twenty-three year old Japanese built Superferry. It is understood that if a new vessel is built for the route, it will provide cabin accommodation for between 700 and 900 passengers, compared to the present vessel which can only sleep 450. The company is also looking to expand its freight operations, if a new vessel is ordered.

During 1995, the Superferry carried more than 190,000 passengers on the ten hour crossing, which is estimated to be worth nearly £10 million a year to the City of Cork.

Meanwhile, on 26th September, Irish Ferries confirmed the order for a second new superferry for their Irish/UK ferry services. The new vessel will be constructed at the Dutch shipbuilding yard of Van der Giessen-de-Noord and will be constructed to accommodate 2,200 passengers with a capacity for 855 cars or 122 freight units. She is due to enter service during January 1997 and is being built at the cost of IR£60 million. She will be placed on the Dublin-Holyhead service in place of the new Isle of Innisfree, which will be transferred to the Rosslare-Pembroke Dock service which has for so many years needed a suitable ship.

The new vessel will be substantially larger than the present Dutch built Isle of Innisfree, with a length of 182.5 metres and an estimated gross tonnage of 33,000 gross tons. She will have an operating speed of 21.5 knots to enable her to operate most crossings in three hours.

Meanwhile, new port facilities at Holyhead were opened for Irish Ferries by Stena Line at the end of 1995, with a double deck ramp.

At Pembroke Dock, in anticipation of the arrival of the Isle of Innisfree from Holyhead, the passenger facilities will be improved during 1996 and a new double-deck linkspan will be constructed for completion by 1998. Meanwhile, the Isle of Innisfree is due to enter service on the southern corridor during late January 1997 and will at last give the route the first suitable ship since it was established in 1981 with the Townsend Thoresen vessel Viking III.

At Fishguard, the charter of the Stena Felicity was extended until April 1997. It had originally been planned that the Stena Jutlandica, from the Gothenburg-Frederikshavn service, would replace her this year but these plans were shelved to allow the Swedish ship to operate on the Dover-Calais route instead as the Stena Empereur from June 1996.

Norstar (Miles Cowsill)

Stena Sealink were to see continued growth and success with their fast ferry service on the Fishguard-Rosslare route. The Stena Sea Lynx was to carry nearly 37% of the total passenger traffic between Pembrokeshire and Ireland. The fast craft also captured 33% of the car traffic on the route. Traffic on the Fishguard-Rosslare link was once again up, with a record season carryings of some 945,000 passengers, 192,300 cars and 42,500 freight units.

At Holyhead, in anticipation of the arrival of the HSS, the Stena Traveller introduced a new freight dedicated service between Holyhead and Dublin on 2nd November.

The Stena Hibernia was renamed Stena Adventurer, following the announcement by the company that she would be retained on the route with the HSS. Meanwhile, the HSS arrived from the builders at the Anglesey port on 26th February and is due enter service on 1st April, on the new 99 minute crossing between Wales and Ireland.

Summer 1995 saw the Isle of Man Steam Packet Co's last traditional car ferry Lady of Mann on charter to Porto Santo Line of Madeira. Meanwhile the two year experiment involving the chartered SeaCat Isle of Man duly finished in violent circumstances on 27th September. Serious structural damage was caused when the craft was hit by a "freak" wave in the Crosby Channel.

The sale-listed Mona's Queen was finally sold to Philippine owners and left the Mersey as the Mary the Queen on 29th November.

Following many months of speculation, Stena Sealink Line announced on 5th September 1995 that they would withdraw their operations from Larne in favour of Belfast. The Stena Galloway completed the final sailing on the route on 11th November and the company transferred to the new £13 million terminal at Belfast the next day with the three existing passenger ships operating on the route. The new HSS craft is due to enter service during July 1996. The anticipated journey times with the HSS between the two ports will be cut to 90 minutes once the new high speed sea

Saint Patrick II (Miles Cowsill)

service is introduced. The Stena Caledonia and Stena Galloway will be maintained on the link in a support role operating as passenger and freight vessels.

An intensive marketing campaign and price war on the North Channel by P&O European Ferries, Stena Line and SeaCat Scotland was immediately started once the Swedish company had moved their operations from Larne to Belfast. The P&O freight vessel European Endeavour was transferred from Dover to support the Pride of Ailsa and Pride of Rathlin. Meanwhile, the company continued to undertake a feasibility study into introducing their own new fast craft between Cairnryan and Larne for 1996. At the time of going to press, no firm announcement had been made by the group.

SeaCat Scotland operations between Stranraer and Belfast continued to have good loadings, despite the intensive price war on the northern channel. The SeaCat Scotland was sent for an upgrading of her passenger areas at the turn of the year.

A new terminal is to be built at Stranraer next year to further improve the company's services. The parent company, Sea Containers, meanwhile have unveiled plans to introduce another craft on the Stranraer-Belfast service as from next year following their order for six mono-hull high-speed ferries from Italian yards. The new craft will be 100 metres in length, and will operate at a service speed of 37.8 knots and will be able to carry 800 passengers and 175 cars.

Pandoro Ferries have also seen continued growth on all their routes from Ireland. Four vessels now maintain the Liverpool-Dublin route and the company hope in the future to introduce a second vessel on the Rosslare-Cherbourg route.

The old-established animal theme of naming ships by P&O was reintroduced by Pandoro at the latter part of the year with the European Clearway, used on the Rosslare-Cherbourg route, becoming the Panther, the Dublin-Liverpool runner Norsky was renamed Ibex and the newly

Merchant Bravery and Peveril (Miles Cowsill)

acquired Merchant Valiant on the Larne-Ardrossan route became the Lion. It is anticipated that the other vessels in the fleet will also be renamed in the near future.

Irish Ferries' operations from Rosslare and Cork to France continued to see continued growth despite aggressive marketing from their rivals Brittany Ferries. Following the unsuccessful plans to establish a new service to Brest by Irish Ferries in 1995, a new route to Roscoff opened on 15th June in place of the planned operation.

Belfast Freight Ferries' Saga Moon, which operates their Belfast-Heysham service, was sent to Tees Dockyard to undergo lengthening operation at the end of the summer.

Norse Irish Ferries introduced their new Norse Mersey at the end of May 1995. The 174 metre vessel has been taken on an eighteen months' charter and can accommodate 64 freight drivers. The main bulk of their passenger operations has now been left in the hands of the Norse Lagan which continues to sail alternative days from Liverpool and Belfast. The previous Norse Mersey was returned to Stena Line at the end of 1994.

Caledonian MacBrayne's new Ullapool – Stornoway (Lewis) vessel Isle of Lewis was launched at Port Glasgow on 18th April and entered service on 31st July. During August, the displaced Suilven duly sailed for further service linking North and South Islands in New Zealand. The order for a new £2.2 million Uist/ Harris ferry was placed in April with McTay on Merseyside.

Meanwhile Western Ferries (Clyde) Ltd introduced their second hand Dutch ferry Sound of Scalpay onto the McInroy's Point to Hunter's Quay link on 12th July. Sadly during the year, their first ship, the historic Sound of Sanda (ex. Lymington) had her accommodation removed on Loch Awe.

Yet another ferry link succumbed on 16th October when the £24 million Skye Bridge was opened.

*Miles Cowsill & John Hendy*

SeaCat Scotland (Sea Containers Ltd)

# NOTES

**Company information** This section gives general information regarding to status of the company ie nationality, whether it is public or private sector and whether it is part of a larger group.

**Management** The managing director and marketing director or manager of each company is listed. Where these posts do not exist, other equivalent people are listed. Where only initials are given, that person is, as far as is know, male.

**Address** This is the address of the company's administrative headquarters. In the case of some international companies, a British and overseas address is given.

**Telephone and Fax**: Numbers Numbers are expressed as follows. ˩ <number> (this is the international dialling code which is dialled in combination with the number dialled to gain access to international calls (00 in UK), it is not used for calling within the country), (<number>) (this is the number which precedes area codes when making domestic calls – it is not dialled when calling from another country (not all countries have this)), <number> (this is the rest of the number including, where appropriate, the area dialling code). In a few cases free or local call rate numbers are used for reservations; note that these are not available from overseas. Telex numbers are also included where applicable; it should be noted that many operators no longer use this service, its role having largely been taken over by fax and a number of operators have ceased their Telex line since the last edition.

**Routes operated** After each route there are, in brackets, details of 1: normal journey time, 2: regular vessel(s) used on the route (number as in list of vessels) and 3: frequencies (where a number per day is given, this relates to return sailings). Please note that frequencies can vary over the year. Freight operations are often restricted at weekends. I have used the 'Cooks European Timetable Convention' in respect of town and country names – local names for towns (eg Göteborg rather than Gothenburg) and English names for countries (eg Germany rather than Deutschland). Many towns in Finland have both Finnish and Swedish names; I have used the Finnish name.

**List of vessels**

| NO | NAME | GROSS TONNAGE (A) | YEAR BUILT | SERVICE SPEED (KNOTS) | NUMBER OF PASSENGERS | VEHICLE (B) DECK CAPACITY | | VEHICLE DECK ACCESS (C) | WHERE BUILT (D) | FLAG (D) |
|----|------|-------------------|------------|------------------------|----------------------|----------------------------|---|--------------------------|-----------------|----------|
| 1 | NAME | 26433t | 87 | 22k | 290P | 650C | 100L | BA2 | Town, GE | GB |

(A) – = measured in accordance with the 1969 Tonnage Convention; c = approximate.

(B) – C = Cars, L = Lorries (15m), T = Trailers (12m), R = Rail wagons, – = No figure quoted, p = passenger only vessel, c = approximate.

(C) – B = Bow, A = Aft, S = Side, Q = Quarterdeck, R = Slewing ramp, 2 = Two decks can be loaded at the same time, C = Cars must be crane loaded aboard, t = turntable ferry.

(D) The following abbreviations are used:

| | | | |
|---|---|---|---|
| AL = Australia | CY = Cyprus | IM = Isle of Man | RU = Russia |
| AN = Antilles | DK = Denmark | IT = Italy | SI = Singapore |
| AU = Austria | ES = Estonia | IR = Irish Republic | SK = South Korea |
| BA = Bahamas | FA = Faroes | JA = Japan | SP = Spain |
| BD = Bermuda | FI = Finland | NL = Netherlands | SV = St Vincent |
| BE = Belgium | FR = France | NO = Norway | SW = Sweden |
| CA = Canada | GB = Great Britain | PA = Panama | UY = Uruguay |
| CH = China | GE = Germany | PL = Portugal | YU = Yugoslavia |
| CI = Caymen Islands | GR = Greece | PO = Poland | |
| CR = Croatia | IC = Iceland | RO = Romania | |

In the notes ships are in CAPITAL LETTERS, shipping lines are in italics.

**Capacity** In this book, capacities shown are the maxima. Sometimes vessels operate at less than their maximum passenger capacity due to reduced crewing or to operating on a route on which they are not permitted to operate above a certain level. Car and lorry/trailer capacities are the maximum for either type. The two figures are not directly comparable; some parts of a vessel may allow cars on two levels to occupy the space that a trailer or lorry occupies on one level, some may not. Also some parts of a vessel many only be accessible to cars. All figures have to be fairly approximate.

**Ownership** The ownership of many vessels is very complicated. Some are actually owned by finance companies and banks, some by subsidiary companies of the shipping lines, some by subsidiary companies of a holding company of which the shipping company is also a subsidiary and some by companies which are jointly owned by the shipping company and other interests like a bank, set up specifically to own one ship or group of ships. In all these cases the vessel is technically chartered to the shipping company. However, in this book, only those vessels chartered from one shipping company to another or from a ship owning company unconnected with the shipping line, are recorded as being on charter. Vessels are listed under the current operator rather than the owner. Charter is 'bareboat' (ie without crew) unless otherwise stated.

**Gross Registered Tonnage** This is a measure of enclosed capacity rather than weight, based on a formula of one gross ton = 100 cubic feet. Even small alterations can alter the gross tonnage. Under old measurement systems, the capacity of enclosed car decks was not included but, under a 1969 convention, all vessels laid down after 1982 have been measured by a new system which includes enclosed vehicle decks as enclosed space, thereby considerably increasing the tonnage of car ferries. Under this convention, from 1st January 1995, all vessels are due to be remeasured under this system; in a few cases, details are not available at the time of going to press. All vessels measured by the old system are indicated with a diamond '◇'. Note that this only applies to larger vessels with enclosed vehicle decks; open decked vessels have generally not been remeasured as the changes that the new formula would make are marginal. Tonnages quoted here are, where possible, those given by the shipping companies themselves.

The following people are gratefully thanked for their assistance with this publication: Brian Rees (Stena Sealink Line), Nick Stevens (P&O European Ferries), Ebbe Pedersen (DFDS), Robert Donaldson (Caledonian MacBrayne), Karen Donovan (Sea Containers), Taru Kaplin (Silja Line), and many others in ferry companies in the UK and abroad, Barry Mitchell, Jack Phelan, Lawrence MacDuff, Ian Smith (Bézier Design), Foto Flite, Haven Colourprint and Pat Sumner (Ferry Publications).

# Section 1 - UK Passenger Operations

# BRITTANY FERRIES

**THE COMPANY** *Brittany Ferries* is the trading name of *BAI SA*, a French private sector company and the operating arm of the *Brittany Ferries* group. The UK operations are run by BAI (UK) Ltd, a UK private sector company, wholly owned by the *Brittany Ferries* Group.

**MANAGEMENT Group Managing Director:** Christian Michielini, **Managing Director UK & Ireland:** Ian Carruthers, **Marketing Director:** David Longden.

**ADDRESS** Millbay Docks, PLYMOUTH, Devon PL1 3EW.

**TELEPHONE Administration:** +44 (0)1705 827701, **Reservations:** All Services: +44 (0)990 360360, Portsmouth: +44 (0)1705 827701, Plymouth: +44 (0)1752 221321, **Fax:** +44 (0)1705 811053, **Telex:** 86878.

**ROUTES OPERATED** Roscoff – Plymouth (6hrs (day), 5 hrs 30 mins – 7 hrs 30 mins (night); *(5,6)*; up to 3 per day), Plymouth – Santander (Spain) (spring, summer, autumn only) (23 hrs – 24 hrs; *(6)*; 2 per week), Portsmouth – Santander (Spain) (winter only) (29 hrs – 33 hrs; *(1)*; 1 per week), Roscoff – Cork (14hrs; *(3,6)*; up to 2 per week), St Malo – Cork (18hrs; *(3)*; 1 per week), St Malo – Portsmouth St (8 hrs 45 mins (day), 9 hrs 30 mins – 10 hrs (night); *(1)*; 1 per day), Caen (Ouistreham) – Portsmouth (6 hrs (day), 6 hrs – 7 hrs (night); *(2,4, winter:6)*; 3 per day), St Malo – Poole (8 hrs; *(3)*; 4 per week), St Malo – Plymouth (8 hrs; *(1)*; 1 per week (winter only)).

## CONVENTIONAL FERRIES

| | | | | | | | | | | |
|---|---|---|---|---|---|---|---|---|---|---|
| 1 | BRETAGNE | 23015t | 89 | 21k | 2030P | 580C | 40L | BA | St Nazaire, FR | FR |
| 2 | DUC DE NORMANDIE | <>9677t | 78 | 21k | 1500P | 350C | 44T | BA | Heusden, NL | FR |
| 3 | DUCHESSE ANNE | <>6812t | 79 | 20k | 1300P | 290C | 39T | BA | Cork, IR | FR |
| 4 | NORMANDIE | 27541t | 92 | 20k | 2263P | 630C | 66T | BA | Turku, FI | FR |
| 5 | QUIBERON | <>8441t | 75 | 20k | 1302P | 300C | 35L | BA2 | Rendsburg, GE | FR |
| 6 | VAL DE LOIRE | 31395t | 87 | 21k | 1800P | 550C | 114T | BA | Bremerhaven, GE | FR |

BRETAGNE Built for the Santander – Plymouth and Roscoff – Cork services (with two trips per week between Roscoff and Plymouth). In 1993 she was transferred to the St Malo – Portsmouth service. She operates the Santander – Portsmouth route during the winter.

DUC DE NORMANDIE Built as the PRINSES BEATRIX for *Stoomvaart Maatschappij Zeeland (Zeeland Steamship Company)* of The Netherlands for their Hoek van Holland – Harwich service. In September 1985 sold to *Brittany Ferries* and chartered back to *SMZ*, continuing to operate for them until the introduction of the KONINGIN BEATRIX in May 1986. In June 1986 delivered to *Brittany Ferries* and inaugurated the Caen – Portsmouth service.

DUCHESSE ANNE Built as the CONNACHT for *B&I Line* and initially used on the Cork – Swansea (from spring 1979, Cork – Pembroke Dock) service. In late 1980 she was transferred to the Dublin – Liverpool service – initially with the MUNSTER (4230t, 1968) and from summer 1981 with the new LEINSTER (now the ISLE OF INISHMORE). Subsequently she also operated between Dublin and Holyhead. In January 1988 she was moved to the reinstated Pembroke Dock – Rosslare service. In late 1988 she was sold to *Brittany Ferries*, renamed the DUCHESSE ANNE, re-registered in France and, in 1989, introduced onto the St Malo – Portsmouth service. In 1993 she moved to operate additional Roscoff – Plymouth services, an additional Roscoff – Cork service and inaugurate a St Malo – Cork service. In summer 1994 she inaugurated a new St Malo – Poole service, which replaced her Plymouth – Roscoff sailings.

NORMANDIE Built for the Caen – Portsmouth route.

# BY FAR THE BEST WAY
# TO HOLIDAY FRANCE & SPAIN

Now, there's no better way to take your car to Holiday France or Spain. Our direct routes to Brittany, Normandy and Santander land you closer to where you want to be.

Our luxury cruise-ferries, with their superb restaurants, value and service, will spoil you the moment you drive on board.

As the leaders in car holidays to France and Spain, our huge range offers by far the best choice.

**Brittany Ferries**
The Holiday Fleet

## BETTER BY FAR

QUIBERON Ordered by *Lion Ferry AB* of Sweden. The contract was sold to *Svenska Lastbils AB (Svelast)* of Sweden (a subsidiary of *Statens Järnvägar (SJ)*, *Swedish State Railways)* before delivery and she was delivered to them as the NILS DACKE. She was initially chartered to *Svenska Rederi AB Öresund* (another *SJ* subsidiary) for their service between Malmö (Sweden) and Travemünde (Germany). Sister vessel the GUSTAV VASA (now NORRÖNA of *Smyril Line*) was owned by *Lion Ferry AB* of Sweden and was also chartered to *SRÖ*. In 1976, Svelast took over the marketing of the service and it was operated under the name *Malmö-Travemünde Line*, with *Lion Ferry AB* operating it as agents. Later in 1976, *Svelast* and *Linjebuss International* (a subsidiary of *Stockholms Rederi AB Svea*) formed a jointly owned subsidiary called *Saga-Linjen* and *Lion Ferry AB* continued as administrative operator. In 1981 a joint marketing agreement was reached with the rival German owned *TT Line*, (running between Travemünde and Trelleborg (Sweden)) and the two services were marketed as *TT-Saga Line*. In April 1982 the NILS DACKE was chartered to *Brittany Ferries* with an option to purchase. She was renamed the QUIBERON and placed on the Santander – Plymouth and Roscoff – Cork services; she also operates between Roscoff and Plymouth. The GUSTAV VASA continued as sole vessel on the Malmö – Travemünde route for a further year until the service was withdrawn. The QUIBERON was purchased by *Brittany Ferries* in 1984 and re-registered in France. Following the delivery of the BRETAGNE in July 1989, she was transferred to the Roscoff – Plymouth service.

VAL DE LOIRE Built as the NILS HOLGERSSON for *TT Line* of Sweden and Germany (jointly owned) for their service between Travemünde and Trelleborg. In 1991 purchased by *Brittany Ferries* for entry into service in spring 1993. After a major rebuild, she was renamed the VAL DE LOIRE and introduced onto the Plymouth – Santander and Roscoff – Plymouth/Cork service. She operates on the Caen – Portsmouth route in the winter.

# COLOR LINE

**THE COMPANY** *Color Line* is the trading name of *Norway Line Ltd*, which is owned by *Color Line A/S*, a Norwegian limited company. Until 1991 it traded as *Norway Line*.

**MANAGEMENT Manager:** Dag Romslo, **Sales Manager:** Mike Wood.

**ADDRESS** International Ferry Terminal, Royal Quays, NORTH SHIELDS NE29 6EE.

**TELEPHONE Administration:** +44 (0)191-296 1313. **Reservations:** +44 (0)191-296 1313. **Fax:** +44 (0)191-296 1540. **Telex:** 537275.

**ROUTES OPERATED** Bergen – Haugesund – Stavanger – Newcastle – Bergen (triangular route), Bergen – Haugesund – Stavanger – Newcastle (Bergen – Stavanger (6 hrs), Stavanger – Newcastle (direct 18 hrs 30 mins, via Bergen 29 hrs 30 mins), Bergen – Newcastle (21 hrs 15 mins); *(1)*; 3 sailings Norway – UK per week).

**CONVENTIONAL FERRY**

| 1 | COLOR VIKING | 20581t | 75 | 19k | 1250P | 285C | 42T | BA | Nantes, FR | NO |
|---|---|---|---|---|---|---|---|---|---|---|

COLOR VIKING Built as the WELLAMO for *EFFOA* of Finland for *Silja Line* services between Helsinki and Stockholm. In 1981 sold to *DFDS*, renamed the DANA GLORIA and placed onto the Göteborg – Newcastle and Esbjerg – Newcastle services. In 1983 she was moved to the København – Oslo service. In 1984 she was chartered to *Johnson Line* of Sweden for *Silja Line* service between Stockholm and Turku and renamed the SVEA CORONA – the name born by her sister vessel. This charter ended in 1985 and she returned to the København – Oslo service and resumed the name DANA GLORIA. During winter 1988/89 she was stretched in Papenburg, Germany and in early 1989 she was renamed the KING OF SCANDINAVIA. She returned to the København – Oslo route; in 1990 a Helsingborg call was introduced. In 1994 she was sold to *Color Line* (as part of a deal which involved *DFDS* buying the VENUS from *Color Line*) and renamed the COLOR VIKING.

Normandie *(Miles Cowsill)*

Havelet *(John Bryant)*

# CONDOR FERRIES

**THE COMPANY** *Condor Ferries* is a Channel Islands private sector company, 50% owned by *The Holyman Group* of Australia and 50% owned by *Commodore Shipping*, Guernsey.

**MANAGEMENT Managing Director:** Bob Adams, **Marketing Manager:** Sam Spindlow.

**ADDRESS** PO Box 10, Commodore House, Bulwer Avenue, St Sampsons, GUERNSEY, Channel Islands GY1 3AF.

**TELEPHONE Administration:** +44 (0)1481 48771, **Reservations:** +44 (0)1305 761551, **Fax:** +44 (0)1481 45049.

**ROUTES OPERATED** *Conventional Ferry:* Weymouth – St Peter Port (Guernsey) – St Helier (Jersey) (Weymouth – Guernsey: 5hrs (day), 11 hrs 45 mins (night (via Jersey)), Guernsey – Jersey: 2 hrs, Weymouth – Jersey: 8 hrs 45 mins (night), 7 hrs 45 mins (day (via Guernsey)); *(1)*; 1 per day).

*Fast Ferry:* Weymouth – St Peter Port (Guernsey) – St Helier (Jersey) (2hrs 15 mins (to Guernsey), 3hrs 30 mins (to Jersey); *(1)*; 2 per day).

## CONVENTIONAL FERRY

| 1 | HAVELET | | 6918t | 77 | 19k | 500P | 200C | 37L | BA2 | Bergen, NO | | BA |
|---|---------|---|-------|----|-----|------|------|-----|-----|------------|---|----|

HAVELET Built as the CORNOUAILLES for *Brittany Ferries* and used mainly on their Roscoff – Plymouth service. In 1984 she was chartered to *SNCF* for use on their Dieppe – Newhaven service. This charter terminated at the end of 1985 and she was transferred to *Truckline Ferries*. From January 1986 she operated on their Cherbourg – Poole freight only service and then, in April, she inaugurated the Caen – Portsmouth service for *Brittany Ferries* on a freight only basis. In June she returned to *Truckline Ferries* and inaugurated a car and passenger service between Cherbourg and Poole . Until 1989 she operated between Cherbourg and Poole all year round, conveying passengers between April and October only. In 1989 she was renamed the HAVELET and sold to *Channel Island Ferries*, holding company of *British Channel Island Ferries*, operating between Poole and the Channel Islands. It was intended that, in 1993, she would be used in a freight only role; however, due to the level of demand it was decided to allow her to carry passengers and she was crewed accordingly. In 1994, *British Channel Island Ferries* ceased operations and she was chartered to *Condor Ferries* to operate between Weymouth and the Channel Islands.

## FAST FERRY

| 2 | CONDOR 12 | | - | 96 | 37k | 700P | 180C | - | BA | Hobart, AL | - |
|---|-----------|---|---|----|-----|------|------|---|----|------------|---|

CONDOR 12 InCat 81m model. On charter for summer 1996 pending delivery of NEWBUILDING in the autumn.

## Under Construction

| 3 | NEWBUILDING | | - | 96 | 39k | 800P | 200C | - | BA | Hobart, AL | - |
|---|-------------|---|---|----|-----|------|------|---|----|------------|---|

NEWBUILDING InCat 84m model. To enter service in the autumn, 1996.

*Condor* also operates high speed passenger only services using: CONDOR 8 (387t, 1988, 300 passengers, catamaran). **Routes operated:** St Malo – Channel Islands and internal services between Jersey, Guernsey and Sark.

# EMERAUDE LINES

**THE COMPANY** *Emeraude Lines* is a French private sector company.

**MANAGEMENT Commercial Manager (St Malo):** Jean-Luc Griffon, **Managing Director (Jersey):** Gordon Forrest.

**ADDRESS** PO Box 16, 35401, St Malo, France.

**TELEPHONE Administration: & Reservations:** St Malo: +33 99 40 48 40, Jersey +44 (0)1534 66566, **Fax:** St Malo: +33 99 81 28 73, Jersey +44 (0)1534 68741.

**ROUTES OPERATED** *Conventional Ferry:* St Malo – St Helier (Jersey) (2 hrs 30 mins – 3 hrs; *(1)*; up to 2 per day). *Fast Ferry:* St Malo – Jersey, (1 hr 10 mins;*(1)*; 3 per day), St Malo – Guernsey (1 hr 50 mins;*1*; 1 per day).

## CONVENTIONAL FERRY

| 1 | SOLIDOR 2 | | 3401t | 77 | 15k | 600P | 90C | 13L | BA | Hoogezand, NL | | SV |
|---|---|---|---|---|---|---|---|---|---|---|---|---|

SOLIDOR 2 Built as the LANGELAND II (registered in Denmark as the LANGELAND TO) for *Langeland – Kiel Linien* of Denmark for their service between Bagenkop (Langeland, Denmark) and Kiel (Germany). In 1989 she was purchased by *Emeraude Lines*, renamed the SOLIDOR II and replaced the SOLIDOR (1000t, 1965) (the same vessel she replaced in 1977 when new since the SOLIDOR was previously the LANGELAND). In 1994 she was renamed the SOLIDOR 2 and in May withdrawn and replaced by the high speed monohull EMERAUDE (900t, 1994). During summer 1994 she was chartered to *Rainbow Lines* of Italy for service between Otranto (Italy) and Albania. She returned to *Emeraude Lines* in March 1995. The EMERAUDE was returned to her builders as unsatisfactory and all vehicle services in 1995 were maintained by the SOLIDOR. In 1996 to be replaced by the SOLIDOR 3.

## FAST FERRY

| 2 | SOLIDOR 3 | | 2100t | 96 | 33k | 450P | 52C | - | BA | Fjellstrand, NO | | FR |
|---|---|---|---|---|---|---|---|---|---|---|---|---|

SOLIDOR 3 Built for *Emeraude Lines* to re-establish fast car ferry services. Enters service in April 1996.

The company also operates catamaran ferries TRIDENT 3 (251t, 1982), TRIDENT 4 (248t, 1981), TRIDENT 5 (251t, 1974), TRIDENT 7 (234t,1979) and PEGASUS (on charter) (249t, 1976) on various routes from France to the Channel Islands. No cars are conveyed.

# EUROLINK FERRIES

**THE COMPANY** *Eurolink Ferries* is a part of the *Mersey Docks and Harbour Company*. Services started in 1994 on a freight only basis, replacing the *Olau Line* service which ceased in May 1994; passenger services were introduced in March 1995 using different vessels.

**MANAGEMENT General Manager:** Laraine Soliman, **Freight Manager:** Nick Kavanagh.

**ADDRESS** Ferry Terminal, Sheerness Dock, SHEERNESS, Kent ME12 1RX.

**TELEPHONE Administration:** +44 (0)1795 581700, **Reservations (Passenger):** +44 (0)1795 581000, **Reservations (Freight):** +44 (0)1795 581600, **Fax:** Admin & Passenger Reservations: +44 (0)1795 581800, Freight Reservations: +44 (0)1795 581818.

**ROUTE OPERATED** Sheerness – Vlissingen (Netherlands) (7 hrs 30 mins (day), 9 hrs 30 mins (night); *(1,2)*; 2 per day).

| 1 | EUROMAGIQUE | 10749t | 77 | 17.5k | 350P | 250C | 80L | A | Lödöse, SW | BA |
| 2 | EUROMANTIQUE | 11591t | 76 | 18.5k | 500P | 250C | 80L | A | Sandefjord, NO | BA |

EUROMAGIQUE Built as the KAPRIFOL, a freight vessel, for the *Johansson Group* of Sweden and chartered out. Early charters included *OT Africa Line* for service between Britain and West Africa and in 1982 she was chartered to the British *Ministry of Defence* to convey supplies to the Falkland Islands. Subsequent charters included *Cobelfret* for service from Belgium and *Trailship* for services from Britain to Spain. In 1988 she was renamed the NAESBORG and in this guise was chartered to *Olau Line* to provide freight backup on the Sheerness – Vlissingen service. In 1990 she was chartered to *DFDS* for North Sea service and renamed the DANA CORONA. The charter ended in the 1991 and she resumed the name NAESBORG before another period on charter to *Cobelfret* which lasted until 1993. In 1994 she was acquired by *AK Ventouris* of Greece and renamed the ATTIKA. They substantially rebuilt her as a freight/passenger vessel. In 1995 chartered to *Eurolink Ferries*, renamed the EUROMAGIQUE and, after further refurbishment, began operation between Sheerness and Vlissingen

EUROMANTIQUE Built as the UNION HOBART for *Union Shipping Australia* freight services between Australia and New Zealand. In 1985 chartered to *Coastal Express Lines* and renamed the SEAWAY HOBART; she was used on services between Australia and Tasmania. In 1993 acquired by *AK Ventouris* of Greece and renamed the SEAWAY I. They substantially rebuilt her as a freight/passenger vessel and, in 1994, renamed her the AGIA METHODIA and introduced her onto the Patras (Greece) – Brindisi (Italy) service. In 1995 chartered to *Eurolink Ferries* and inaugurated the new service (without being renamed). On the arrival of the EUROMAGIQUE she returned to Greece where further work was done to her and she was renamed the EUROMANTIQUE. She then returned and inaugurated two ship working on the service.

Euromantique *(John Hendy)*

# IRISH FERRIES

**THE COMPANY** *Irish Ferries* is the trading name of *Irish Continental Line*, an Irish Republic private sector company, part of the *Irish Continental Group*. It was originally mainly owned by the state owned *Irish Shipping* and partly by *Lion Ferry AB of Sweden*. *Lion Ferry* participation ceased in 1977 and the company was sold into the private sector in 1987. *B&I Line* was taken over in 1991 and from 1995 all operations were marketed as a single entity.

**MANAGEMENT Group Managing Director:** Eamon Rothwell, **Group Marketing Director:** Frank Carey.

**ADDRESS** 2 Merrion Row, DUBLIN 2, Republic of Ireland.

**TELEPHONE Administration:** +353 (0)1 855 2222. **Reservations:** Dublin +353 (0)1 661 0511, Cork +353 (0)21 504333, Rosslare Harbour +353 (0)53 33158, Holyhead +44 (0)1407 760222, Pembroke Dock +44 (0)1646 684161, National: +44 (0)990 171717. **Fax:** Dublin +353 (0)1 661 0743, Cork +353 (0)21 504651. **24 hour information:** +353 (0)1 661 0715.

**ROUTES OPERATED** All year: Dublin – Holyhead (3 hrs 30 mins; *(2)*; 2 per day). Rosslare – Pembroke Dock (4 hrs 15 mins; *(1)*; 2 per day). Rosslare – Cherbourg (17 hrs; *(3,4)*; up to 2 per week), Rosslare – Le Havre (21 hrs; *(3,4)*; up to 3 per week), Summer only: Cork – Le Havre (21 hrs 30 mins; *(3,4)*; 1 per week, Cork – Roscoff (14 hrs; *(3,4)*; 1 per week), Rosslare – Roscoff (14 hrs; *(3,4)*; up to 2 per week).

## CONVENTIONAL FERRIES

| | | | | | | | | | | |
|---|---|---|---|---|---|---|---|---|---|---|
| 1 | ISLE OF INISHMORE | 9700t | 81 | 20k | 1500P | 326C | 39T | BA | Cork, IR | IR |
| 2 | ISLE OF INNISFREE | 22365t | 95 | 21.5k | 1700P | 600C | 142T | BA | Crepelle, NL | IR |
| 3 | SAINT KILLIAN II | 13638t | 73 | 20.5k | 2000P | 380C | 36L | BA | Kraljevica, YU | IR |
| 4 | SAINT PATRICK II | 11481t | 73 | 20.5k | 1630P | 300C | 31L | BA | Hamburg, GE | IR |

ISLE OF INISHMORE Built as the LEINSTER for *B&I Line* for the Dublin – Liverpool service. Between 1982 and 1988 she operated between Dublin and both Liverpool and Holyhead. After 1988 she operated on the Dublin – Holyhead service. In 1993 she was renamed the ISLE OF INISHMORE and transferred to the Rosslare – Pembroke Dock route.

ISLE OF INNISFREE Built for *Irish Ferries* to operate on the Holyhead – Dublin service from June 1995.

SAINT KILLIAN II Built as the STENA SCANDINAVICA for *Stena Line AB* of Sweden for their service from Göteborg to Kiel (with day-time return trips from Kiel to Korsør or Nyborg in Denmark and from Göteborg to Frederikshavn, Denmark). In 1978 she was purchased by *Irish Continental Line* in order to inaugurate a new service between Rosslare and Cherbourg in addition to their Rosslare – Le Havre service. She was renamed the SAINT KILLIAN. In 1980 she was chartered back to *Stena Line* for two months to operate between Göteborg and Kiel and Frederikshavn. After the 1981 summer season a new 32m section was added amidships, raising passenger capacity from 1500 to 2000. On return to service in early 1982 she was renamed the SAINT KILLIAN II. She operates on all routes.

SAINT PATRICK II Built as the AURELLA for *SF Line* of Finland (a member of *Viking Line*) for services between Naantali (Finland), Mariehamn (Åland) and Kapellskär (Sweden). In 1982 she was acquired by *Irish Continental Line*, renamed the SAINT PATRICK II and replaced the SAINT PATRICK (5285t, 1973), which had been transferred to *Belfast Car Ferries* (an associated company which used to operate between Liverpool and Belfast) and renamed the SAINT COLUM I (5284t, 1973). She also substituted for the SAINT COLUM I on the Liverpool – Belfast service. In 1987 she was transferred to *Belfast Car Ferries* but returned to *Irish Ferries* in spring 1988 as it was not possible to find a replacement for her. She is generally not required during the winter (except when the SAINT KILLIAN II is being overhauled) and is usually chartered out. Charterers have included *B&I Line*,

King Orry *(Miles Cowsill)*

Isle of Inishmore *(Miles Cowsill)*

*North Sea Ferries, P&O European Ferries* and *Stena Line*. During winter 1993/94 she was chartered to *Tallink* of Estonia to operate between Helsinki (Finland) and Tallinn (Estonia); she was temporarily re-registered in Estonia but nor renamed. During the first half of 1995 she operated between Dublin and Holyhead, replacing the previous ISLE OF INNISFREE which had been returned to *Stena Line* at the end of her charter in early 1995.

### Under Construction

| 5 | NEWBUILDING | | c33000t | 97 | 21.5k | 2200P | 855C | 122T | BA2 | Crepelle, NL | IR |
|---|---|---|---|---|---|---|---|---|---|---|---|

NEWBUILDING This vessel will replace the ISLE OF INNISFREE on the Dublin – Holyhead service. This vessel will then move to the Rosslare – Pembroke Dock service, replacing the ISLE OF INISHMORE.

# ISLE OF MAN STEAM PACKET COMPANY

**THE COMPANY** The *Isle of Man Steam Packet Company*, is an Isle of Man registered company. A 42.93% share in the company is owned by *Sea Containers*.

**MANAGEMENT Managing Director:** David Dixon, **Passenger Services Manager:** Mark Woodward.

**ADDRESS** PO Box 5, Imperial Buildings, DOUGLAS, Isle of Man, IM99 1AF.

**TELEPHONE Administration:** +44 (0)1624 645645, **Reservations:** +44 (0)1624 661661, **Fax (Admin):** +44 (0)1624 661065, **Fax (Reservations):** +44 (0)1624 645697.

**ROUTES OPERATED** All year: Douglas (Isle of Man) – Heysham (3 hrs 45 mins; *(1)*; up to 2 per day), Douglas – Liverpool (4 hrs 30 mins; *(1,2)*; irregular). Summer only: Douglas – Belfast (4hrs 30mins/4hrs 45 mins; *(1,2)*; irregular, Douglas – Dublin (5hrs; *(1,2)*; irregular), Douglas – Ardrossan (8 hrs; *(CalMac vessel)*; weekly June to mid August)(joint service with *Caledonian MacBrayne*).

### CONVENTIONAL FERRIES

| 1 | KING ORRY | 7555t | 75 | 19.5k | 1100P | 170C | 34T | AS | Genova, IT | IM |
|---|---|---|---|---|---|---|---|---|---|---|
| 2 | LADY OF MANN | 4482t | 76 | 21k | 1000P | 130C | 0L | S | Troon, GB | IM |

KING ORRY Built as the SAINT ELOI for *ALA (Société Anonyme de Navigation Angleterre Lorraine-Alsace)*, a wholly owned subsidiary of *Sealink UK Ltd* registered in France, for the Dover – Dunkerque train ferry service. Although built in 1973 she did not enter service until 1975. She ceased carrying passengers and accompanied cars in September 1985 and replaced on the Dunkerque Ouest – Dover service by the NORD PAS-DE-CALAIS in May 1988. In summer 1988 she resumed passenger service and operated sailings primarily for rail connected foot passengers between Calais and Dover (Western Docks) on charter to *Sealink – SNCF*. In summer 1989 she was renamed the CHANNEL ENTENTE; she operated the same services as 1988 but for *Sealink British Ferries*. In 1990 she was purchased by *IOMSP*, re-registered in the Bahamas and took up service on the Douglas – Heysham service. Following a major refurbishment in the autumn 1990, she was renamed the KING ORRY. She was re-registered in the Isle of Man during 1995.

LADY OF MANN Built for the *IOMSP*. Cars and small vans are side loaded but no RO/RO freight is conveyed. In 1994 replaced by the SEACAT ISLE OF MAN (see the SEACAT NORGE, *ColorSeaCat*) and laid up for sale. She was used in 1995 during the period of the 'TT' motor cycle races between 26 May to 12 June. Later in 1996 she was chartered to *Porto Santo Line* of Madeira for a service to Tenerife. In 1996 she will operate throughout the summer, as the SEACAT ISLE OF MAN will not be chartered.

# NORSE IRISH FERRIES

**THE COMPANY** *Norse Irish Ferries* is a British private sector company. It started as a freight only operation but passenger facilities were established in 1992.

**MANAGEMENT Managing Director:** Phillip Shepherd, **Marketing Manager:** Diane Parry.

**ADDRESS** Belfast: Victoria Terminal 2, West Bank Road, BELFAST BT3 9JN, Liverpool: North Brocklebank Dock, BOOTLE, Merseyside L20 1BY.

**TELEPHONE Administration:** Belfast: +44 (0)1232 779090, Liverpool: +44 (0)151-944 1010, **Reservations (Passenger):** Belfast: +44 (0)1232 779090/779191, Liverpool: +44 (0)151-944 1010, **Fax:** Belfast: +44 (0)1232 775520, Liverpool: +44 (0)151-922 0344.

**ROUTE OPERATED** Liverpool – Belfast (11 hrs; *(1)*; alternate days (other days freight only – see Section 3).

## CONVENTIONAL FERRIES

| 1 | NORSE LAGAN | 22508t | 68 | 18.5k | 200P | 360C | 140T | AS2 | Lauzon, CA | NL |
|---|---|---|---|---|---|---|---|---|---|---|

NORSE LAGAN Built as the FREDERICK CARTER and used on freight services in Canada. In 1986 renamed the FRED and sold to *Anco Ferries* of Greece who renamed her the FLAVIA II. In 1987 chartered to *Olympic Ferries* who renamed her the ATHENIA. In 1988 renamed the THENIA and sold to *Nordö Link* of Sweden who renamed her the HANSA LINK and used her on their service between Malmö and Travemünde. During winter 1989-90 she was lengthened and an extra vehicle deck added. In 1991 chartered to *Norse Irish Ferries*, renamed the NORSE LAGAN and introduced on their Liverpool – Belfast freight service. In 1992 she began carrying cars and passengers.

# NORTH SEA FERRIES

**THE COMPANY** *North Sea Ferries* is a private sector international company jointly owned by *The P&O Group* of Great Britain and *The Royal Nedlloyd Group* of The Netherlands.

**MANAGEMENT Managing Director:** Peter van den Brandhof, **Marketing Managers:** UK: Tony Farrell, Netherlands: Hans van Dijck, Belgium: Christian Berkein.

**ADDRESS** UK: King George Dock, Hedon Road, HULL HU9 5QA, Netherlands: Beneluxhaven, Rotterdam (Europoort), Postbus 1123, 3180 Rozenburg ZH, Netherlands, Belgium: Leopold II Dam 13, Havendam, B-8380, Zeebrugge, Belgium.

**TELEPHONE Administration:** UK: +44 (0)1482 795141, Netherlands: +31 (0)181 255500, Belgium: +32 (0)50 54 34 11. **Reservations:** UK: +44 (0)1482 77177, Netherlands: +31 (0)181 255555, Belgium: +32 (0)50 54 34 30. **Fax:** UK: +44 (0)1482 706438, Netherlands: +31 (0)181 355215, Belgium: +32 (0)50 54 71 12.

**ROUTES OPERATED** Hull – Rotterdam (Europoort) (14 hrs; *(2,4)*; 1 per day), Hull – Zeebrugge (14 hrs; *(1,3)*; 1 per day).

## CONVENTIONAL FERRIES

| 1 | NORLAND | 26290t | 74 | 18.5k | 881P | 500C | 134T | A | Bremerhaven, GE | GB |
|---|---|---|---|---|---|---|---|---|---|---|
| 2 | NORSEA | 31785t | 87 | 18.5k | 1250P | 850C | 180T | A | Glasgow, GB | GB |
| 3 | NORSTAR | 26919t | 74 | 18.5k | 881P | 500C | 134T | A | Bremerhaven, GE | NL |
| 4 | NORSUN | 31598t | 87 | 18.5k | 1250P | 850C | 180T | A | Tsurumi, JA | NL |

NORLAND Built for the Hull – Rotterdam service. She is owned by *P&O*. In April 1982 she was requisitioned for the Falkland Islands Task Force by the Ministry of Defence. She took part in the invasion of the Islands, disembarking troops and equipment at San Carlos. After the cessation of hostilities she made trips to Argentina and Uruguay and was then employed on a shuttle service between Port Stanley and Ascension. She returned to Hull on 1st February 1983 and re-entered service on the Rotterdam service on 19th April. In 1987 she was 'stretched' and refurbished to a similar standard to the NORSEA. She replaced the NORWAVE (3450t, 1965) on the Hull – Zeebrugge service.

NORSEA, NORSUN Built for the Hull – Rotterdam service. The NORSEA is owned by *P&O* and the NORSUN is owned by *Nedlloyd*.

NORSTAR Built for *North Sea Ferries* for the Hull – Rotterdam service. She is owned by *Nedlloyd*. In 1987 she was 'stretched' and replaced the NORWIND (3692t, 1966) on the Hull – Zeebrugge service.

# OOSTENDE LINES

**THE COMPANY** *Oostende Lines* is the trading name of *RMT (Regie voor Maritiem Transport – Maritime Transport Authority (RTM – Regie des Transports Maritimes in French))*, an agency of the Belgian Government. Until 1985 operations were part of the *Sealink* pool but from January 1986 services were operated as part of the *Townsend Thoresen* network and the ships received *Townsend Thoresen* orange hulls and 'TOWNSEND THORESEN' lettering. With the change to *P&O European Ferries* there was a reversion to plain hulls (albeit blue rather than the previous black) but services continued to be marketed in the UK by *P&O*. The trading name of *Dover – Ostend Line (Oostende – Dover Line* in Belgium), together with new livery and logo, was adopted in 1991. In 1994 services were transferred to Ramsgate in conjunction with *Sally Ferries* and the trading name changed to *Oostende Lines*.

**MANAGEMENT Managing Director:** Eric Depraetere, **Commercial Director:** Francis Engelen, **Technical Director:** Roland Beyen.

**ADDRESS** Natienkaai 5, 8400 Oostende, Belgium.

**TELEPHONE Administration:** +32 (0)59 55 91 11, **Reservations:** Belgium: +32 (0)59 55 99 55, **Fax:** Admin: +32 (0)59 80 86 56, Reservations: +32 (0)59 80 94 17, U.K: See *Sally Ferries*.

**ROUTE OPERATED** Oostende – Ramsgate (4 hrs – 4 hrs, 45 mins; *(2,3,4)*; 6 per day).

**CONVENTIONAL FERRIES**

| 1 | PRINCESSE MARIE-CHRISTINE | 6276t | 76 | 22k | 1200P | 354C | 68T | BA2 | Hoboken, BE | BE |
|---|---|---|---|---|---|---|---|---|---|---|
| 2 | PRINS ALBERT | 6612t | 78 | 22k | 1200P | 354C | 68T | BA2 | Hoboken, BE | BE |
| 3 | PRINS FILIP | 28838t | 91 | 21k | 1350P | 710C | 145T | BAS | Temse, BE | BE |
| 4 | REINE ASTRID | 11717t | 75 | 17k | 1000P | 450C | 66T | BA2 | Bremerhaven, GE | BE |

PRINCESSE MARIE-CHRISTINE Built for the Oostende – Dover service. During 1985 she had an extra vehicle deck added, increasing vehicle capacity. Passenger capacity was increased by 200 by the conversion of an upper deck 'garage' into passenger accommodation. Operated during the early part of 1994 whilst additional dredging took place to enable the PRINS FILIP to use the port. Later in 1994 chartered to *Sally Ferries* to replace the SALLY STAR, following a fire on that vessel. Now a spare and relief vessel.

PRINS ALBERT Built for the Oostende – Dover service. During 1986 she had an additional vehicle deck added.

PRINS FILIP Built for the Oostende – Dover service. Although completed in 1991, she did not enter service until May 1992.

REINE ASTRID Built as the STENA NORDICA for *Stena Line AB* of Sweden, one of four similar vessels built for chartering. In 1978 she was chartered to *Soutos Hellas* of Greece, renamed the HELLAS and used on services between Volas (Greece) and Latakia (Syria). In 1979 she resumed her original

# We now OFFER the LUXURY of lower prices from HULL.

The most convenient port for Cruising to the continent, by far is Hull.

Cruise?

With the most luxurious cruiseferries sailing daily to Rotterdam (ideal for Holland and Germany) and Zeebrugge (just 35 miles from the French border we offer you so much more.

It's not surprising that for two consecutive years, readers of The Observer have voted us "Best Ferry Company."

### LUXURY AT
### NEW LOWER PRICES.

With many fares lower in 1996, cruising from Hull is a luxury you really can afford.

See your travel agent or call 01482 707770 for more information on *The Overnight Sensation.*

**NORTH SEA FERRIES**

## A CRUISE FOR THE PRICE OF A FERRY

name for a short time but later in the year she returned to *Soutos Hellas* and was again named the HELLAS. In 1980 she resumed the name STENA NORDICA again. Subsequent charters included *B&I Line* for the Rosslare – Pembroke Dock service, *CN Marine* for the service between North Sydney (Nova Scotia) and Port-aux-Basques (Newfoundland) and *Sealink* UK for the Fishguard – Rosslare service. After her return from Canada in 1981 she underwent a refit in the Clyde and then went for a further period of charter with *Soutos Hellas*. On return in 1982, she was renamed the STENA NAUTICA (taking the name of her sister vessel which had been sold to *CN Marine* of Canada and renamed the MARINE NAUTICA) and, after another brief period on charter to *CN Marine*, chartered to *RMT*. Ownership was transferred to a *Stena Line* subsidiary in Belgium called *Nautica (Belgium) NV* and registry was transferred to Belgium. In March 1983 she was purchased by *RMT* and renamed the REINE ASTRID. She is slower than other vessels and, when operating from Dover, was only used on Eastern Docks services.

*Oostende Lines* also operate two Boeing Jetfoils of 289t, built in Seattle, USA in 1981 and carrying 280 passengers at 42k between Oostende and Ramsgate. They are named the PRINCESSE CLEMENTINE and PRINSES STEPHANIE. No cars are conveyed.

# P&O EUROPEAN FERRIES

**THE COMPANY** *P&O European Ferries* Ltd is the trading name of *P&O European Ferries* (Dover), *P&O European Ferries* (Portsmouth) and *P&O European Ferries* (Felixstowe), British private sector companies, part of the *P&O Group*. These companies were, until 1987, respectively: *Townsend Car Ferries*, *Thoresen Car Ferries* and *Atlantic Steam Navigation*, all part of *European Ferries* and trading as *Townsend Thoresen*. *European Ferries* was taken over by the *P&O Group* in January 1987 and the trading name was changed in October 1987.

**MANAGEMENT Chairman:** Graeme Dunlop, **Managing Director:** Russ Peters, **Passenger Marketing & Sales Director:** Peter Stratton.

**ADDRESS** Channel House, Channel View Road, DOVER, Kent CT17 9TJ.

**TELEPHONE Administration:** +44 (0)1304 223000 **Reservations:** 44 (0)990 980111, +44 (0)1304 203388 (Portsmouth – Bilbao service: +44 (0)1304 240077), **Fax:** +44 (0)1304 223457, **Telex:** 965104.

**ROUTES OPERATED** Cairnryan – Larne (2 hrs 15 mins; *(1,12)*; up to 6 per day), Portsmouth – Cherbourg (5 hrs (day), 7 hrs – 8 hrs 15 mins (night); *(2,6,8 (2 once weekly))*; 2 day crossings, one night crossing per day), Portsmouth – Le Havre (5hrs 30 mins (day), 7 hrs 30 mins – 8 hrs (night); *(10,11)*; 2 day crossings, one night crossing per day), Portsmouth – Bilbao (Santurzi) (35 hrs (UK-Spain), 30 hrs (Spain-UK); *(2)*; 2 per week), Dover – Calais (1 hr 15 mins; *(3,4,5,7,9)*; up 25 per day).

## CONVENTIONAL FERRIES

| | | | | | | | | | | |
|---|---|---|---|---|---|---|---|---|---|---|
| 1 | PRIDE OF AILSA | 12503t | 72 | 19.3k | 1041P | 340C | 60L | BA2 | Schiedam, NL | GB |
| 2 | PRIDE OF BILBAO | 37583t | 86 | 22k | 2500P | 600C | 90T | BA | Turku, FI | BA |
| 3 | PRIDE OF BRUGES | 13601t | 80 | 23k | 1326P | 330C | 48L | BA2 | Bremerhaven, GE | GB |
| 4 | PRIDE OF BURGUNDY | 28138t | 93 | 21k | 1420P | 600C | 148T | BA2 | Bremerhaven, GE | GB |
| 5 | PRIDE OF CALAIS | 26433t | 87 | 22k | 2290P | 650C | 100L | BA2 | Bremen-Vegesack, GE | GB |
| 6 | PRIDE OF CHERBOURG | 14760t | 75 | 18k | 1200P | 380C | 53L | BA2 | Aalborg, DK | GB |
| 7 | PRIDE OF DOVER | 26433t | 87 | 22k | 2290P | 650C | 100L | BA2 | Bremen-Vegesack, GE | GB |
| 8 | PRIDE OF HAMPSHIRE | 14760t | 75 | 18k | 1200P | 380C | 53L | BA2 | Aalborg, DK | GB |
| 9 | PRIDE OF KENT | 20446t | 80 | 21k | 1825P | 460C | 64L | BA2 | Bremerhaven, GE | GB |
| 10 | PRIDE OF LE HAVRE | 33336t | 89 | 21k | 1600P | 575C | 118T | BA | Bremerhaven, GE | GE |
| 11 | PRIDE OF PORTSMOUTH | 33336t | 89 | 21k | 1600P | 575C | 118T | BA | Bremerhaven, GE | GE |
| 12 | PRIDE OF RATHLIN | 12503t | 73 | 19.3k | 1035P | 340C | 60L | BA2 | Schiedam, NL | GB |

PRIDE OF AILSA Built as the FREE ENTERPRISE VI for Dover – Calais and Dover – Zeebrugge services. After 1980 she was generally used on the Dover – Zeebrugge service. In 1985/86 she was 'stretched' in Bremerhaven, Germany, through the placing of the existing superstructure and rear part of hull on a new front part of hull. She was renamed the PRIDE OF SANDWICH in 1988. In 1992 she was transferred to the Cairnryan – Larne route and renamed the PRIDE OF AILSA.

PRIDE OF BILBAO Built as the OLYMPIA for *Rederi AB Slite* of Sweden for *Viking Line* service between Stockholm and Helsinki. In 1993 she was chartered to *P&O European Ferries* to inaugurate a new service between Portsmouth and Bilbao. During the summer period she also operates, at weekends, a round trip between Portsmouth and Cherbourg. In 1993 she was purchased by the *Irish Continental Group* and re-registered in the Bahamas. However, she is expected to remain on charter to *P&O European Ferries* until 2003 at least.

PRIDE OF BRUGES Built as the PRIDE OF FREE ENTERPRISE for the Dover – Calais service, also operating on the Dover – Zeebrugge service during the winter. She was renamed the PRIDE OF BRUGES in 1988 and, following the delivery of the new PRIDE OF CALAIS, she was transferred all year to the Dover – Zeebrugge service. In 1992 she returned to the Dover – Calais route.

PRIDE OF BURGUNDY Built for the Dover – Calais service. When construction started she was due to be a sister vessel to the EUROPEAN CLEARWAY, EUROPEAN HIGHWAY and EUROPEAN PATHWAY (see Section 4) called the EUROPEAN CAUSEWAY and operate on the Zeebrugge freight route. However, it was decided that should be completed as a passenger/freight vessel (the design allowed for conversion) and she was launched as the PRIDE OF BURGUNDY.

PRIDE OF CALAIS Built for the Dover – Calais service.

PRIDE OF CHERBOURG Built as the VIKING VALIANT. Details otherwise as the PRIDE OF HAMPSHIRE. In 1989 she was renamed the PRIDE OF LE HAVRE. In 1994 transferred to the Portsmouth – Cherbourg service and renamed the PRIDE OF CHERBOURG.

PRIDE OF DOVER Built for the Dover – Calais service.

PRIDE OF HAMPSHIRE Built as the VIKING VENTURER for Southampton (from 1976 Southampton/Portsmouth and 1984 Portsmouth only) – Cherbourg/Le Havre services. Extensively rebuilt in Bremerhaven in 1986 to increase vehicle capacity in a similar way to the PRIDE OF AILSA and generally operated Portsmouth – Le Havre only. She was renamed the PRIDE OF HAMPSHIRE in 1989. In 1995 she was transferred to the Portsmouth – Cherbourg service.

PRIDE OF LE HAVRE Built as the OLAU HOLLANDIA for *Olau Line* of Germany, operating between Sheerness (Great Britain) and Vlissingen (Netherlands). In May 1994 the service ceased and she was chartered from her owners *TT Line* of Germany to *P&O European Ferries*, re-registered in Great Britain and renamed the PRIDE OF LE HAVRE. After a brief period on the Portsmouth – Cherbourg service she became a regular vessel on the Portsmouth – Le Havre service.

PRIDE OF KENT Built as the SPIRIT OF FREE ENTERPRISE for the Dover – Calais service, also operating on the Dover – Zeebrugge service during the winter. She was renamed the PRIDE OF KENT in 1987. Sister vessel of the PRIDE OF BRUGES. During winter 1991/92 she was 'stretched' in Palermo, Italy to give her similar capacity to the PRIDE OF CALAIS and the PRIDE OF DOVER. Now operates Dover – Calais only.

PRIDE OF PORTSMOUTH Built as the OLAU BRITANNIA for *Olau Line*. In 1994 she was chartered from her owners *TT Line* of Germany to *P&O European Ferries* and renamed the PRIDE OF PORTSMOUTH. After a brief period on the Portsmouth – Cherbourg service she became a regular vessel on the Portsmouth-Le Havre service from June 1994.

PRIDE OF RATHLIN Built as the FREE ENTERPRISE VII for Dover – Calais and Dover – Zeebrugge services. After the delivery of new vessels in 1980 she was generally used on the Dover – Zeebrugge

service. 'Stretched' in Bremerhaven in 1985/6 in a similar way to the PRIDE OF AILSA. She was renamed the PRIDE OF WALMER in 1988. In summer 1992 she was transferred to the Cairnryan – Larne route and renamed the PRIDE OF RATHLIN.

# SALLY FERRIES

**THE COMPANY** *Sally Ferries* is the trading name of *Sally Line Limited*, a British subsidiary of *Silja Oy Ab*, a Finnish/Swedish company. Until 1987 *Sally Line Limited* was owned by *Rederi AB Sally* of Finland. This company was named 'Sally' by its founder Algot Johansson after Åland Islands writer Sally Salminen; it became part of the *Effjohn* group (from 1/9/95 *Silja Oy Ab*) in 1987.

**MANAGEMENT Group Chief Executive:** Bill Moses, **Passenger Director:** Linda McLeod, **Finance Director:** Paul Pascan.

**ADDRESS** Argyle Centre, York Street, RAMSGATE, Kent CT11 9DS.

**TELEPHONE Administration:** +44 (0)1843 595566. **Reservations:** +44 (0)1843 595522. **Fax:** +44 (0)1843 589329. **Telex:** 965979.

**ROUTE OPERATED** Ramsgate – Dunkerque Ouest (2 hrs 30 mins; *(1,2)*; 8 per day (includes 1 freight only sailing using passenger vessels)).

**CONVENTIONAL FERRIES**

| 1 | SALLY SKY | 14458t | 76 | 17.5k | 1150P | 323C | 58L | BA2 | Bremerhaven, GE | BA |
| 2 | SALLY STAR | 16829t | 81 | 19k | 1800P | 550C | 71L | BA2 | Helsinki, FI | BA |

SALLY SKY Built as the GEDSER for *Gedser-Travemünde Ruten* of Denmark for their service between Gedser (Denmark) and Travemünde (Germany). In 1986 she was purchased by *Thorsviks Rederi A/S* of Norway and chartered to *Sally Ferries*, re-registered in the Bahamas, renamed the VIKING 2 and entered service on the Ramsgate – Dunkerque service. In early 1989 she was renamed the SALLY SKY and during winter 1989/90 she was 'stretched' to increase vehicle capacity.

SALLY STAR Built as the TRAVEMÜNDE for *Gedser-Travemünde Ruten* of Denmark for their service between Gedser (Denmark) and Travemünde (Germany). In 1986 the company's trading name was changed to *GT Linien* and in 1987, following the take-over by *Sea-Link AB* of Sweden, it was further changed to *GT Link*. The vessel's name was changed to the TRAVEMÜNDE LINK. In 1988 she was purchased by *Gotlandsbolaget* of Sweden, although remaining in service with *GT Link*. Later in 1988 she was chartered to *Sally Ferries* and entered service in December on the Ramsgate – Dunkerque service. She was renamed the SALLY STAR.

# SCANDINAVIAN SEAWAYS

**THE COMPANY** *Scandinavian Seaways Ltd* is the passenger division of the *DFDS Group*, a Danish private sector company which operates in the UK through its subsidiary company *DFDS plc*. In 1981 *Tor Line* of Sweden and *Prinzen Linie* of Germany were taken over.

**MANAGEMENT Managing Director (DFDS plc):** Ebbe Pedersen, **Managing Director (Scandinavian Seaways Ltd):** John Crummie.

**ADDRESS** Scandinavia House, Parkeston Quay, HARWICH, Essex CO12 4QG.

**TELEPHONE Administration:** +44 (0)1255 243456, **Reservations:** Harwich: +44 (0)1255 240240, Newcastle: +44 (0)191-293 6262. **Fax:** . 0255 244370, **Telex:** 987542.

**ROUTES OPERATED** (All North Sea services). All year: Harwich – Esbjerg (19 hrs 45 mins; *(1)*; 3 per week or alternate days), Harwich – Göteborg (24 hrs; *(5)*; 2 per week), Harwich – Hamburg (20 hrs 30 mins; *(2)*; alternate days). Summer only: Newcastle – Hamburg (23 hrs 30 mins; *(3)*; every 4 days), Newcastle – Göteborg (21 hrs; *(5)*; 1 per week), Newcastle – Ijmuiden (Amsterdam) (15 hrs; *(3)*; every 4 days).

*Pride of Le Havre (FotoFlite)*

*Hamburg (Miles Cowsill)*

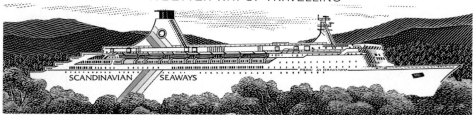
## CONVENTIONAL FERRIES

| | | | | | | | | | | | |
|---|---|---|---|---|---|---|---|---|---|---|---|
| 1 | DANA ANGLIA | | 19321t | 78 | 21k | 1372P | 470C | 45L | BA | Aalborg, DK | DK |
| 2 | HAMBURG | | 18888t | 76 | 21k | 1132P | 400C | 45L | BA | Rendsburg, GE | BA |
| 3 | KING OF SCANDINAVIA | | 13336t | 74 | 22.5k | 1100P | 300C | 38L | BA | Turku, FI | DK |
| 4 | PRINCE OF SCANDINAVIA | | 21545t | 75 | 23k | 1692 | 385 | 70T | AS | Lübeck, GE | DK |
| 5 | PRINCESS OF SCANDINAVIA | | 21545t | 76 | 23k | 1704 | 385 | 70T | AS | Lübeck, GE | DK |

DANA ANGLIA Built for the Harwich – Esbjerg service.

HAMBURG Built as the KRONPRINS HARALD for *Jahre Line* of Norway and used on their service between Oslo and Kiel (Germany). Acquired by *DFDS* in 1987, renamed the HAMBURG, re-registered in the Bahamas and replaced the PRINS HAMLET (5830t, 1973) on the Harwich – Hamburg service.

KING OF SCANDINAVIA Built as the PRINSESSAN BIRGITTA for *Göteborg – Frederikshavnlinjen* and *Ragne Rederi AB* of Sweden (trading as *Sessan Line*) for their alternate day Göteborg – Travemünde service. The company was taken over by rival *Stena Line AB* in 1981 and later that year she was transferred to their Göteborg – Kiel route, the Travemünde route becoming freight only. In 1982 a new PRINSESSAN BIRGITTA was delivered (see the STENA NORMANDY, *Stena Line*) and she was renamed the STENA SCANDINAVICA. She remained on the Göteborg – Kiel route until 1987 when she was replaced by the new STENA GERMANICA. During summer 1987 she was chartered to *Cotunav*, the Tunisian state shipping concern, and used on their service between Tunis and Marseilles (France) and Genova (Italy). In early 1988 a new STENA SCANDINAVICA was delivered and she was further renamed the SCANDINAVICA. In June 1988 she was taken on four months charter by *Sealink British Ferries* and used on additional sailings between Dover (Eastern Docks) and Calais (passenger and freight services) and Zeebrugge (freight only services). In 1989, after further charter to *Cotunav*, being renamed the TARAK L, she was sold to *Norway Line*. In 1990 she was renamed the VENUS, re-registered in Norway and took over the Bergen/Stavanger – Newcastle service from the JUPITER (9499t, 1966). In 1994 she was sold to *DFDS*, renamed the KING OF SCANDINAVIA and, in 1995, replaced the WINSTON CHURCHILL on the Newcastle – Esbjerg/Hamburg services. In 1996 she will operate alternate sailings from Newcastle to Hamburg and Ijmuiden.

PRINCE OF SCANDINAVIA Built as the TOR BRITANNIA for *Tor Line* of Sweden for their Amsterdam – Göteborg and Felixstowe – Göteborg services. She was acquired by *DFDS* in 1981 and subsequently re-registered in Denmark. Since winter 1983/4 she also operated on the Harwich – Esbjerg service with the DANA ANGLIA. She has also operated Newcastle – Esbjerg and Amsterdam – Göteborg. During winter 1989/90 she was used as an accommodation ship for refugees in Malmö. In 1991 renamed the PRINCE OF SCANDINAVIA following a major refurbishment. In summer 1994 and 1995 she operated on the Ijmuiden (Netherlands) – Göteborg (Sweden) and Ijmuiden – Kristiansand (Norway) service and did not serve the UK. In 1996 she was chartered to *Cotunav* of Tunisia for service between Tunisia and France.

PRINCESS OF SCANDINAVIA Built as the TOR SCANDINAVIA for *Tor Line* of Sweden for their Amsterdam – Göteborg and Felixstowe – Göteborg services. In 1979 she was used on a world trade cruise and was temporarily renamed the HOLLAND EXPO. Similar exercises were undertaken in 1980, 1982 and 1984, but on these occasions the name was the WORLD WIDE EXPO. She was acquired by *DFDS* in 1981 and subsequently re-registered in Denmark. She has also operated on the Harwich – Esbjerg service with the DANA ANGLIA although this arrangement has now ceased. Since summer 1989 she has also operated Newcastle – Esbjerg and Amsterdam – Göteborg services. In 1991 renamed the PRINCESS OF SCANDINAVIA following a major refurbishment. During summer 1994 and 1995 she operated on the Harwich – Göteborg and Newcastle – Göteborg services; this will be repeated in 1996.

# SEA CONTAINERS FERRIES

**THE COMPANY** *Sea Containers Ferries Ltd* is a British private sector company, part of the *Sea Containers Group.*

**MANAGEMENT Vice President Ferries & Ports:** David Benson.

**ADDRESS** 20 Upper Ground, LONDON SE1 9PF.

**TELEPHONE Administration:** +44 (0)171-805 5000, **Fax:** +44 (0)171-805 5900.

Fast ferry services in the UK are operated through two subsidiaries – *Hoverspeed Ltd* and *Sea Containers Ferries Scotland Ltd* (trading as *SeaCat Scotland*).

## HOVERSPEED

**THE COMPANY** *Hoverspeed Ltd* is a British private sector company. It was formed in October 1981 by the merger of *Seaspeed*, a wholly owned subsidiary of the *British Railways Board*, operating between Dover and Calais and Dover and Boulogne and Hoverlloyd, a subsidiary of *Broström AB* of Sweden, operating between Ramsgate (Pegwell Bay) and Calais. The Ramsgate – Calais service ceased after summer 1982. In early 1984 the company was sold by its joint owners to a management consortium. In 1986 the company was acquired by *Sea Containers*. It was retained by *Sea Containers* in 1990 following the sale of most of *Sealink British Ferries* to *Stena Line*. Hovercraft services were supplemented by wave piercing catamarans (SeaCats) in 1991 and during winter 1991/92 no hovercraft services were operated. However, since summer 1992, an all year hovercraft service (excluding winter refits) has run between Dover Hoverport and Calais with the SeaCat operating

*Hoverspeed Great Britain (FotoFlite)*

between Folkestone and Boulogne except for a brief period during the winter when the hovercraft are being overhauled and the SeaCat operates between Dover and Calais.

**MANAGEMENT Managing Director:** Geoffrey Ede, **Marketing Director:** John Smith.

**ADDRESS** International Hoverport, Western Docks, DOVER, Kent CT17 9DG.

**TELEPHONE Administration:** +44 (0)1304 240101, **Reservations:** +44 (0)1304 240241. **Fax: (Admin):** +44 (0)1304 202029, **Fax: (Reservations):** +44 (0)1304 240088.

**ROUTES OPERATED** SeaCat: Folkestone – Boulogne (55 mins; up to 6 per day), Hovercraft: Dover – Calais (35 mins; *(5,6)*; up to 14 per day).

## SEACAT SCOTLAND

**THE COMPANY** *SeaCat Scotland* is the trading name of *Sea Container Ferries Scotland Ltd*, a subsidiary of *Sea Container Ferries Ltd*.

**MANAGEMENT Managing Director:** Hamish Ross, **Route General Manager:** John Burrows.

**ADDRESS** 34 Charlotte Street, STRANRAER DG9 7EF.

**TELEPHONE Administration:** +44 (0)1776 702755, **Reservations:** From UK: 0345 523523, From elsewhere: +44 (0)1232 313543, **Fax:** +44 (0)1776 705894.

**ROUTE OPERATED** Stranraer – Belfast (1 hrs 30 mins; up to 5 per day).

**FAST FERRIES**

**Special Note** In view of the frequent interchange between companies and routes, all SeaCats owned by the *Sea Containers Ferries Ltd* (including those, at the time of going to print, not operating

# When you're crossing the water, you could just follow the herd...

## or you could try a more civilised approach.

on UK routes) and not listed elsewhere in this book have been listed together. The SEACAT DANMARK and SEACAT NORGE are listed in Section 6.

| 1 | HOVERSPEED GREAT BRITAIN | 3003t | 90 | 37k | 600P | 80C | - | BA | Hobart, AL | BA |
|---|---|---|---|---|---|---|---|---|---|---|
| 2 | SEACAT SCOTLAND | 3003t | 91 | 37k | 432P | 80C | - | BA | Hobart, AL | BA |
| 3 | THE PRINCESS ANNE | - | 69 | 60k | 390P | 55C | - | BA | Cowes, GB | GB |
| 4 | THE PRINCESS MARGARET | - | 68 | 60k | 390P | 55C | - | BA | Cowes, GB | GB |

HOVERSPEED GREAT BRITAIN InCat 74m model. Launched as the CHRISTOPHER COLUMBUS but renamed before entering service. During delivery voyage from Australia, won the Blue Riband Trophy for the fastest commercial crossing of the Atlantic. Built for *Hoverspeed* to inaugurate a new car and passenger service between Portsmouth and Cherbourg. This service was suspended in early 1991 and later that year she was, after modification, switched to a new service between Dover (Eastern Docks) and Boulogne/Calais, replacing hovercraft. In 1992 operated on Channel routes. During winter 1992/3 she was chartered to *Ferry Lineas* of Argentina, operating between Buenos Aires (Argentina) and Montevideo (Uruguay). In early 1994 passenger capacity was increased to 600. She now operates mainly between Folkestone and Boulogne.

SEACAT SCOTLAND InCat 74m model, the fifth SeaCat to be built. She was used on the Stranraer – Belfast route. In autumn 1994 chartered to *Q-Ships* of Qatar for services between Doha (Qatar) and Bahrain and Dubai and renamed the Q-SHIP EXPRESS. In spring 1995 returned to the Stranraer – Belfast service and resumed the name SEACAT SCOTLAND.

THE PRINCESS ANNE Hovercraft built for *Seaspeed*. BHC (British Hovercraft Corporation) SRN4 type. Built to Mark I specification. In 1978 stretched to Mark III specification. Underwent complete refurbishment at the beginning of 1995.

THE PRINCESS MARGARET Hovercraft built for *Seaspeed*. BHC SRN4 type. Built to Mark I specification. In 1979 stretched to Mark III specification. Underwent complete refurbishment at the beginning of 1995.

**Under Construction**

| | | | | | | | | | |
|---|---|---|---|---|---|---|---|---|---|
| NEWBUILDING 1 | - | 97 | 37.8k | 800P | 175C | - | A | Genova, IT | - |
| NEWBUILDING 2 | - | 97 | 37.8k | 800P | 175C | - | A | La Spezia, IT | - |
| NEWBUILDING 3 | - | 98 | 37.8k | 800P | 175C | - | A | Genova, IT | - |
| NEWBUILDING 4 | - | 98 | 37.8k | 800P | 175C | - | A | La Spezia, IT | - |
| NEWBUILDING 5 | - | 98 | 37.8k | 800P | 175C | - | A | Genova, IT | - |
| NEWBUILDING 6 | - | 98 | 37.8k | 800P | 175C | - | A | La Spezia, IT | - |

NEWBUILDINGS 1-6 Under construction to replace all *Sea Containers'* InCat vessels by the end of 1998. They are to be monohull vessels and the builders *Fincanteri* of Italy have split the order between their Sestri Levante yard at Genova and their yard at La Spezia.

# SEAFRANCE

**THE COMPANY** SeaFrance SA (previously *SNAT (Société Nouvelle Armement Transmanche)* is a French company. It is jointly owned by *Société National des Chemins de fer Français (French Railways)*, *Compagnie Générale Maritime Français (French National Shipping Company)* and *Stena Line*. SNAT was established in 1990 to take over the services of *SNCF Armement Naval*, a wholly owned division of *SNCF*. At the same time a similarly constituted body called *Société Proprietaire Navires (SPN)* was established to take over ownership of the vessels. Joint operation of services with *Stena Line* ceased at the end of 1995 and *SeaFrance SA* was formed.

**MANAGEMENT Président du Directoire:** M Bonnet, **Managing Director (UK):** Pat Williams.

**ADDRESS France:** 3 rue Ambroise Paré, 75475, PARIS Cedex 10, France, **UK:** Room 106, East Camber Office, Eastern Docks, DOVER, Kent CT16 1JA.

**TELEPHONE Administration:** +33 1 49 95 58 92. **Reservations:** France: +33 21 96 70 70, UK: +44 (0)1304 212696, **Fax:** France: +33 1 48 74 62 37, UK: +44 (0)1304 212726. **Telex:** 280549.

**ROUTE OPERATED** Calais – Dover (1 hr 30 mins; *(1,2,3)*; up to 14 per day).

**CONVENTIONAL FERRIES**

| 1 | SEAFRANCE CEZANNE | 25122t | 80 | 19.5k | 1800P | 600C | 150T | BA2 | Malmö, SW | FR |
|---|---|---|---|---|---|---|---|---|---|---|
| 2 | SEAFRANCE NORD PAS-DE-CALAIS | 13727t | 87 | 21.5k | 80P | - | 114T | BA2 | Dunkerque, FR | FR |
| 3 | SEAFRANCE RENOIR | 15207t | 81 | 18k | 1600P | 330C | 54T | BA2 | Le Havre, FR | FR |
| 4 | STENA LONDONER | 12962t | 74 | 22k | 1800P | 425C | 51L | BA2 | Trogir, YU | BA |

SEAFRANCE CEZANNE Built as the ARIADNE for *Rederi AB Nordö* of Sweden. Renamed SOCA before entering service on *UMEF* freight services (but with capacity for 175 drivers) in the Mediterranean. In 1981 she was sold to *SO Mejdunaroden Automobilen Transport (SOMAT)* of Bulgaria and renamed the TRAPEZITZA. She operated on Medlink services between Bulgaria and the Middle East. In 1988 she was acquired by *Sealink*, re-registered in the Bahamas and in 1989 renamed the FANTASIA. Later in 1989 she was modified in Bremerhaven, renamed the CHANNEL SEAWAY and, in May, she inaugurated a new freight only service between Dover (Eastern Docks) and Calais. During winter 1989/90 she was modified in Bremerhaven to convert her for passenger service. In spring 1990 she was renamed the FIESTA, transferred to *SNAT*, re-registered in France and replaced the CHAMPS ELYSEES (see the STENA PARISIEN, *Stena Line*) on the Dover – Calais service. In 1996 she was renamed the SEAFRANCE CEZANNE.

SEAFRANCE NORD PAS-DE-CALAIS Built for *SNCF* for the Dunkerque Ouest – Dover train ferry service to replace the SAINT ELOI (see the KING ORRY, *Isle of Man Steam Packet Company*) and SAINT-GERMAIN (3492t, 1951). Before being used on the train ferry service (which required the

*Stena Challenger (FotoFlite)*

*SeaFrance Nord Pas de Calais (FotoFlite)*

construction of a new berth at Dover (Western Docks)) in May 1988, she operated road freight services from Calais to Dover Eastern Docks. She continued to operate following the opening of the Channel Tunnel in 1994 to convey road vehicles and dangerous loads which are banned from the tunnel. However, the train ferry service ceased in December 1995 and, after a substantial refit, in February 1996 she was renamed the SEAFRANCE NORD PAS-DE-CALAIS and switched to the Calais – Dover service, primarily for road freight vehicles and drivers but also advertised as carrying up to 50 car passengers.

SEAFRANCE RENOIR Built as the COTE D'AZUR for the Dover – Calais service. Also operated Boulogne – Dover in 1985. In 1996 she was renamed the SEAFRANCE RENOIR.

STENA LONDONER Built as the STENA DANICA for *Stena Line AB* of Sweden for their Göteborg – Frederikshavn service. In 1982, in anticipation of the delivery of a new STENA DANICA, being built in France, she was renamed the STENA NORDICA. In June 1983 she was taken by *RMT* on a three year charter, introduced onto *RMT's* Oostende – Dover service and re-registered in Belgium. In March 1984 she was renamed the STENA NAUTICA. The charter ended in June 1986 when the PRINS ALBERT re-entered service; she returned to *Stena Line* and was re-registered in The Bahamas. In 1987 she was sold to *SNCF*, re-registered in France, renamed the VERSAILLES and introduced onto the Dieppe – Newhaven service. In May 1992 she was chartered to *Stena Sealink Line*, re-registered in The Bahamas, renamed the STENA LONDONER and relaunched the service abandoned by *SNAT* earlier that year. In March 1996 she was returned to *SeaFrance* but will probably be disposed of.

# STENA LINE (NETHERLANDS)

**THE COMPANY** *Stena Line* is the trading name of *Stena Line* bv of The Netherlands, a wholly owned subsidiary of *Stena Line AB* of Sweden. *Stena Line* acquired the previous operator of this route, the Dutch *Stoomvaart Maatschappij Zeeland (Zeeland Steamship Company)* (which had since the start of 1989 traded as *Crown Line*) in summer 1989. Joint operation of the route with *Sealink* ceased in 1990, although *Stena Line Ltd* continue to market the service in the UK and Irish Republic.

**MANAGEMENT Managing Director:** Jan Heppener, **Marketing and Sales Director:** Harry Betist.

**ADDRESS** PO Box 2, 3150 AA, Hoek van Holland.

**TELEPHONE Administration:** +31 (0)1747 89333. **Reservations:** +31 (0)1747 84140, **Fax:** +31 (0)1747 87047. **Telex:** 31272.

**ROUTE OPERATED** Hoek van Holland (Netherlands) – Harwich (6 hrs 30 mins (day), 8 hrs 30 mins (night); *(1,2)*; 2 per day).

**CONVENTIONAL FERRIES**

| 1 | KONINGIN BEATRIX | 31189t | 86 | 21k | 2100P | 200C | 96L | BA | Krimpen, NL | NL |
|---|------------------|--------|----|-----|-------|------|-----|-----|-------------|-----|
| 2 | STENA EUROPE | 24828t | 81 | 20.4k | 2076P | 500C | 78T | BA2 | Göteborg, SW | SW |

KONINGIN BEATRIX Built for *Stoomvaart Maatschappij Zeeland* for the Hoek van Holland – Harwich service.

STENA EUROPE Built as the KRONPRINSESSAN VICTORIA for *Göteborg – Frederikshavnlinjen* of Sweden (trading as *Sessan Line*) for their Göteborg – Frederikshavn service. Shortly after delivery, the company was taken over by *Stena Line* and services were marketed as *Stena – Sessan Line* for a period. In 1982 she was converted to an overnight ferry by the conversion of one vehicle deck to two additional decks of cabins and she was switched to the Göteborg – Kiel route (with, during the summer, daytime runs from Göteborg to Frederikshavn and Kiel to Korsør (Denmark)). In 1989 she was transferred to the Oslo – Frederikshavn route and renamed the STENA SAGA. In 1994, transferred to *Stena Line bv* and renamed the STENA EUROPE. She replaced the STENA

BRITANNICA, which had been transferred to *Stena Line AB* to operate between Oslo and Frederikshavn and renamed the STENA SAGA (see Section 5).

**Under Construction**

| | | | | | | | | | | |
|---|---|---|---|---|---|---|---|---|---|---|
| 3 | STENA HSS3 | - | 97 | 40k | 1500P | 375C | 50L | BA | Rauma, FI | - |

STENA HSS3 Under construction to replace both the KONINGIN BEATRIX and the STENA EUROPE on the Hoek van Holland – Harwich service.

# STENA LINE (UK)

**THE COMPANY** *Stena Line* is the trading name of *Stena Line Ltd*, a British private sector company. It was purchased (as *Sealink UK Ltd*) from the state owned *British Railways Board* in summer 1984 by *British Ferries Ltd*, a wholly owned subsidiary of *Sea Containers of Bermuda*. In 1990 most services and vessels were purchased from *Sea Containers* by *Stena Line AB* of Sweden – although the Isle of Wight vessels and services were excluded. In late 1990 the trading name was changed to *Sealink Stena Line*, in 1993 changed to *Stena Sealink Line* and in 1996 to *Stena Line*. *Stena Line* is named after its founder, Sten A Olsson.

**MANAGEMENT Managing Director:** W Gareth Cooper, **Marketing Director:** John Govett.

**ADDRESS** Charter House, Park Street, ASHFORD, Kent TN24 8EX.

**TELEPHONE Administration:** +44 (0)1233 647022, **Reservations:** +44 (0)1233 647047, +44 (0)990 707070.

**ROUTES OPERATED** *Conventional Ferries:* Stranraer – Belfast (3 hrs; *(2,3,9)*; 8 per day until 31 May, 4 per day from 1 June), Holyhead – Dun Laoghaire (3hrs 30 mins; *(1 or 4)*; 2 per day); Fishguard – Rosslare (3 hrs 30 mins; *(8)*; 2 per day), Newhaven – Dieppe (4 hrs; *(12)*; 2 per day), Southampton – Cherbourg (5 hrs; *(11)*; 1 or 2 per day), Dover – Calais (1 hr 30 mins; *(1 or 4,5,6,7,10)*; up to 20 per day).

*Fast Ferries:* Stranraer – Belfast (1 hrs 30 mins; *(14)*; 5 per day (from 1 June)), Holyhead – Dun Laoghaire (1 hr 39 mins; *(13)*; up to 5 per day), Fishguard – Rosslare (1 hr 39 mins; *(15)*; up to 5 per day), Dover – Calais (45 mins; *(16,17)*; up to 7 per day); Newhaven – Dieppe (2 hrs 15 mins; *(18)*; up to 4 per day).

**CONVENTIONAL FERRIES**

| 1 | STENA ADVENTURER | 11690t | 77 | 19.5k | 1700P | 310C | 28T | BA | Aalborg, DK | GB |
|---|---|---|---|---|---|---|---|---|---|---|
| 2 | STENA ANTRIM | 12711t | 81 | 19.5k | 1350P | 310C | 62T | BA2 | Belfast, GB | GB |
| 3 | STENA CALEDONIA | 12619t | 81 | 19.5k | 1000P | 310C | 62T | BA2 | Belfast, GB | GB |
| 4 | STENA CAMBRIA | 12705t | 80 | 19.5k | 1350P | 310C | 62T | BA2 | Belfast, GB | GB |
| 5 | STENA CHALLENGER | 18523t | 90 | 18k | 500P | - | 100L | BA2 | Fevag, NO | GB |
| 6 | STENA EMPEREUR | 28727t | 83 | 20k | 2300P | 630C | 136T | BA2 | Dunkerque, FR | SW |
| 7 | STENA FANTASIA | 25122t | 80 | 19.5k | 1800P | 600C | 150T | BA2 | Malmö, SW | BA |
| 8 | STENA FELICITY | 23775t | 80 | 21k | 1800P | 515C | 45L | BAS | Landskrona, SW | SW |
| 9 | STENA GALLOWAY | 12175t | 80 | 19.0k | 1000P | 296C | 62T | BA2 | Belfast, GB | GB |
| 10 | STENA INVICTA | 19763t | 85 | 19.3k | 2000P | 400C | 50T | BA2 | Nakskov, DK | GB |
| 11 | STENA NORMANDY | 24872t | 82 | 20.4k | 2100P | 480C | 52L | BA2 | Göteborg, SW | BA |
| 12 | STENA PARISIEN | 15093t | 84 | 18k | 1800P | 330C | 54T | BA2 | Nantes, FR | FR |

STENA ADVENTURER Built as the ST COLUMBA for the Holyhead – Dun Laoghaire service to replace separate classic and car ferry services with a single multi-purpose vessel, performing two round trips per day. She has also been used on the Fishguard – Rosslare service. During winter 1982/3 she was modified to change her from a two-class to a single class vessel. She was further extensively rebuilt over winter 1990/91 and was renamed the STENA HIBERNIA. In 1996 she was renamed the

# Less haste, more speed

Next time you're off to France, there's no need to rush: for 1996 Stena Line has up to 27 sailings a day, so you're sure to find a convenient departure.

But, if speed is important to you, board Stena Line's fast ferry service which takes you from Dover to Calais in just 45 minutes.

So for the best in travel - and a wide range of duty-free shopping and on board entertainment - the choice is yours. Less haste AND more speed, from Stena Line on

*Holiday and ferry bookings, call*
## *0990 70 70 70*
*or see your travel agent or motoring organisation*

*The world's leading ferry company*

STENA ADVENTURER. Her deployment after the HSS service starts is currently uncertain. She may remain on this route or she may be moved to the Dover – Calais route, being replaced by the STENA CAMBRIA. This will depend on the level and mix of advance bookings.

STENA ANTRIM Built as the ST CHRISTOPHER for the Dover – Calais service. Before taking up duty on that route she substituted on the Fishguard – Rosslare service. Subsequent refits have increased passenger capacity and improved passenger facilities. In 1991 she was renamed the STENA ANTRIM and later transferred to the Stranraer – Larne (now Belfast) route. The deployment of this vessel in summer 1996 is currently uncertain.

STENA CALEDONIA Built as the ST DAVID for the Holyhead – Dun Laoghaire and Fishguard – Rosslare services. It was originally planned that she would replace the chartered STENA NORMANDICA (5607t, 1975 – the vessel which subsequently became the ST BRENDAN) but it was subsequently decided that an additional large vessel (which could deputise for the ST COLUMBA and the STENA NORMANDICA) was required for the Irish Sea routes. Until 1985 her normal use was, therefore, to substitute for other Irish Sea vessels as necessary (including the Stranraer – Larne route) and also to operate additional summer services on the Holyhead – Dun Laoghaire route. During the spring of 1983 she operated on the Dover – Calais service while the ST CHRISTOPHER (now the STENA ANTRIM) was being modified. From March 1985 she operated between Dover and Oostende, a service which ceased in December 1985 with the decision of *RMT* to link up with *Townsend Thoresen*. During the early part of 1986 she operated between Dover and Calais and then moved to the Stranraer – Larne route where she has become a regular vessel. In 1990 she was renamed the STENA CALEDONIA. She will continue to operate on this route, at least in the short term.

STENA CAMBRIA Built as the ST ANSELM for the Dover – Calais service. During winter 1982/3 she was modified to increase passenger capacity from 1200 to 1400 and improve passenger facilities. In February 1990 she replaced the HORSA (5496t, 1972) on the Folkestone – Boulogne service. In 1991 she was renamed the STENA CAMBRIA and was moved to the Irish Sea to operate between Holyhead and Dun Laoghaire. In winter 1996 she was moved to the Dover – Calais route. Her deployment in spring/summer 1996, before the arrival of the STENA EMPEREUR in June is uncertain. She may remain at Dover; alternately she may return to the Holyhead – Dun Laoghaire route and be replaced by the STENA ADVENTURER. This will depend on the level and mix of advance bookings.

STENA CHALLENGER Built for *Stena Rederi AB* of Sweden and chartered to *Stena Sealink Line* for Dover – Calais and Dover – Dunkerque freight services. Her hull was constructed and launched in Landskrona, Sweden and towed to Norway for fitting out. In 1992 she was switched to the Dover – Dunkerque freight services, operating with the NORD PAS-DE-CALAIS. From summer 1994 she has operated passenger services between Dover and Calais.

STENA EMPEREUR Built as the STENA JUTLANDICA for *Stena Line* for the Göteborg – Frederikshavn service. In 1996 to be transferred to the Dover-Calais route and renamed the STENA EMPEREUR.

STENA FANTASIA Built as the SCANDINAVIA for *Rederi AB Nordö* of Sweden. After service in the Mediterranean for UMEF, she was, in 1981, sold to SOMAT of Bulgaria, renamed the TZAREVETZ and used on *Medlink* services between Bulgaria and the Middle East and later on other routes. In 1986 she was chartered to *Callitzis* of Greece for a service between Italy and Greece. In 1988 she was sold to *Sealink*, re-registered in the Bahamas and renamed the FIESTA. She was then chartered to *OT Africa Line*. During autumn 1989 she was modified in Bremerhaven to convert her for passenger use and in March 1990 she was renamed the FANTASIA and placed her on the Dover – Calais service. Later in 1990 she was renamed the STENA FANTASIA.

STENA FELICITY Built as the VISBY for *Gotlandsbolaget* of Sweden for their services between the island of Gotland and the Swedish mainland. In 1987, the franchise to operate these services was lost by the company and awarded to *Nordström & Thulin* of Sweden. A subsidiary called *Gotlandslinjen* was formed to operate the service. The VISBY was chartered to this company and managed by *Johnson Line*, remaining owned by *Gotlandsbolaget*. In early 1990 she was chartered to *Sealink* and renamed the FELICITY. After modifications at Tilbury, she was, in March 1990, introduced onto the Fishguard – Rosslare route. Later in 1990 she was renamed the STENA FELICITY.

STENA GALLOWAY Built as the GALLOWAY PRINCESS for the Stranraer – Larne service. In 1990 renamed the STENA GALLOWAY. She will continue to operate on this route (now Stranraer – Belfast) at least in the short term.

STENA INVICTA Built as the PEDER PAARS for *DSB (Danish State Railways)* for their service between Kalundborg (Sealand) and Aarhus (Jutland). In 1990 purchased by *Stena Line AB* of Sweden for delivery in 1991. In 1991 renamed the STENA INVICTA and entered service on the Dover – Calais service, replacing the STENA CAMBRIA.

STENA NORMANDY One of two vessels ordered by *Göteborg – Frederikshavnlinjen* of Sweden (trading as *Sessan Line*) before the take over of their operations by *Stena Line AB* in 1981. Both were designed for the Göteborg – Frederikshavn route (a journey of about three hours). However, *Stena Line* decided in 1982 to switch the first vessel, the KRONPRINSESSAN VICTORIA (now the STENA EUROPE of *Stena Line bv*), to their Göteborg – Kiel (Germany) route since their own new tonnage for this route, being built in Poland, had been substantially delayed. She was modified to make her more suitable for this overnight route. Work on the second vessel – provisionally called the DROTTNING SILVIA – was suspended for a time but she was eventually delivered, as designed, in late 1982 and introduced onto the Göteborg – Frederikshavn route on a temporary basis pending delivery of new *Stena Line* ordered vessels. She was named the PRINSESSAN BIRGITTA, the existing ex *Sessan Line* vessel of the same name being renamed the STENA SCANDINAVICA (see the KING OF SCANDINAVIA, *Scandinavian Seaways*). In early 1983 she was substantially modified in a similar way to her sister. In June 1983 she was renamed the ST NICHOLAS, re-registered in Great Britain and entered service on five year charter to *Sealink* UK on the Harwich – Hoek van Holland route. In 1988 she was purchased and re-registered in The Bahamas. In 1989 she was sold to *Gotlandsbolaget* of Sweden and then chartered back. In 1991 she was renamed the STENA NORMANDY and inaugurated a new service between Southampton and Cherbourg.

STENA PARISIEN Built for *SNCF* as the CHAMPS ELYSEES to operate Calais – Dover and Boulogne – Dover services, later operating Calais – Dover only. In 1990 transferred to the Dieppe – Newhaven service. Chartered to *Stena Sealink Line* in June 1992, and renamed the STENA PARISIEN; she has a French crew. She is likely to continue on this route throughout 1996, operating with the STENA LYNX IV.

## FAST FERRIES

| 13 | STENA EXPLORER | - | 95 | 40k | 1500P | 375C | 50L | A | Rauma, FI | GB |
|----|----------------|-------|----|-----|-------|------|-----|----|-----------|----|
| 14 | STENA HSS2 | - | 96 | 40k | 1500P | 375C | 50L | A | Rauma, FI | GB |
| 15 | STENA LYNX I | 3231t | 93 | 35k | 450P | 90C | - | BA | Hobart, AL | BA |
| 16 | STENA LYNX II | 3989t | 94 | 38k | 600P | 130C | - | BA | Hobart, AL | BA |
| 17 | STENA LYNX III | - | 96 | 37k | 600P | 181C | - | BA | Hobart, AL | BA |
| 18 | STENA LYNX IV | 3000t | 95 | 32k | 631P | 150C | - | BA | Henderson, AL | GB |

STENA EXPLORER (HSS 1) ('High Speed Ship') built for *Stena Line*. In 1996 introduced onto the Holyhead – Dun Laoghaire route.

STENA HSS2 Second HSS built for *Stena Line*. In Summer 1996 to be introduced onto the Stranraer – Belfast route.

STENA LYNX I InCat 74m model. Second of two vessels ordered for *Condor*. Whilst the first became the CONDOR 10, the option on the second (intended to be the CONDOR 11) was cancelled and she was instead chartered to *Stena Sealink Line* named the STENA SEA LYNX and, in July 1993, she started a new high speed service between Holyhead and Dun Laoghaire. In 1994, she was moved to inaugurate a fast ferry service between Fishguard and Rosslare and renamed the STENA SEA LYNX I. In 1996 she was renamed the STENA LYNX I.

STENA LYNX II InCat 78m model (updated and enlarged version of 74m version). Chartered by *Stena Sealink Line* and, in 1994, introduced onto the Holyhead – Dun Laoghaire service as the STENA SEA LYNX II. In 1996 she was renamed the STENA LYNX I. In February 1996 she was transferred to the Dover – Calais route. When STENA LYNX III is delivered she will probably return to the Irish Sea.

STENA LYNX III InCat 81m model. To be chartered to *Stena Line* in June 1996 for the Dover – Calais service, replacing the STENA LYNX II.

STENA LYNX IV Austal Ships 78m model ordered by *Sea Containers* and launched as the SUPER SEACAT FRANCE. However, due to a dispute between *Sea Containers* and the builders, delivery was not taken and she was instead sold to *Stena Rederi* of Sweden and chartered to *Stena Line*, for the Newhaven – Dieppe service.

# STRANDFARASKIP LANDSINS

**THE COMPANY** *Strandfaraskip Landsins* is the Faroe Islands state shipping company. It ceased services to the UK when *Smyril Line* was established in 1983 but re-established sailings during summer 1989.

**MANAGEMENT Managing Director:** Thomas Arabo, **Marketing Manager:** Ms Unn á Lad.

**ADDRESS** Postboks 88, FR-110, Tórshavn, Faroe Islands.

**TELEPHONE Administration:** +298-14550, **Reservations:** Faroe Islands: +298-14550, UK: +44 (0)1224 572615 (*P&O Scottish Ferries*), **Fax:** +298-16000, **Telex:** 81295.

**ROUTE OPERATED** Tórshavn (Faroes) – Aberdeen (21 hrs; *(2)*; 1 per week (2 per week mid June to mid August)).

## CONVENTIONAL FERRY

| 1 | SMYRIL | | 3937t | 69 | 18k | 500P | 120C | 16L | BA | Aalborg, DK | FA |
|---|--------|--|-------|----|----|------|------|-----|----|-------------|----|

SMYRIL Built as the MORTEN MOLS for *Mols Linien A/S* of Denmark (a subsidiary of *DFDS*) for their internal Danish service between Ebeltoft (Jutland) and Sjaellands Odde (Sealand). She was purchased by *Strandfaraskip Landsins* in 1975 to inaugurate RO/RO services to and from the Faroe islands and the UK, Denmark and Norway and renamed the SMYRIL. Used only on inter-island services between 1983 and 1989. In 1989 international services were resumed. She was chartered out in 1991 and the service was operated by sister vessel the TEISTIN (4269t, 1969 (ex MIKKEL MOLS 1975)). She resumed the service in March 1992.

# SWANSEA CORK FERRIES

**THE COMPANY** *Swansea Cork Ferries* is a company established in 1987 to re-open the Swansea – Cork service abandoned by *B&I Line* in 1979. It was jointly owned by West Glamorgan County Council, Cork Corporation, Cork County Council and Kerry County Council. The service did not operate in 1989 but resumed in 1990. In 1993 it was acquired by *Strintzis Lines* of Greece.

**MANAGEMENT Managing Director:** Thomas Hunter McGowan, **Marketing Manager:** Desmond Donnelly.

**ADDRESS** 52 South Mall, CORK, Republic of Ireland.

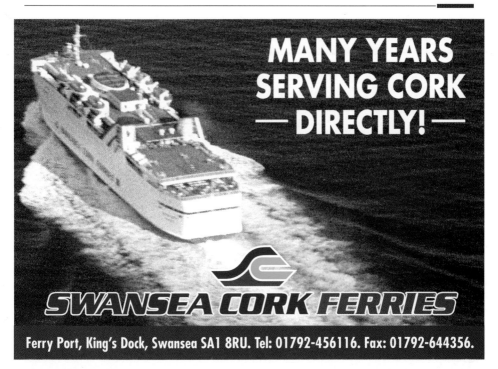
**TELEPHONE Administration:** Head Office: +353 (0)21 276000, Cork Ferry Port: +353 (0)21 378036, **Reservations:** IR: +353 (0)21 271166, UK: +44 (0)1792 456116, **Fax:** IR (Admin). +353 (0)21 275814, IR (Reservations): +353 (0)21 275061, UK: +44 (0)1792 644356.

**ROUTE OPERATED** Swansea – Cork (10 hrs; *(1)*; 1 per day or alternate days, according to season). NOTE: Due to tidal restrictions at Swansea, the service operates to Pembroke Dock a few days each year.

**CONVENTIONAL FERRY**

| | | | | | | | | | | |
|---|---|---|---|---|---|---|---|---|---|---|
| 1 | SUPERFERRY | 14797t | 72 | 21k | 1400P | 350C | 50L | BA2 | Hashihama, JA | GR |

SUPERFERRY Built as the CASSIOPEIA for *Ocean Ferry KK* of Japan. In 1976 the company became *Ocean Tokyu Ferry KK* and she was renamed the IZU NO 3. She was used on the service between Tokyo (Honshu) – Tokushima (Shikoko) – Kokura (Kyshu). In 1991 she was sold to *Strintzis Lines* and briefly renamed the IONIAN EXPRESS. Following major rebuilding, she was renamed the SUPERFERRY and used on their services between Greece and the Greek islands. In 1993 chartered to *Swansea Cork Ferries*.

# TRUCKLINE FERRIES

**THE COMPANY** *Truckline Ferries* is the freight division of *Brittany Ferries*. However, it also operates passenger services.

**MANAGEMENT** As *Brittany Ferries*.

**TELEPHONE Administration:** +44 (0)1202 667388. **Reservations:** +44 (0)1202 666466.

**ROUTE OPERATED** Cherbourg – Poole (4 hrs 15 mins; *(1)*; 2 per day).

## CONVENTIONAL FERRY

| 1 | BARFLEUR | | 20500t | 92 | 19k | 1173P | 550C | 125T | BA | Helsinki, FI | | FR |
|---|----------|---|--------|-----|------|-------|------|------|-----|--------------|---|-----|

BARFLEUR Built for the Cherbourg – Poole service to replace two passenger vessels – the CORBIERE (see the APOLLO, *Eestin-Linjat*) and the TREGASTEL (see the ST CLAIR, *P&O Scottish Ferries*) – and to inaugurate a year round passenger service.

# SECTION 2 - Domestic Services

# ARGYLL & BUTE COUNCIL

**THE COMPANY** *Argyll & Bute Council* is a British local government authority. It took over the operation of the service from *Strathclyde Regional Council* on 1st April 1996.

**MANAGEMENT Network Manager:** James C Tolmie.

**ADDRESS** Kilbowie House, Gallanach Road, OBAN PA34 4PF.

**TELEPHONE Administration:** +44 (0)1631 562125. **Reservations:** +44 (0)1374 750873, **Fax:** +44 (0)1631 566728.

**ROUTE OPERATED** Seil – Luing (5 mins; *(1)*; frequent service).

## VESSEL

| 1 | BELNAHUA | | 35t | 72 | 8k | 40P | 5C | 1L | BA | Campbeltown, GB | | GB |
|---|----------|---|-----|-----|------|------|-----|-----|-----|-----------------|---|-----|

BELNAHUA Built for *Argyll County Council* for the Seil – Luing service. In 1975, following local government reorganisation, transferred to *Strathclyde Regional Council*. In 1996, transferred to *Argyll and Bute Council*.

# ARRANMORE ISLAND FERRY SERVICES

**THE COMPANY** *Arranmore Island Ferry Services* is an Irish Republic Company, supported by *Údarás na Gaeltachta (The Gaeltacht Authority)*, a semi-state body responsible for tourism and development in the Irish speaking areas of The Irish Republic. The operation is also known as *Maoin-Na-Farraige* (literally 'sea treasure' or 'sea wealth').

**MANAGEMENT Managing Director:** Cornelius Bonner.

**ADDRESS** Bridge House, Leabgarrow, ARRANMORE, County Donegal, Republic of Ireland.

**TELEPHONE Administration: & Reservations:** +353 (0)75 20532, **Fax:** + 353 (0)75 20750.

**ROUTE OPERATED** Burtonport (County Donegal) – Leabgarrow (Arranmore Island) (20 mins; *(1)*; up to 8 per day (summer), 5 per day (winter)).

## VESSEL

| 1 | ÁRAINN MHÓR | 64t | 72 | 8k | 138P | 4C | - | B | Port Glasgow, GB | | GB |
|---|-------------|-----|-----|------|------|-----|-----|-----|------------------|---|-----|
| 2 | MORVERN | 64t | 73 | 8k | 138P | 4C | - | B | Port Glasgow, GB | | GB |

ÁRAINN MHÓR Built as the KILBRANNAN for *Caledonian MacBrayne*. Used on a variety of routes until 1977, she was then transferred to the Scalpay (Harris) – Kyles Scalpay service. In 1990 she was replaced by the CANNA and, in turn, replaced the CANNA in her reserve/relief role. In 1992 sold to *Arranmore Island Ferry Services* and renamed the ÁRAINN MHÓR.

MORVERN Built for *Caledonian MacBrayne*. After service on a number of routes she was, after 1979, the main vessel on the Fionnphort (Mull) – Iona service. In 1992 replaced by the LOCH BUIE and became a spare vessel. In 1995 sold to *Arranmore Island Ferry Services* and, in the summer, operates alongside the ÁRAINN MHÓR.

# BERE ISLAND FERRIES

**THE COMPANY** *Bere Island Ferries Ltd* is an Irish Republic private sector company.

**MANAGEMENT Operator:** C Harrington.

**ADDRESS** Ferry Lodge, West End, Bere Island, County Cork, Republic of Ireland.

**TELEPHONE Administration:** +353 (0)27 75009. **Reservations:** Not applicable.

**ROUTE OPERATED** Castletownbere (County Cork) – Bere Island (10 mins; *(1)*; up to 10 per day).

**VESSEL**

| 1 | MISNEACH | 30t | 78 | 7k | 80P | 4C | - | B | New Ross, IR | IR |
|---|----------|-----|----|----|-----|-----|---|---|--------------|-----|

MISNEACH Built for *Arranmore Island Ferry Services* of the Irish Republic and used on their Burtonport – Arranmore service. In 1992 sold to *Bere Island Ferries*. In 1993 inaugurated a car ferry service between Castletownbere and Bere Island.

# CALEDONIAN MACBRAYNE

**THE COMPANY** *Caledonian MacBrayne* is a British state owned company, the responsibility of the Secretary of State for Scotland. Until 1st April 1990 it was part of the state owned *Scottish Transport Group* (formed in 1969). *Caledonian MacBrayne* as such was formed in 1973 by the merger of the *Caledonian Steam Packet Company* (which had been formed in 1889) and *David MacBrayne Ltd* (whose origins go back to 1851). *CalMac* (as the company is often called locally) has more vessels sailing under the British flag than any other company.

**MANAGEMENT Managing Director:** C S Paterson CBE, **Marketing Officer:** W J H Bowie.

**ADDRESS** The Ferry Terminal, GOUROCK PA19 1QP.

**TELEPHONE Administration:** +44 (0)1475 650100, **Reservations:** +44 (0)1475 650000, **Fax:** +44 (0)1475 637607.

**ROUTES OPERATED** Ardrossan – Brodick (Arran) (55 mins; *(2)*; up to 6 per day), Ardrossan – Douglas (Isle of Man) (in partnership with the *Isle of Man Steam Packet Company*) (8 hrs; *(5)*; 1 per week), Claonaig – Lochranza (Arran) (30 mins; *(24)*; up to 10 per day), Largs – Cumbrae Slip (Cumbrae) (10 mins; *(20,23)*; every 30 or 15 mins), Wemyss Bay – Rothesay (Bute) (30 mins; *(14,15,27,30)*; up to 22 per day), Rothesay (Bute) – Brodick (Arran) (1 hr 30 mins; *(27)*; 2 per week), Colintraive – Rhubodach (Bute) (5 mins; *(22)*; frequent service), Tarbert (Loch Fyne) – Portavadie (20 mins; *(29)*; up to 11 per day), Gourock – Dunoon (20 mins; *(14,15,30)*; hourly service with extras at peaks), Kennacraig – Port Ellen (Islay) (2 hrs 15 mins; *(10)*; 1 or 2 per day), Kennacraig – Port Askaig (Islay) (2 hrs; *(10)*; 1 or 2 per day), Kennacraig – Port Askaig – Colonsay – Oban (3 hrs 35 mins; *(10)*; 1 per week), Tayinloan – Gigha (20 mins; *(21)*; hourly with some gaps), Oban – Lismore (50 mins; *(7)*; up to 4 per day), Oban – Colonsay (2 hrs 10 mins; *(10,13)*; 3 per week), Oban – Craignure (Mull) (40 mins; *(13)*; two hourly), Oban – Coll (2 hrs 45 mins (direct), 4 hrs 50 mins (via Tiree); *(26)*; up to 5 per week), Oban – Tiree (3 hrs 30 mins (direct), 4 hrs 15 mins (via Coll); *(26)*; up to 5 per week), Oban – Castlebay (Barra) (5 hrs (direct); *(26)*; 4 per week), Oban – Lochboisdale (South Uist) (5 hrs (direct), 7hrs (via Barra); *(26)*; 5 per week), Otternish (North Uist) – Berneray – Leverburgh (Harris) (1 hr 10 mins ; *(16)*; 4 per day), Lochaline – Fishnish (Mull) (15 mins; *(11)*; up to 16 per day), Fionnphort (Mull) – Iona (5 mins; *(17)*; frequent) (passengers only; residents' private cars and service vehicles conveyed by special arrangement), Tobermory (Mull) – Kilchoan (35 mins; *(6)*; up to 11 per day), Mallaig – Armadale (Skye)(cars and passengers – summer only) (30 mins; *(9)*; up to 7 per day), Mallaig – Armadale (Skye)(passenger only October – Easter) (30 mins; *(25)*; up to 2 per day), Mallaig – Eigg – Muck – Rum – Canna – Mallaig (passenger only) (round trip 7 hrs (all islands); *(25)*; at least 1 sailing per day – most islands visited daily), Mallaig – Kyle of Lochalsh (passenger only) (2 hrs; *(25)*; 1 per week), Mallaig – Lochboisdale (South Uist) (3 hrs 30 mins; *(9)*; 2 per week), Mallaig – Castlebay (Barra) (via Lochboisdale) (5 hrs 30 mins; *(9)*; 2 per week), Sconser (Skye) – Raasay (15 mins; *(28)*; up to 10 per day), Uig (Skye) – Tarbert (Harris) (1 hr 45 mins; *(8)*; 1 or 2 per day), Uig (Skye) – Lochmaddy (North Uist) (1 hr 45 mins; *(8)*; 1 or 2 per day), Kyles Scalpay (Harris) – Scalpay (10 mins; *(4)*; up to 13 per day), Ullapool – Stornoway (Lewis) (2 hrs 30 mins; *(12)*; up to 3 per day), **Clyde Cruising** In addition to normal car and passenger service, the following cruises are operated in the Clyde; parts of these cruises are sometimes normal car/passenger services: Gourock – Dunoon – Largs – Rothesay – Tighnabruaich (*(14,15,30)*; 2 per week), Dunoon – Gourock – Rothesay – Largs – Brodick (*(27)*; 2 per week) (with connections from Gourock and Dunoon). Gourock-Dunoon-Rothesay-Tarbert (*(14,15,30*; 1 per week)

## VESSELS

| 1 | BRUERNISH | 69t | 73 | 8k | 164P | 6C | - | B | Port Glasgow, GB | GB |
|----|-----------------|-------|----|------|-------|------|---|-----|-------------------|----|
| 2 | CALEDONIAN ISLES | 5221t | 93 | 15k | 1000P | 120C | - | BA | Lowestoft, GB | GB |
| 4 | CANNA | 69t | 73 | 8k | 50P | 6C | - | B | Port Glasgow, GB | GB |
| 5 | CLAYMORE | 1871t | 78 | 14k | 500P | 50C | - | AS | Leith, GB | GB |
| 6 | COLL | 69t | 74 | 8k | 152P | 6C | - | B | Port Glasgow, GB | GB |
| 7 | EIGG | 69t | 75 | 8k | 75P | 6C | - | B | Port Glasgow, GB | GB |
| 8 | HEBRIDEAN ISLES | 3040t | 85 | 15k | 507P | 68C | - | BAS | Selby, GB | GB |
| 9 | IONA | 1908t | 70 | 16k | 554P | 47C | - | BAS | Troon, GB | GB |
| 10 | ISLE OF ARRAN | 3296t | 84 | 15k | 800P | 76C | - | BA | Port Glasgow, GB | GB |
| 11 | ISLE OF CUMBRAE | 169t | 77 | 8.5k | 99P | 15C | - | BA | Troon, GB | GB |
| 12 | ISLE OF LEWIS | 6753t | 95 | 18k | 1000P | 123C | - | BA | Port Glasgow, GB | GB |
| 13 | ISLE OF MULL | 4719t | 88 | 15k | 968P | 80C | - | BA | Port Glasgow, GB | GB |
| 14 | JUNO | 902t | 74 | 14k | 531P | 40C | - | AS | Port Glasgow, GB | GB |
| 15 | JUPITER | 898t | 74 | 14k | 531P | 40C | - | AS | Port Glasgow, GB | GB |
| 16 | LOCH BHRUSDA | - | 96 | 8k | 150P | 15C | - | BA | Liverpool, GB | GB |
| 17 | LOCH BUIE | 295t | 92 | 8k | 250P | 9C | - | BA | St Monans, GB | GB |
| 18 | LOCH DUNVEGAN | 550t | 91 | 9k | 250P | 36C | - | BA | Port Glasgow, GB | GB |
| 19 | LOCH FYNE | 550t | 91 | 9k | 250P | 36C | - | BA | Port Glasgow, GB | GB |
| 20 | LOCH LINNHE | 206t | 86 | 8k | 199P | 12C | - | BA | Hessle, GB | GB |
| 21 | LOCH RANZA | 206t | 87 | 8k | 199P | 12C | - | BA | Hessle, GB | GB |
| 22 | LOCH RIDDON | 206t | 86 | 8k | 199P | 12C | - | BA | Hessle, GB | GB |
| 23 | LOCH STRIVEN | 206t | 86 | 8k | 199P | 12C | - | BA | Hessle, GB | GB |
| 24 | LOCH TARBERT | 211t | 92 | 8k | 149P | 18C | - | BA | St Monans, GB | GB |
| 25 | LOCHMOR | 175t | 79 | 10k | 130P | 1C | - | C | Troon, GB | GB |
| 26 | LORD OF THE ISLES | 3504t | 89 | 16k | 506P | 60C | - | BAS | Port Glasgow, GB | GB |
| 27 | PIONEER | 1088t | 74 | 16k | 356P | 32C | - | AS | Leith, GB | GB |
| 28 | RAASAY | 69t | 76 | 8k | 75P | 6C | - | B | Port Glasgow, GB | GB |
| 29 | RHUM | 69t | 73 | 8k | 164P | 6C | - | B | Port Glasgow, GB | GB |
| 30 | SATURN | 899t | 78 | 14k | 531P | 40C | - | AS | Troon, GB | GB |

BRUERNISH Until 1980 she served on a variety of routes. In 1980 she inaugurated RO/RO working between Tayinloan and the island of Gigha and served this route until June 1992 when she was replaced by the LOCH RANZA and became a relief vessel. In summer 1994 she operated as secondary vessel on the Tobermory (Mull) – Kilchoan service. She now acts as a general relief vessel.

CALEDONIAN ISLES Built for the Ardrossan – Brodick (Arran) service. Entered service on 25th August 1993.

CANNA She was the regular vessel on the Lochaline – Fishnish (Mull) service. In 1986 she was replaced by the ISLE OF CUMBRAE and until 1990 she served in a relief capacity in the north, often assisting the MORVERN on the Iona service. In 1990 she replaced the KILBRANNAN (see theÁRAINN

*Isle of Lewis* (Lawrence MacDuff)

*Claymore* (Lawrence MacDuff)

MHÓR, *Arranmore Island Ferry Services*) on the Kyles Scalpay (Harris) – Scalpay service. The service is to be replaced by a bridge in late 1996/early 1997; when this happens she will be redeployed elsewhere.

CLAYMORE She was built for the Oban – Castlebay/ Lochboisdale service, also serving Coll and Tiree between October and May, replacing the IONA. In 1989 she was transferred to the Kennacraig – Port Ellen/Port Askaig (Islay) route, replacing the IONA. In summer she also operated a weekly service from Port Askaig (Islay) to Colonsay and Oban. She relieved on the Ardrossan – Brodick service during winter 1990. In autumn 1993 she was replaced by the ISLE OF ARRAN and became a spare vessel. Her summer duties in 1994 and 1995 included 15 Saturday sailings from Ardrossan to Douglas (Isle of Man), returning on Sundays. During the winter she is general relief vessel, spending several months on Islay sailings. In summer 1996 she will operate the Isle of Man service on seven weekends and will also serve as standby/relief vessel.

COLL For several years she was employed mainly in a relief capacity. In 1986 she took over the Tobermory (Mull) – Kilchoan service from a passenger only vessel; the conveyance of vehicles was not inaugurated until 1991.

EIGG Since 1976 she has been employed mainly on the Oban – Lismore service.

HEBRIDEAN ISLES Built for the Uig – Tarbert/Lochmaddy service. She entered service in December 1985 and was used initially on the Ullapool – Stornoway and Oban – Craignure/Colonsay services pending installation of link-span facilities at Uig, Tarbert and Lochmaddy. She took up her regular role in May 1986. From May 1996 she will no longer operate direct services between Tarbert and Lochmaddy; this role will be taken on by the new LOCH BHRUSDA.

IONA Built for *David MacBrayne* (the only vessel now in the fleet not built for *Caledonian MacBrayne*). She was actually built to operate the Islay service. However, as plans to built a new pier further down West Loch Tarbert were abandoned, she was not able to operate on this route until the *Western Ferries'* pier in deeper water at Kennacraig was acquired in 1978. She operated on the Gourock – Dunoon service in 1970 and 1971, between Mallaig and Kyle of Lochalsh and Stornoway in 1972 and between Oban and Craignure in 1973. From 1974 until 1978 she operated mainly on the Oban to Castlebay/Lochboisdale service and in addition the winter Oban – Coll/Tiree route. From 1978 until 1989 she operated mainly on the Islay service. In 1989 she was replaced by the CLAYMORE and then replaced the PIONEER as the summer Mallaig – Armadale vessel. Full RO/RO working was introduced on the route in 1994 and she also operated new twice weekly sailing between Mallaig, Lochboisdale and Castlebay. She is now a standby vessel in winter and is likely to be replaced in 1997.

ISLE OF ARRAN Built for the Ardrossan – Brodick service. In 1993 transferred to the Kennacraig – Port Ellen/Port Askaig service, also undertaking the weekly Port Askaig – Colonsay – Oban summer service. She has also relieved on other routes during the winter.

ISLE OF CUMBRAE Built for the Largs – Cumbrae Slip (Cumbrae) service. In 1986 she was replaced by the LOCH LINNHE and the LOCH STRIVEN and transferred to the Lochaline – Fishnish (Mull) service. She used to spend most of the winter as secondary vessel on the Kyle of Lochalsh – Kyleakin service; however this no longer happens following the opening of the Sky Bridge in 1994.

ISLE OF LEWIS Built to replace the SUILVEN on the Ullapool – Stornoway service. Largest vessel ever to operate on Clyde or Western Isles routes.

ISLE OF MULL Built to replace the CALEDONIA (1157t, 1966) on the Oban – Craignure (Mull) service. She also operates the Oban – Colonsay service and is the usual relief vessel on the Ullapool – Stornoway service. She has also relieved on the Oban – Castlebay/Lochboisdale route.

JUNO, JUPITER, SATURN Built for the Gourock – Dunoon, Gourock – Kilcreggan and Wemyss Bay – Rothesay services. The JUPITER has been upgraded to Class III standard for the Ardrossan – Brodick service. Before 1986, the JUNO and JUPITER operated mainly on the Gourock – Dunoon and Kilcreggan services and the SATURN on the Wemyss Bay – Rothesay service. Since 1986 they usually rotated on a four weekly basis on the three services. They are all used on the summer cruise programme. In 1996 they will rotate weekly on the Dunoon and Rothesay services plus cruising.

LOCH BHRUSDA Built to inaugurate a new Otternish (North Uist) – Berneray – Leverburgh (Harris) service. Due to enter service in May 1996.

LOCH BUIE Built for the Fionnphort (Mull) – Iona service to replace the MORVERN and obviate the need for a relief vessel in the summer. Due to height restrictions, loading arrangements for vehicles taller than private cars are bow only. Only islanders cars and service vehicles (eg mail vans, police) are carried. No tourist vehicles are conveyed.

LOCH DUNVEGAN, LOCH FYNE Built for the Kyle of Lochalsh – Kyleakin service, replacing the KYLEAKIN and the LOCHALSH (see *Cross River Ferries*). On the opening of the Skye Bridge in October 1995 they were withdrawn from service and put up for sale.

LOCH LINNHE Used mainly on the Largs – Cumbrae Slip (Cumbrae) service. Until winter 1994/95 she was usually used on the Lochaline – Fishnish service.

LOCH RANZA Built for the Claonaig – Lochranza (Arran) seasonal service and used a relief vessel in the winter. In 1992 she was replaced by the LOCH TARBERT and transferred to the Tayinloan – Gigha service.

LOCH RIDDON Used mainly on the Colintraive – Rhubodach (Bute) service.

LOCH STRIVEN Used mainly on the Largs – Cumbrae Slip (Cumbrae) service. Since winter 1994/5 she has been a spare vessel in the winter.

LOCH TARBERT Built for the Claonaig – Lochranza (Arran) service. She has been the regular winter vessel on the Largs – Cumbrae Slip route since winter 1994/5.

LOCHMOR Built for the passenger only 'small isles' service from Mallaig to Eigg, Muck, Rum and Canna with summer cruises to Kyle of Lochalsh and also maintains the winter restricted passenger only service between Mallaig and Armadale (Skye). She can convey a small vehicle for the islands as cargo but this service is not available to tourists.

LORD OF THE ISLES Built to replace the CLAYMORE on the Oban – Castlebay (Barra) and Lochboisdale (South Uist) services and also the COLUMBA (1420t, 1964) on the Oban – Coll and Tiree service.

PIONEER Built to operate on the West Loch Tarbert – Port Ellen service (see the IONA). When the IONA was at last able to operate this service in 1978 (following the move to Kennacraig) the PIONEER was transferred to the Mallaig – Armadale service, operating as a relief vessel in the winter on Upper Clyde and Small Isles routes. In 1989 she was replaced at Mallaig by the IONA and became the company's spare vessel, replacing the GLEN SANNOX (1269t, 1957). In summer 1996 she will undertake Wemyss Bay and Rothesay services and Rothesay – Largs – Brodick cruises. She serves as a Clyde and small isles relief vessel in the winter.

RAASAY Built for and used primarily on the Sconser (Skye) – Raasay service.

RHUM Until 1987, used primarily on the Claonaig – Lochranza (Arran) service. Since that time she has served on various routes. In 1994 she inaugurated a new service between Tarbert (Loch Fyne) and Portavadie.

SATURN See above with the JUPITER and JUNO.

# CROSS RIVER FERRIES

**THE COMPANY** *Cross River Ferries Ltd* is an Irish Republic company, jointly owned by *Marine Transport Services Ltd* of Cobh and *Arklow Shipping Ltd* of Arklow, County Wicklow.

**MANAGEMENT Operations Manager:** Edward Perry.

**ADDRESS** Atlantic Quay, Cobh, County Cork, Republic of Ireland.

**TELEPHONE Administration:** +353 (0)21 811223, **Reservations:** Not applicable, **Fax:** +353 (0)21 812645.

**ROUTE OPERATED** Carrigaloe (near Cobh, on Great Island) – Glenbrook (Co Cork) (4 mins; *(1,2)*; frequent service (one or two vessels used according to demand).

**VESSELS**

| 1 | CARRIGALOE | 225t | 70 | 8k | 200P | 27C | - | BA | Newport (Gwent), GBIR |
|---|------------|------|----|----|------|-----|---|----|-----------------------|
| 2 | GLENBROOK  | 225t | 71 | 8k | 200P | 27C | - | BA | Newport (Gwent), GBIR |

CARRIGALOE, GLENBROOK Built as the KYLEAKIN and the LOCHALSH for *David MacBrayne Ltd* (later *Caledonian MacBrayne*) for the Kyle of Lochalsh – Kyleakin service. In 1991 replaced by the LOCH DUNVEGAN and the LOCH FYNE and sold to *Marine Transport Services Ltd* who renamed them the CARRIGALOE and the GLENBROOK respectively. They entered service in March 1993.

# DOE (NORTHERN IRELAND)

**THE COMPANY** *DOE (Department of the Environment) (Northern Ireland)* is a UK Department of State.

**MANAGEMENT Ferry Manager:** D Pedlow.

**ADDRESS** Strangford Ferries, STRANGFORD, Co Down BT30 7NE.

**TELEPHONE Administration:** +44 (0)1396 881637 **Reservations:** Not applicable. **Fax:** +44 (0)1396 881249.

**ROUTE OPERATED** Strangford – Portaferry (County Down) (10 mins; *(1,2)*; half hourly).

**VESSELS**

| 1 | PORTAFERRY FERRY | 151t | 62 | 9k  | 200P | 22C | - | BA | Pembroke, GB | GB |
|---|------------------|------|----|-----|------|-----|---|----|--------------|----|
| 2 | STRANGFORD FERRY | 186t | 69 | 10k | 263P | 22C | - | BA | Cork, IR     | GB |

PORTAFERRY FERRY Built as the CLEDDAU KING for *Pembrokeshire County Council* (from 1974 *Dyfed County Council*) for their service between Hobbs Point (Pembroke Dock) and Neyland. Following the opening of a new bridge, the service ceased and in 1976 she was sold to *DOE Northern Ireland* and renamed the PORTA FERRY. In 1990 she was renamed the PORTAFERRY FERRY.

STRANGFORD FERRY Built for *Down County Council*. Subsequently transferred to *DOE Northern Ireland*.

# GLENELG – KYLERHEA FERRY

**THE COMPANY** The *Glenelg – Kylerhea Ferry* is privately operated.

**MANAGEMENT Ferry Master:** R MacLeod.

**ADDRESS** Corriehallie, Inverinate, KYLE IV40 8HD.

**TELEPHONE Administration:** +44 (0)1599 511302, **Reservations:** +44 (0)1599 511302, **Fax:** +44 (0)1599 511302.

**ROUTE OPERATED** Glenelg – Kylerhea (Skye) (summer only) (10 mins; *(1)*; frequent service).

**VESSEL**

| 1 | GLENACHULISH | 44t | 69 | 9k | 12P | 6C | - | BSt | Troon, GB | GB |
|---|---|---|---|---|---|---|---|---|---|---|

GLENACHULISH Built for the *Ballachulish Ferry Company* for the service between North Ballachulish and South Ballachulish, across the mouth of Loch Leven. In 1975 the ferry was replaced by a bridge and she was sold to *Highland Regional Council* and used on a relief basis on the North Kessock – South Kessock and Kylesku – Kylestrome routes. In 1984 she was sold to the operator of the Glenelg – Kylerhea service. She is the last turntable ferry in operation.

# HIGHLAND COUNCIL (THE)

**THE COMPANY** The *Highland Council* (previously *Highland Regional Council*) is a British local government authority.

**MANAGEMENT Ferry Manager:** J McAuslane.

**ADDRESS** Ferry Cottage, Ardgour, Fort William.

**TELEPHONE Administration:** +44 (0)1855 841243, **Reservations:** Not applicable. **Fax:** +44 (0)1855 841243.

**ROUTE OPERATED** Corran – Ardgour (5 mins; *(1 or 2)*; half hourly).

**VESSELS**

| 1 | MAID OF GLENCOUL | 166t | 75 | 8k | 116P | 16C | - | BA | Ardrossan, GB | GB |
|---|---|---|---|---|---|---|---|---|---|---|
| 2 | ROSEHAUGH | 150t | 67 | 8.5k | 150P | 18C | - | BA | Berwick on Tweed, GB | GB |

MAID OF GLENCOUL Built for *Highland Regional Council* for the service between Kylesku and Kylestrome. In 1984 the ferry service was replaced by a bridge and she was transferred to the Corran – Ardgour service. In April 1966, ownership transferred to *The Highland Council*.

ROSEHAUGH Built for *Ross and Cromarty County Council* for the service between South Kessock and North Kessock (across the Beauly Firth, north of Inverness). In 1975, ownership was transferred to *Highland Regional Council*. In 1982 a bridge was opened and she was transferred to the Corran – Ardgour route. Following the arrival of the MAID OF GLENCOUL in 1984 she has been the reserve vessel. In April 1966, ownership transferred to *The Highland Council*.

*The Highland Council* also operate a 26 passenger vessel on the ten minute crossing of Loch Linnhe between Fort William and Camusnagaul. She is called the CAILIN AN AISEAG, was built at Buckie, Scotland in 1980 and her service speed is 7.5k. No cars are conveyed. Enquiries to the ferryman, +44 (0)1397 772483.

# ISLES OF SCILLY STEAMSHIP COMPANY

**THE COMPANY** The *Isles of Scilly Steamship Company* is a British private sector company.

**MANAGEMENT Managing Director:** K N Christopher, **Marketing Manager:** R Johns.

**ADDRESS** Scilly: PO Box 10, Hugh Town, St Mary's, Isles of Scilly TR21 0LJ, Penzance: Steamship House, Quay Street, PENZANCE, Cornwall, TR18 4BD.

**TELEPHONE Administration: & Reservations:** Scilly: +44 (0)1720 422357, Penzance: +44 (0)1736 64290, **Fax:** Scilly: +44 (0)1720 422192, Penzance: +44 (0)1736 51223.

**ROUTE OPERATED** Penzance – St Mary's (Isles of Scilly) (2 hrs 40 mins; *(1,3)*; 1 per day). Freight services St Mary's – Tresco/St Martin's/St Agnes/Bryher; *(2)*; irregular).

## VESSELS

| 1 | GRY MARITHA | 550t | 81 | 10.5k | 12P | 5C | 1L | C | Kolvereid, NO | GB |
|---|---|---|---|---|---|---|---|---|---|---|
| 2 | LYONESSE LADY | 50t | 91 | 9k | 12P | 1C | 0L | A | Fort William, GB | GB |
| 3p | SCILLONIAN III | 1256t | 77 | 15.5k | 600P | - | - | C | Appledore, GB | GB |

GRY MARITHA Built for *Gjofor* of Norway. In design she is a coaster rather than a ferry. In 1990 sold to *The Isles of Scilly Steamship* Company. She operates a freight and passenger service all year (conveying all residents' cars and other vehicles to and from the islands – tourist cars are not conveyed). During the winter she provides the only passenger service to the islands, the SCILLONIAN III being laid up.

LYONESSE LADY Built for inter-island ferry work.

SCILLONIAN III Built for the Penzance – St Mary's service. She operates from Easter to late autumn and is laid up in the winter. Last major conventional passenger/cargo ferry built for UK waters and probably Western Europe.

# ORKNEY FERRIES

**THE COMPANY** *Orkney Ferries Ltd* (previosely the *Orkney Islands Shipping Co.*) is a British company, owned by *The Orkney Islands Council.*

**MANAGEMENT Operations Director:** R C Sclater, **Ferry Services Manager:** A Learmonth.

**ADDRESS** Shore Street, KIRKWALL, Orkney KW15 1QLG.

**TELEPHONE Administration:** +44 (0)1856 872044, **Reservations:** +44 (0)1856 872044, **Fax:** +44 (0)1856 872921, **Telex:** 75475.

**ROUTES OPERATED** Kirkwall (Mainland) to Eday, (1 hr, 15 mins) Westray (1 hr 25 mins), Sanday (1 hr 25 mins), Stronsay (1 hr 35 mins), Westray (1 hr 25 mins), North Ronaldsay (2 hrs 30 mins) ('North Isles service')(timings are direct from Kirkwall – sailings via other islands take longer; *(1,2,7)*; daily except Papa Westray which is twice weekly and North Ronaldsay which is weekly), Kirkwall to Shapinsay (25 mins; *(6)*; 6 daily), Houton (Mainland) to Lyness (Hoy) (35 mins; *(4)*; 5 daily), Flotta (35 mins; *(4)*; 4 daily) and Graemsay (25 mins; *(4)*; weekly)('South Isles service') (timings are direct from Houton – sailings via other islands take longer), Tingwall (Mainland) to Rousay (20 mins; *(3)*; 6 daily), Egilsay (30 mins; *(3)*; 5 daily) and Wyre (20 mins; *(3)*; 5 daily) (timings are direct from Tingwall – sailings via other islands take longer).

## VESSELS

| 1 | EARL SIGURD | 771t | 90 | 12k | 145P | 26C | - | BA | Bromborough, GB | GB |
|---|---|---|---|---|---|---|---|---|---|---|
| 2 | EARL THORFINN | 771t | 90 | 12k | 145P | 26C | - | BA | Bromborough, GB | GB |
| 3 | EYNHALLOW | 79t | 87 | 9.5k | 95P | 8C | - | BA | Bristol, GB | GB |
| 4 | HOY HEAD | 358t | 94 | 9.8k | 125P | 18C | - | BA | Bideford, GB | GB |
| 5 | SHAPINSAY | 199t | 89 | 9.5k | 91P | 12C | - | BA | Hull, GB | GB |
| 6 | THORSVOE | 400t | 91 | 10.5k | 96P | 16C | - | BA | Campbletown, GB | GB |
| 7 | VARAGEN | 950t | 89 | 12k | 150P | 33C | 5L | BA | Selby, GB | GB |

EARL SIGURD, EARL THORFINN Built to inaugurate RO/RO working on the 'North Isles' service.

EYNHALLOW Built to inaugurate RO/RO services from Tingwall (Mainland) to Rousay, Egilsay and Wyre. In 1991 she was lengthened by 5 metres, to increase car capacity.

HOY HEAD Built to replace the THORSVOE on the 'South Isles' service (see above).

SHAPINSAY Built for the service from Kirkwall (Mainland) to Shapinsay.

THORSVOE Built for the 'South Isles' service (see above). In 1994 replaced by new HOY HEAD and became the main reserve vessel for the fleet.

VARAGEN Built for *Orkney Ferries*, a private company established to start a new route between Gills Bay (Caithness, Scotland) and Burwick (South Ronaldsay, Orkney). However, due to problems with the terminals it was not possible to establish regular services. In 1991, the company was taken over by *OISC* and the VARAGEN became part of their fleet, sharing 'North Isles' services with the EARL SIGURD and the EARL THORFINN and replacing the freight vessel ISLANDER (494t, 1969).

Services are also operated by the GOLDEN MARIANA (33t, 1973), a small passenger vessel.

**Under Construction**

| 8 | GRAEMSAY | - | 96 | 10k | 73P | 1C | - | C | Troon, GB | GB |
|---|----------|---|----|-----|-----|----|----|----|-----------|----|

GRAEMSAY Under construction to operate between Hoyness (Mainland), Moness (Hoy) and Graemsay. Designed to offer an all year round service to these islands, primarily for passengers and cargo.

# P&O SCOTTISH FERRIES

**THE COMPANY** *P&O Scottish Ferries* is British private sector company, part of the *P&O Group*. The name was changed from *P&O Ferries* to *P&O Scottish Ferries* in 1989.

**MANAGEMENT Managing Director:** Terry Cairns, **Marketing Director:** Scott Colegate.

**ADDRESS** PO Box 5, Jamieson's Quay, ABERDEEN AB9 8DL.

**TELEPHONE Administration:** +44 (0)1224589111 **Reservations:** +44 (0)1224 572615, **Fax:** +44 (0)1224 574411. **Telex:** 73344.

**ROUTES OPERATED** Scrabster – Stromness (Orkney) (1 hr 45 mins; *(2)*; up to 3 per day)), Aberdeen – Lerwick (Shetland) (14 hrs; *(1)*; up to 6 per week), Aberdeen – Stromness (8 hrs (day), 14 hrs (night)) – Lerwick (8 hrs; *(3)*; 1 per week (2 per week June, July and August)), Lerwick – Bergen (Norway) (13 hrs; *(1)*;1 per week (June, July and August)).

**VESSELS**

| 1 | ST CLAIR | 8696t | 71 | 19k | 600P | 160C | 30L | A | Bremerhaven, GE | GB |
|---|----------|-------|----|-----|------|------|-----|----|-----------------|----|
| 2 | ST OLA | 4833t | 71 | 16k | 500P | 140C | 12L | BA | Papenburg, GE | GB |
| 3 | ST SUNNIVA | 6350t | 71 | 16k | 407P | 199C | 28L | A | Helsingør, DK | GB |

ST CLAIR Built as the TRAVEMÜNDE for *Gedser-Travemünde Ruten* for their service between Gedser (Denmark) and Travemünde (Germany). In 1981 she was sold to *Prekookeanska Plovidba* of Yugoslavia, renamed the NJEGOS and used on their services between Yugoslavia, Greece and Italy. In 1984 chartered to *Sally Line* for use on their Ramsgate – Dunkerque service. In 1985 she was taken on a two year charter by *Brittany Ferries*, renamed the TREGASTEL and moved to the Plymouth – Roscoff service. In 1987 she was purchased and re-registered in France. In 1989 she was replaced by the QUIBERON and transferred to *Truckline Ferries* for their Poole – Cherbourg service. In 1991 she was sold to *P&O Scottish Ferries* and renamed the TREG. Following a major refit she was, in 1992, renamed the ST CLAIR and in March 1992 introduced onto the Aberdeen – Lerwick service, replacing the previous ST CLAIR (4468t, 1965). In addition to operating between Aberdeen and Lerwick, in 1993 she inaugurated a weekly peak season Lerwick – Bergen (Norway) service.

ST OLA Built as the SVEA SCARLETT for *Stockholms Rederi AB Svea* of Sweden and used on the *SL (Skandinavisk Linjetrafik)* service between København (Tuborg Havn) and Landskrona (Sweden). In 1980 she was sold to *Scandinavian Ferry Lines* of Sweden and *Dampskibsselskabet Øresund A/S* of Denmark (jointly owned). Initially she continued to serve Landskrona but later that year the Swedish terminal became Malmö. In 1981 she operated on the Helsingborg – Helsingør service for a short while, after which she was withdrawn and laid up. In 1982 she was sold to *Eckerö Line* of Finland, renamed the ECKERÖ and used on services between Grisslehamn (Sweden) and Eckerö (Åland Islands). In 1991 she was sold to *P&O Scottish Ferries* and renamed the ST OLA. In March 1992 she replaced the previous ST OLA (1345t, 1974) on the Scrabster – Stromness service.

ST SUNNIVA Built as the DJURSLAND for *Jydsk Faergefart* of Denmark for their service between Grenaa (Jutland) and Hundested (Sealand). In 1974 she was replaced by a larger vessel called DJURSLAND II (4371t, 1974) and switched to the company's other route, between Juelsminde (Jutland) and Kalundborg (Sealand), being renamed the LASSE II. In 1979 she was sold to *P&O Ferries*, renamed the N F PANTHER ('N F' standing for *'Normandy Ferries'*) and became the third vessel on the Dover – Boulogne service. Sold to *European Ferries* in 1985 and in summer 1986 replaced (with sister vessel NF TIGER (4045t, 1972)) by the FREE ENTERPRISE IV (5049t, 1969) and FREE ENTERPRISE V (5044t, 1970). In 1987 sold to *P&O Ferries*, renamed the ST SUNNIVA, converted to an overnight ferry and introduced onto the Aberdeen – Lerwick service, supplementing ST CLAIR and also providing a weekly Aberdeen – Stromness – Lerwick – and return service (twice weekly in high summer).

# PASSAGE EAST FERRY

**THE COMPANY** *Passage East Ferry Company Ltd* is an Irish Republic private sector company.

**MANAGEMENT Managing Director:** Derek Donnelly. **Operations Manager:** Conor Gilligan.

**ADDRESS** Barrack Street, Passage East, Co Waterford, Republic of Ireland.

**TELEPHONE Administration:** +353 (0)51 382480. **Reservations:** Not applicable. **Fax:** +353 (0)51 382598.

**ROUTE OPERATED** Passage East (County Waterford) – Ballyhack (County Wexford) (7 mins; *(1)*; frequent service).

**VESSEL**

| 1 | F.B.D. DUNBRODY | 139t | 60 | 8k | 107P | 18C | - | BA | Hamburg, GE | IR |
|---|----------------|------|----|----|------|-----|---|----|-------------|-----|

F.B.D. DUNBRODY Built as the BERNE-FARGE for the service between Berne and Farge, across the River Weser in Germany. Subsequently she was sold to *Elbe Clearing* of Germany, renamed the ELBE CLEARING 12 and used as a floating platform for construction works in the Elbe. In 1979 she was sold to *Passage East Ferry Company* and renamed the F.B.D. DUNBRODY. Passenger capacity is 72 in the winter.

# RED FUNNEL FERRIES

**THE COMPANY** *Red Funnel Ferries* is the trading name of the *Southampton Isle of Wight and South of England Royal Mail Steam Packet Public Limited Company*, a British private sector company. The company was acquired by *Associated British Ports* (owners of Southampton Docks) in 1989.

**MANAGEMENT Managing Director:** A M Whyte, **Marketing Director:** Ms O H Glass.

**ADDRESS** 12 Bugle Street, SOUTHAMPTON SO14 2JY.

**TELEPHONE Administration:** +44 (0)1703 333042, **Reservations:** +44 (0)1703 330333, **Fax:** +44 (0)1703 639438.

**ROUTE OPERATED** Southampton – East Cowes (55 mins; *(1,2,3,4)*; hourly).

**VESSELS**

| 1 | NETLEY CASTLE | 1858t | 74 | 12k | 713P | 70C | 12L | BA | Wallsend, GB | GB |
|---|---------------|-------|----|-----|------|------|------|----|--------------|-----|
| 2 | RED EAGLE | c3000t | 96 | 13k | 900P | 140C | 16L | BA | Port Glasgow, GB | GB |

# Superior accommodation with spectacular sea views.

When you sail to Orkney and Shetland with P&O Scottish Ferries you'll be spoilt with the high standards of comfort and service on the way to these unspoilt islands as well as by spectacular views from the sea of the coastline, wild yet gentle and inviting in its solitude.

Our vessels St Clair and St Ola, like their sister ship St Sunniva are as much a part of the local scene as the seabirds and the seals and ensure the perfect start to your island adventure.

You can choose from hotel inclusive holidays, mini-cruises, motorist holidays or day excursions. Our regular sailing prices start from £13.00.

Whichever you decide, you'll find us more than accommodating.

For further information see your local travel agent or contact P&O Scottish Ferries, Jamieson's Quay, Aberdeen, AB9 8DL. Tel: (01224) 572615.

**P&O**
Scottish Ferries

| 3 | RED FALCON | 2881t | 94 | 13k | 900P | 140C | 16L | BA | Port Glasgow, GB | GB |
|---|---|---|---|---|---|---|---|---|---|---|
| 4 | RED OSPREY | 2881t | 94 | 13k | 900P | 140C | 16L | BA | Port Glasgow, GB | GB |

NETLEY CASTLE Built for the Southampton – Cowes – East Cowes service (now Southampton – East Cowes). Although largely built at Wallsend, she was completed at Southampton as her original builders went bankrupt. Following delivery of the RED EAGLE she may be retained as a spare/relief vessel.

RED EAGLE, RED FALCON, RED OSPREY Built for the Southampton – East Cowes service.

*Red Funnel Ferries* also operate two 67 passenger hydrofoils named the SHEARWATER 5 (62t, 1980) and the SHEARWATER 6 (62t, 1982) and two 138 passenger catamarans named the RED JET 1 (168t, 1991) and the RED JET 2 (168t, 1991). They operate between Southampton and West Cowes; journey time is 20 minutes.

# SEABOARD MARINE (NIGG)

**THE COMPANY** *Seaboard Marine (Nigg)* is a British private company.

**MANAGEMENT Managing Director:** Andrew Thoms, **Marketing Manager:** Robert McCrae.

**ADDRESS** Cliff House, Cadboll, TAIN, Ross-shire.

**TELEPHONE Administration:** +44 (0)1862 871254, **Reservations:** +44 (0)1862 871254, **Fax:** +44 (0)1862 871231.

**ROUTE OPERATED** Cromarty – Nigg (Ross-shire) (10 mins; *(1)*; half hourly).

**VESSEL**

| 1 | CROMARTY ROSE | 28t | 87 | 8k | 50P | 2C | - | B | Ardrossan, GB | GB |
|---|---|---|---|---|---|---|---|---|---|---|

CROMARTY ROSE Built for *Seaboard Marine (Nigg)*.

# SHANNON FERRY LTD

**THE COMPANY** *Shannon Ferry Ltd* is an Irish Republic private company owned by six families on both sides of the Shannon Estuary.

**MANAGEMENT Managing Director:** J J Meehan.

**ADDRESS** Killimer, County Clare, Republic of Ireland.

**TELEPHONE Administration:** +353 (0)65 53124. **Reservations:** Not applicable. **Fax:** +353 (0)65 53125.

**ROUTE OPERATED** Killimer (County Clare) – Tarbert (County Kerry) (20 mins; *(1,2,3)*; hourly (half hourly during July and August).

**VESSELS**

| 1 | SHANNON DOLPHIN | 501t | 95 | 10k | 350P | 52C | - | BA | Appledore, GB | IR |
|---|---|---|---|---|---|---|---|---|---|---|
| 2 | SHANNON HEATHER | 300t | 68 | 9k | 250P | 30C | - | BA | Dartmouth, GB | IR |
| 3 | SHANNON WILLOW | 360t | 78 | 10k | 300P | 44C | - | BA | Bowling, GB | IR |

SHANNON DOLPHIN, SHANNON HEATHER, SHANNON WILLOW Built for *Shannon Ferry Ltd*.

# SHETLAND ISLANDS COUNCIL

**THE COMPANY** *Shetland Islands Council* is a British Local Government authority.

**MANAGEMENT Director of Marine Operations:** Capt G H Sutherland, FNI MRIN, **Divisional Manager, Ferry Operations:** M J Hogan.

**ADDRESS** Port Administration: Building, Sella Ness, MOSSBANK, Shetland ZE2 9QR.

**TELEPHONE Administration:** +44 (0)1806 244216, 244262, 244252, **Reservations:** +44 (0)1957 722259, **Fax:** +44 (0)1806 242237. **Voice Bank:** +44 (0)1426 986763, **Telex:** 75142 Sulvoe G.

**ROUTES OPERATED** Toft (Mainland) – Ulsta (Yell) (20 mins; *(1,5)*; up to 26 per day), Gutcher (Yell) – Belmont (Unst) (10 mins; *(3)*; 30 per day), Gutcher (Yell) – Oddsta (Fetlar) (25 mins; *(4)*; 6 per day), Lerwick (Mainland) – Bressay (5 mins; *(11)*; 19 per day), Laxo (Mainland) – Symbister (Whalsay) (30 mins; *(8,9)*; 17 per day), Vidlin (Mainland) – Symbister (Whalsay) (30-45 mins; *(8,9)*; operates when weather conditions preclude using Laxo), Lerwick (Mainland) – Out Skerries (3 hrs; *(2)*; 2 per week), Vidlin (Mainland) – Out Skerries (1 hrs 30 mins; *(2)*; 7 per week), Grutness (Mainland) – Fair Isle (3 hrs; *(6)*; 2 per week), West Burrafirth (Mainland) – Papa Stour (40 mins; *(10)*; 7 per week), Foula – Mainland (port varies)(3 hrs; *(13)*; 2 per week).

## VESSELS

| 1 | BIGGA | 274t | 91 | 11k | 96P | 21C | 4L | BA | St Monans, GB | GB |
|---|-------|------|----|----|-----|-----|----|----|---------------|-----|
| 2 | FILLA | 130t | 83 | 9k | 12P | 6C | 1T | A | Flekkefjord, NO | GB |
| 3 | FIVLA | 230t | 85 | 11k | 95P | 15C | 4L | BA | Troon, GB | GB |
| 4 | FYLGA | 147t | 75 | 8.5k | 93P | 10C | 2L | BA | Tórshavn, FA | GB |
| 5 | GEIRA | 226t | 88 | 10.8k | 95P | 15C | 4L | BA | Hessle, GB | GB |
| 6 | GOOD SHEPHERD IV | 76t | 86 | 10k | 12P | 1C | 0L | C | St Monans, GB | GB |
| 7 | GRIMA | 147t | 74 | 8.5k | 93P | 10C | 2L | BA | Bideford, GB | GB |
| 8 | HENDRA | 225t | 82 | 11k | 100P | 18C | 4L | BA | Bromborough, GB | GB |
| 9 | KJELLA | 158t | 57 | 10.5k | 63P | 12C | 2L | BA | Harstad, NO | GB |
| 10 | KOADA | 35t | 69 | 8k | 12P | 1C | 0L | C | Bideford, GB | GB |
| 11 | LEIRNA | 420t | 93 | 10k | 100P | 20C | 4L | BA | Greenock, GB | GB |
| 12 | THORA | 147t | 75 | 8.5k | 93P | 10C | 2L | BA | Tórshavn, FA | GB |

BIGGA Used on the Toft (Mainland ) – Ulsta (Yell) service.

FILLA Used on the Lerwick (Mainland) – Out Skerries and Vidlin (Mainland) – Out Skerries services. At other times she operates freight services around the Shetland Archipelago. She resembles a miniature oil rig supply vessel.

FIVLA Used on the Gutcher (Yell) – Belmont (Unst) service.

FYLGA Used on the Gutcher (Yell) – Oddsta (Fetlar) service.

GEIRA Used on the Toft (Mainland ) – Ulsta (Yell) service.

GOOD SHEPHERD IV Used on the service between Grutness (Mainland) and Fair Isle. Vehicles conveyed by special arrangement and generally consist of agricultural vehicles for the islanders.

GRIMA Used on the Lerwick (Mainland) – Maryfield (Bressay) service until 1992 when she was replaced by the LEIRNA and became a spare vessel.

HENDRA Used on the Laxo (Mainland) – Symbister (Whalsay) service.

KJELLA Built for *A/S Torghatten Trafikkselskap* of Norway for Norwegian fjord services. In 1980 purchased by *Shetland Islands Council*. She operates on the Laxo (Mainland) – Symbister (Whalsay) service.

*St Sunniva (Lawrence MacDuff)*

*Earl Sigurd* and *Earl Thorfinn* *(Lawrence MacDuff)*

KOADA Built as an inshore trawler and bought by the shareholders on Fair Isle to operate to Shetland and named the GOOD SHEPHERD III. In 1986 the service was taken over by *Shetland Islands Council* and she was replaced by GOOD SHEPHERD IV. She was however acquired by the Council and renamed the KOADA. She now operates between West Burrafirth (Mainland) and Papa Stour and Foula. Car carrying capacity used occasionally.

LEIRNA Built for *Shetland Islands Council* for the Lerwick – Maryfield (Bressay) service. She is of similar design to *Caledonian MacBrayne's* LOCH DUNVEGAN and LOCH FYNE.

THORA Now a spare vessel. Sister vessel to the FYLGA and the GRIMA.

**Under Construction**

| 13 | NEWBUILDING | - | 96 | 12P | 1C | - | C | Penryn, GB | GB |
|----|-------------|---|----|-----|----|---|---|-----------|-----|

NEWBUILDING Under construction for the Foula service. She has a Cygnus Marine GM38 hull and is to be based on the island where she will be lifted out of the water. She is due to enter service in May 1996. Vehicle capacity is to take new vehicles to the island – not for tourist vehicles. Mainland ports to be used are Walls, Scalloway or West Burrafirth. The KOADA will then operate to Papa Stour only.

# WESTERN FERRIES (ARGYLL)

**THE COMPANY** *Western Ferries (Argyll)* is a British private sector company, a subsidiary of *Harrisons (Clyde) Ltd.*

**MANAGEMENT Director:** Kenneth C Cadenhead.

**ADDRESS** 16 Woodside Crescent, GLASGOW G3 7UT.

**TELEPHONE Administration:** +44 (0)141-332 9766. **Reservations:** Not applicable. **Fax:** +44 (0)141-332 0267, **Telex:** 77203.

**ROUTE OPERATED** Port Askaig (Islay) – Feolin (Jura) (5 mins; *(1)*; approx hourly).

**VESSEL**

| 1 | SOUND OF GIGHA | 65t | 66 | 7.5k | 28P | 8C | - | B | Bideford, GB | GB |
|---|----------------|-----|----|------|-----|----|---|---|-------------|-----|

SOUND OF GIGHA Built as the ISLE OF GIGHA for *Eilean Sea Service*. She was built as small 'landing-craft' type vessel, conveying lorries around the west coast of Scotland. In 1969, purchased by *Western Ferries*, converted to a car and passenger vessel, renamed the SOUND OF GIGHA and put onto the Port Askaig (Islay) – Feolin (Jura) service.

# WESTERN FERRIES (CLYDE)

**THE COMPANY** *Western Ferries (Clyde)* is a British private sector company. The company broke away from *Western Ferries (Argyll)* following a management 'buy out' in 1985.

**MANAGEMENT Managing Director:** Alan Bradley.

**ADDRESS** Hunter's Quay, DUNOON PA23 8HY.

**TELEPHONE Administration:** +44 (0)1369 4452, **Reservations:** Not applicable, **Fax:** +44 (0)1369 6020, **Telex:** 77203 H Clyde G.

**ROUTE OPERATED** McInroy's Point, Gourock – Hunter's Quay, Dunoon (20 mins; *(1,2,3,4)*; half hourly).

## VESSELS

| 1 | G24 | - | 61 | 10k | 200P | 37C | - | BA | - | GB |
|---|---|---|---|---|---|---|---|---|---|---|
| 2 | SOUND OF SCALPAY | 549t | 61 | 10k | 200P | 37C | - | BA | Arnhem, NL | GB |
| 3 | SOUND OF SCARBA | 175t | 60 | 7k | 200P | 22C | - | BA | Åmål, SW | GB |
| 4 | SOUND OF SEIL | 363t | 59 | 10.5k | 620P | 26C | - | BA | Troon, GB | GB |
| 5 | SOUND OF SHUNA | 244t | 62 | 7k | 200P | 25C | - | BA | Åmål, SW | GB |
| 6 | SOUND OF SLEAT | 466t | 61 | 10k | 296P | 30C | - | BAS | Hardinxveld, NL | GB |

G24 Built for *Amsterdam City Council* for services across the harbour. In 1996 purchased by *Western Ferries* to replace the SOUND OF SEIL. Although similar to the SOUND OF SCALPAY she is not a sister vessel. New name not available at time of going to print.

SOUND OF SCALPAY Built as the G23 for *Amsterdam City Council* for services across the harbour. In 1995 sold to *Western Ferries* and renamed the SOUND OF SCALPAY.

SOUND OF SCARBA Built as the ÖLANDSSUND III for *Rederi AB Ölandssund* of Sweden for service between Revsudden on the mainland and Stora Rör on the island of Öland. Following the opening of a new bridge near Kalmar, about 4 miles to the South, the ferry service ceased. In 1973 she was sold to *Western Ferries*, renamed the SOUND OF SCARBA and joined the SOUND OF SHUNA their Gourock – Dunoon service. Now relief vessel and also used on contract work in the Clyde estuary.

SOUND OF SEIL Built as the FRESHWATER for *British Railways* for their Lymington – Yarmouth (Isle of Wight) service. In 1983 sold to Lebanese interests for an undisclosed purpose but remained laid up at Portsmouth until 1985 when she was sold to *Western Ferries*. In 1986 she was renamed the SOUND OF SEIL and introduced on the Gourock – Dunoon service.

SOUND OF SHUNA Built as the ÖLANDSSUND IV for *Rederi AB Ölandssund* of Sweden (see the SOUND OF SCARBA above). In 1973 she was sold to *Western Ferries*, renamed the SOUND OF SHUNA and, with the SOUND OF SCARBA, inaugurated the Gourock – Dunoon service.

SOUND OF SLEAT Built as the DE HOORN for the service between Maassluis and Rozenburg, across the 'Nieuwe Waterweg' (New Waterway) in The Netherlands. In 1988 she was purchased by *Western Ferries (Clyde)*, renamed the SOUND OF SLEAT and introduced onto the Gourock – Dunoon service.

# WESTERN ISLES ISLANDS COUNCIL

**THE COMPANY** *Western Isles Islands Council* is a British municipal authority.

**ADDRESS** Council Offices, Sandwick Road, STORNOWAY, Isle of Lewis HS1 2BW.

**TELEPHONE Administration:** +44 (0)1851 703773, Extn 496 **Reservations:** Berneray Ferry: +44 (0)1876 540230, Eriskay Ferry: +44 (0)1878 720261, **Fax:** +44 (0)1851 705349.

**ROUTE OPERATED** Ludaig (South Uist) – Eriskay (30 mins; *(2)*; 3 per day (minimum)), Newtonferry (North Uist) – Berneray (15 mins; *(1)*; 5 per day). Additional services operate during the summer.

## VESSELS

| 1 | EILEAN BHEARNARAIGH | 67t | 83 | 7k | 35P | 4C | 1T | BA | Glasgow, GB | GB |
|---|---|---|---|---|---|---|---|---|---|---|
| 2 | EILEAN NA H-OIGE | 69t | 80 | 7k | 35P | 4C | 1T | BA | Stornoway, GB | GB |

EILEAN BHEARNARAIGH Built for *Western Isles Islands Council* for their Newtonferry (North Uist) – Berneray service. When the new *Caledonian MacBrayne* service starts in spring 1996 she will continue to provide a limited service as backup. When a causeway between North Uist and Berneray is built in about two years' time she will probably be withdrawn.

EILEAN NA H-OIGE Built for *Western Isles Islands Council* for their Ludaig (South Uist) – Eriskay service.

# WIGHTLINK

**THE COMPANY** *Wightlink* is a British private sector company, owned by *ClNVen Ltd*, a venture capital company. The routes and vessels were previously part of *Sealink* but were excluded from the purchase of most of the *Sealink* operations by *Stena Line AB* in 1990.

**MANAGEMENT Executive Chairman:** Michael Aiken, **Managing Director:** Michael Mulvey, **Head of Marketing:** Janet Saville.

**ADDRESS** PO Box 59, PORTSMOUTH PO1 2XB.

**TELEPHONE Administration:** +44 (0)1705 812011, **Reservations:** +44 (0)1705 827744, **Fax:** +44 (0)1705 855257, **Telex:** 86440 WIGHTLG.

**ROUTES OPERATED** Lymington – Yarmouth (Isle of Wight) (approx 30 mins; *(1,2,3)*; half hourly), Portsmouth – Ryde (Isle of Wight)(passenger only) (approx 15mins; *(4,5)*; half hourly/hourly), Portsmouth – Fishbourne (Isle of Wight) (approx 35 mins; *(6,7,8,9)*, half hourly/hourly).

**VESSELS**

| 1 | CAEDMON | 763t | 73 | 9.5k | 756P | 58C | 6L | BA | Dundee, GB | GB |
|---|---------|------|----|------|------|-----|----|----|-----------|----|
| 2 | CENRED | 761t | 73 | 9.5k | 756P | 58C | 6L | BA | Dundee, GB | GB |
| 3 | CENWULF | 761t | 73 | 9.5k | 756P | 58C | 6L | BA | Dundee, GB | GB |
| 4p | OUR LADY PAMELA | 312t | 86 | 28.5k | 410P | - | - | - | Hobart, AL | GB |
| 5p | OUR LADY PATRICIA | 312t | 86 | 28.5k | 410P | - | - | - | Hobart, AL | GB |
| 6 | ST CATHERINE | 2036t | 83 | 12.5k | 1000P | 142C | 12L | BA | Leith, GB | GB |
| 7 | ST CECILIA | 2968t | 87 | 12.5k | 1000P | 142C | 12L | BA | Selby, GB | GB |
| 8 | ST FAITH | 3009t | 90 | 12.5k | 1000P | 142C | 12L | BA | Selby, GB | GB |
| 9 | ST HELEN | 2983t | 83 | 12.5k | 1000P | 142C | 12L | BA | Leith, GB | GB |

CAEDMON Built for Portsmouth – Fishbourne service. In 1983 transferred to the Lymington – Yarmouth service.

CENRED, CENWULF Built for Lymington – Yarmouth service.

OUR LADY PAMELA, OUR LADY PATRICIA Built for the Portsmouth – Ryde service. Passenger only catamarans.

ST CATHERINE, ST CECILIA, ST FAITH, ST HELEN Built for the Portsmouth – Fishbourne service.

# WOOLWICH FREE FERRY

**THE COMPANY** The *Woolwich Free Ferry* is operated by the *London Borough of Greenwich*, a British municipal authority.

**MANAGEMENT Principal Engineer (Ferry):** C Thew, **Ferry Manager:** Capt P Deeks.

**ADDRESS** New Ferry Approach, Woolwich, LONDON SE18 6DX.

**TELEPHONE Administration:** +44 (0)181-312 5574, **Reservations:** Not applicable, **Fax:** +44 (0)181-316 6096.

**ROUTE OPERATED** Woolwich – North Woolwich (free ferry) (5 mins; *(1,2,3)*; 5 mins (weekdays), 10 mins (weekends)).

**VESSELS**

| 1 | ERNEST BEVIN | 738t | 63 | - | 300P | 32C | 6L | BA | Dundee, GB | GB |
|---|--------------|------|----|---|------|-----|----|----|-----------|----|
| 2 | JAMES NEWMAN | 738t | 63 | - | 300P | 32C | 6L | BA | Dundee, GB | GB |
| 3 | JOHN BURNS | 738t | 63 | - | 300P | 32C | 6L | BA | Dundee, GB | GB |

ERNEST BEVIN, JAMES NEWMAN, JOHN BURNS Built for the *London County Council* who operated the service in 1963. In 1965 ownership was transferred to the *Greater London Council*. Following the abolition of the *GLC* in April 1986, ownership was transferred to the *Department of Transport*. The *London Borough of Greenwich* operate the service on their behalf.

# SECTION 3 - Freight only Ferries

# BELFAST FREIGHT FERRIES

**THE COMPANY** *Belfast Freight Ferries* is a British private sector company owned by *Scruttons plc* of London.

**MANAGEMENT Operations Director:** Trevor Wright. **Commercial Director:** Alan Peacock.

**ADDRESS** Victoria Terminal 1, Dargan Road, BELFAST BT3 9LJ.

**TELEPHONE Administration:** +44 (0)1232 770112. **Reservations:** +44 (0)1232 770112. **Fax:** +44 (0)1232 781217.

**ROUTE OPERATED** Heysham – Belfast; (8 hrs; *(1,2,3)*; 3 daily).

**VESSELS**

| 1 | RIVER LUNE | 7756t | 83 | 15k | 12P | - | 80T | A | Galatz, RO | BA |
|---|------------|-------|----|-----|-----|---|-----|---|------------|----|
| 2 | SAGA MOON  | 7746t | 84 | 15k | 12P | - | 72T | A | Travemünde, GE | GI |
| 3 | SPHEROID   | 7171t | 71 | 16k | 12P | - | 57T | A | Sharpsborg, NO | IM |

RIVER LUNE Built for chartering as the BALDER VIK and initially used on services between Italy and the Middle East. Subsequently she was employed on a number of charters including *North Sea Ferries* and *Norfolk Line*. In 1986 she was sold to *Navrom* of Romania, renamed the BAZIAS 7 and initially used on their Mediterranean and Black Sea services. In 1987 she was chartered to *Kent Line* for service between Chatham and Zeebrugge. In 1988 she was sold to *Stena AB* of Sweden and chartered for service between Finland and Germany. In 1989 she was briefly renamed the STENA TOPPER before being further renamed the SALAR. During the ensuing years she undertook a number of charters. In 1993 chartered to *Belfast Freight Ferries* and renamed the RIVER LUNE.

SAGA MOON Built as the LIDARTINDUR for *Trader Line* of the Faroe Islands for services between Tórshavn and Denmark. In 1986 chartered to *Belfast Freight Ferries* renamed the SAGA MOON. In 1990 she was sold to *Belfast Freight Ferries*. In 1995 she was stretched to increase trailer capacity from 52 to 72 units, the separate carriage of 50 trade cars and the replacement of a lift by a ramp.

SPHEROID Built as the STARMARK for *Avermoi Oy* of Finland. In 1981 sold to *Manta Line* of Greece for Mediterranean and deep sea service and renamed the RORO TRADER. In 1985 she was sold to *Oceanwide Shipping* for charter and renamed the NIEKIRK. In 1986 chartered to *Belfast Freight Ferries* and in 1987 sold to them and renamed the SPHEROID.

# COBELFRET RO/RO SERVICES

**THE COMPANY** *Cobelfret RO/RO Services* is a Belgian private sector company, a subsidiary of *Cobelfret nv* of *Antwerp*.

**MANAGEMENT Managing Director (Belgium):** George Bruers, **Managing Director (UK):** Mike Gray, **UK Agents:** Ronnie Daelman and Peter Mann (Purfleet Agencies).

**ADDRESS** Belgium: Sneeuwbeslaan 14 B2610, ANTWERP, Belgium, UK: Purfleet Thames Terminal Ltd, London Road, PURFLEET, Essex RM16 1RT.

**TELEPHONE Administration:** Belgium: +32 (0)3 829 9011, UK: +44 (0)1708 865522, **Reservations** Belgium: +32 (0)50 547200, UK (Purfleet Services): +44 (0)1708 891199, (Immingham Services): +44 (0)1469 571711, **Fax:** Belgium (Admin): +32 (0)3 237 7646, Belgium (Reservations): +32 (0)50 545348, UK (Admin): +44 (0)1708 866418, UK (Reservations – Purfleet): +44 (0)1708 890853, (Reservations – Immingham) +44 (0)1469 573739, **Telex:** Belgium: 32600, UK (Admin): 897854, UK (Reservations): 911683.

**ROUTES OPERATED** Zeebrugge – Purfleet (8 hrs; 4 per day), Zeebrugge – Immingham (14 hrs; 9 per week). Vessels are switched between routes (and other *Cobelfret* services not serving the UK), so it is not possible so say which vessels serve on which routes at any particular time.

**VESSELS**

| 1 | BELVAUX | 6832t | 79 | 14k | 12P | 520C | 100T | R | Hoboken, BE | PA |
|---|---------|-------|----|-----|-----|------|------|----|-------------|-----|
| 2 | CYMBELINE | 11886t | 92 | 14.5k | 10P | 790C | 130T | A2 | Dalian, CH | PA |
| 3 | EGLANTINE | 10035t | 89 | 14.5k | 10P | 790C | 120T | A2 | Dalian, CH | PA |
| 4 | LOVERVAL | 10931t | 78 | 17k | 12P | 675C | 112T | A2 | Lödöse, SW | PA |
| 5 | SYMPHORINE | 10030t | 88 | 14.5k | 10P | 790C | 130T | A2 | Dalian, CH | PA |
| 6 | UNDINE | 11854t | 91 | 14.5k | 10P | 790C | 130T | A2 | Dalian, CH | PA |

BELVAUX Built for *Cobelfret*.

CYMBELINE Built for *Cobelfret*.

EGLANTINE Built by *Cobelfret*.

LOVERVAL Built as the VALLMO for the *Johansson Group* of Sweden and undertook a variety of charters. In 1982 she was sold *Cobelfret* and renamed the MATINA. In 1984 renamed the LOVERVAL.

SYMPHORINE Built *Cobelfret*.

UNDINE Built for *Cobelfret*.

**Under Construction**

| 7 | CELESTINE | c25000t | 96 | 18k | 0P | 400C | 160T | A | Kavasaki, JA | PA |
|---|-----------|---------|----|-----|-----|------|------|----|--------------|-----|
| 8 | CLEMENTINE | c25000t | 96 | 18k | 0P | 400C | 160T | A | Kavasaki, JA | PA |

CELESTINE, CLEMENTINE Under construction for *Cobelfret*.

# COMMODORE FERRIES

**THE COMPANY** *Commodore Ferries (CI) Ltd* is a Guernsey private sector company.

**MANAGEMENT Managing Director:** Jeff Vidamour.

**ADDRESS** Commodore House, Bulwer Avenue, St Sampson's, GUERNSEY, Channel Islands GY2 4JN.

**TELEPHONE Administration:** +44 (0)1481 46841 **Reservations:** +44 (0)1481 46841. **Fax:** +44 (0)1481 49543.

**ROUTE OPERATED** Portsmouth – Channel Islands (9 hrs; *(1,2)*; 2 per day).

**VESSELS**

| 1 | COMMODORE GOODWILL | 11166t | 96 | 18.3k | 12P | - | 95T | A | Vlissingen, NL | BA |
|---|--------------------|--------|----|-------|-----|---|-----|----|----------------|-----|
| 2 | ISLAND COMMODORE | 11166t | 95 | 18.3k | 12P | - | 95T | A | Vlissingen, NL | BA |

COMMODORE GOODWILL, ISLAND COMMODORE Built for *Commodore Ferries*.

*Island Commodore (Commodore Ferries)*

# DART LINE

**THE COMPANY** *Dart Line Ltd* is a British private sector company owned by *Jacobs Holdings plc.* They took over the Dartford – Vlissingen service from *Sally Ferries* in 1996.

**MANAGEMENT Managing Director:** Simon Taylor, **Marketing Manager** Kevin Miller.

**ADDRESS** Crossways Business Park, Thames Europort, DARTFORD, Kent DA2 6PJ.

**TELEPHONE Administration: & Reservations:** +44 (0) 1322 281122, **Fax:** +44 (0) 1322 281133.

**ROUTE OPERATED** Dartford – Vlissingen (8/9 hrs; *(1,2)*; 2 per day).

**VESSELS**

| 1 | DART 2 | 2846t | 84 | 15k | 0P | - | 100T | A | Galatz, RO | RO |
|---|--------|-------|----|----|----|---|------|---|-----------|-----|
| 2 | DART 5 | 2831t | 86 | 15k | 0P | - | 100T | A | Galatz, RO | RO |

DART 2 Built as the BALDER HAV for *Parley Augustsson*. In 1986 sold to *Navrom* of Romania, renamed the BAZIAS 2 and used on Mediterranean services. In 1996 chartered to *Dart Line* and renamed the DART 2.

DART 5 Launched as the BALDER RA. On completion sold to *Navrom* of Romania, renamed the BAZIAS 5 and used on Mediterranean services. In 1996 chartered to *Dart Line* and renamed the DART 5.

# DFDS

**THE COMPANY** *DFDS* is one of the trading names of the freight division of *DFDS* A/S, a Danish private sector public company. See also *Tor Line* (Swedish services).

**MANAGEMENT Managing Director UK:** Ebbe Pedersen.

**ADDRESS** Scandinavia House, Parkeston Quay, HARWICH CO12 4QG.

**TELEPHONE Administration & Reservations:** +44 (0)1255 242242, **Fax:** +44 (0)1255 244310, **Telex:** 98582.

**ROUTES OPERATED** Immingham – Esbjerg (20 hrs; *(1,3)*; 4/5 per week), North Shields – Esbjerg (24 hrs; *(1,3)*; 2/3 per week), Immingham – Cuxhaven (22 hrs; *(4)* 3 per week) (under the name of *Elbe – Humber RoLine*), Harwich – Esbjerg (20 hrs;*(2)*; 6 per week (including sailings by passenger vessel DANA ANGLIA)).

**VESSELS**

| 1 | DANA CIMBRIA | 12189t | 86 | 17k | 12P | - | 150T | A | Frederikshavn, DK | DK |
|---|--------------|--------|----|------|-----|------|------|----|------------------|-----|
| 2 | DANA HAFNIA | 11125t | 79 | 16k | 12P | 400C | 121T | A2 | Lödöse, SW | DK |
| 3 | DANA MAXIMA | 17068 | 78 | 17 | 12P | - | 210T | A | Osaka | DK |
| 4 | DANA MINERVA | 3973t | 75 | 18.5k | 12P | - | 94T | A | Kristiansand, NO | GE |

DANA CIMBRIA Launched as the MERCANDIAN EXPRESS II and immediately chartered to *DFDS* for their North Sea freight services, being renamed the DANA CIMBRIA. Generally used on the Immingham and North Shields – Esbjerg services.

DANA HAFNIA Built as the LINNÉ and chartered to *OT Africa Line* for services between Italy and Libya. In 1985 sold and renamed the BELINDA; she was employed on a variety of charters including *DFDS* and *Stena Line* until 1988 when she was sold to *Dannebrog* of Denmark and renamed the NORDBORG. Chartering continued, including *Kent Line* and *DFDS* again, and in 1993 she was chartered to *Cobelfret*. In 1994 she was sold to *DFDS* and renamed the DANA HAFNIA. Initially operated on Tor Line services but in 1995 transferred to *DFDS* to operate between Harwich and Esbjerg.

DANA MAXIMA Built for *DFDS* for their North Sea services. Generally used on the Immingham and North Shields services. In summer 1995 she was lengthened to increase trailer capacity.

DANA MINERVA Launched as the TOR CALEDONIA for *Tor Line* of Sweden for North Sea service. In 1978 sold to *DSR Line* of the former DDR and renamed the FICHTELBERG. She was used on services between the DDR and Cuba and also performed a number of charters. In 1991 she was chartered to *Dublin Ferries* for a new Dublin-Liverpool service and in 1992 she was renamed the SPIRIT OF DUBLIN. Later in 1992 the service ceased and, after a brief period with her owners, resuming the name FICHTELBERG, she was chartered to *North Sea Ferries* and placed on the Hull – Rotterdam service, being renamed NORCLIFF. In 1993 the charter was ended and she returned to her owners and resumed her name. In 1994 chartered to *DFDS* to provide additional capacity on the Immingham – Cuxhaven service following the ending of *DSR Line's* service between Hull and Hamburg. In 1995 renamed the DANA MINERVA. In 1995 transferred to *Dan-Liet Line* (71% owned by *DFDS*) in 1995 to operate between Fredericia (Denmark) and Klaipeda (Lithuania) but returned at the end of the year and in 1996 operates on the Hull – Cuxhaven service.

**Under Construction**

| | | | | | | | | | |
|---|---|---|---|---|---|---|---|---|---|
| DANA FUTURA | 14820t | 96 | 19.7k | 12P | - | 156T | AS | Donanda, IT | DK |

DANA FUTURA Built for *DFDS* to operate between Harwich and Esbjerg. Due to enter service in June 1996.

# EIMSKIP

**THE COMPANY** *Eimskip* is an Icelandic private sector company.

**MANAGEMENT Managing Director:** Mr Sigurgestsson, **Marketing Manager:** Gudjón Audunsson.

**ADDRESS** PO Box 220, 121 Reykjavik, Iceland.

**TELEPHONE Administration:** +354 (0)5257000. **Reservations:** Iceland: +354 (0)5257000, UK: +44 (0)1469 571880, **Fax:** Iceland: +354 (0)5257179, UK: +44 (0)1469 571878, **Telex:** Iceland: 2022, UK: 527179.

**ROUTE OPERATED** Reykjavik – Immingham (1 per week). Immingham – Hamburg – Rotterdam – Immingham (circular service) (1 per week).

**VESSELS**

| 1 | BRUARFOSS | 14714t | 78 | 14.5k | 12P | - | 230T | A | Kiel, GE | IC |
|---|---|---|---|---|---|---|---|---|---|---|
| 2 | LAXFOSS | 12817t | 78 | 15k | 12P | - | 115T | A | Kiel, GE | IC |

BRUARFOSS Built as the MERZARIO PERSIA for *Merzario Line* of Italy and used on services between Italy and the Middle East. In 1986 she was chartered to *Grimaldi Line* of Italy and renamed the PERSIA, continuing on Middle East services. In 1988 she was sold to *Eimskip* and renamed the BRUARFOSS.

LAXFOSS Built as the MERZARIO ARABIA for *Merzario Line* of Italy and used on services between Italy and the Middle East. In 1986 she was chartered to *Ignazio Messina* of Italy and renamed the JOLLY OCRA, continuing on Middle East services. In 1987, she was chartered to *Lloyd Triestino Line* of Italy and renamed the DUINO. In 1988 she was sold to *Eimskip* and renamed the LAXFOSS.

# EUROAFRICA SHIPPING LINE

**THE COMPANY** *Euroafrica Shipping Line* is a Polish private sector company.

**MANAGEMENT Managing Director:** Wlodzimierz Matuszewski, **Deputy Managing Director:** Zbigniew Ligierko.

**ADDRESS** Poland: Energetyków 3/4, 70-952, Szczecin, Poland. UK: Gdynia-America Shipping Lines (London) Ltd, 238 City Road, LONDON EC1V 2QL.

**TELEPHONE Administration & Reservations:** Poland: +48 (0)91 623 806. UK: +44 (0)171-253 9561, **Fax:** Poland: +48 (0)91 623 183, 623 140, UK: +44 (0)171-250 3625, **Telex:** Poland: 422387 & 422396, UK: 23256.

**ROUTE OPERATED** Gdynia – Felixstowe – Middlesbrough – Gdynia (3/4 days; *(1)*; 2 per week). Note: triangular service, operating in a clockwise direction.

**VESSEL**

| 1 | INOWROCŁAW | 14786t | 80 | 15k | 12P | - | 116T | A | Rauma, FI | PO |
|---|---|---|---|---|---|---|---|---|---|---|

INOWROCŁAW Built for *Polish Ocean Lines*, previously a state owned company. Now owned by *Euroafrica Shipping Line*.

# EXXTOR FERRIES

**THE COMPANY** *Exxtor Ferries* is a British private sector company

**MANAGEMENT Line Manager:** Jeffe Bake.

**ADDRESS** PO Box 40, Manby Road, IMMINGHAM, South Humberside DN40 3EG.

**TELEPHONE Administration & Reservations:** +44 (0)1469 571711 x 314.

**ROUTE OPERATED** Immingham – Rotterdam (14 hours; *(1,2)*; 1 daily)

| 1 | ENDEAVOUR | 9963t | 76 | 16k | 12P | - | 95T | A | Brevik, NO | BA |
|---|---|---|---|---|---|---|---|---|---|---|
| 2 | EXCALIBUR | 9963t | 76 | 16k | 12P | - | 95T | A | Brevik, NO | BA |

ENDEAVOUR Built as the SEASPEED DORA. In 1980 chartered to *Roto Line*, renamed the INGER EXPRESS and used on services between Sweden and the UK. In 1981 she was chartered to *Cobelfret*, renamed the MARCEL C and used on their services between the UK and Belgium. In 1989 she was renamed the BASSRO STAR embarked on a series of charters including *Belfast Freight Ferries* and a number of Mediterranean operators. In 1995 she was sold to *Exxtor Ferries* and renamed the ENDEAVOUR.

EXCALIBUR Built as the SEASPEED DANA. In 1980 chartered to *Roto Line*, renamed the DANA and used on services between Sweden and the UK. In 1983 she was sold to *Stena Line* and embarked on a number of charters, mainly in the Caribbean. In 1990 she was chartered to *CoTuNav* of Tunisia, renamed the SALAH L and used on services from Tunisia to Southern Europe. In 1993 she was chartered to *Olympic Ferries* of Greece, renamed the SENATOR, operating between Greece and Italy. In 1995 she was sold to *Exxtor Ferries* and renamed the EXCALIBUR.

# FINANGLIA FERRIES

**THE COMPANY** *Finanglia Ferries* is a joint operation between *Finncarriers Oy Ab*, a Finnish private sector company and *United Baltic Corporation*, a British private sector company.

**MANAGEMENT Managing Director:** J Ashley, **Marketing Manager:** Miss C M Cotton.

**ADDRESSES** UK: 5th Floor, Banksede House, 107/112 Leadenhall Street, LONDON EC3A 4AP,

Finland: Porkkalankatu 7, 00181 Helsinki, Finland.

**TELEPHONE Reservations and Administration:** UK: +44 (0)171-397 0500, Finland: +358 (0) 134311, **Fax:** UK: +44 (0)171-488 4450, Finland: +358 (0) 13431200, **Telex:** UK: 887002, Finland: 1001743.

**ROUTES OPERATED** Felixstowe – Helsinki (Finland) – Hamina (Finland) (4 days; 2 per week northbound, 3 per week southbound), Hull – Helsinki – Hamina (5 days; 1 per week). Note: Finland – Hull service operates via Felixstowe on southward journey giving additional southward sailing. Vessels operate on weekly, two and three weekly cycles and are frequently moved between routes. *Finncarriers* has a very large fleet of vessels operating between Finland and other European destinations and vessels are subject to change

## VESSELS

| 1 | BALTIC EAGLE | 14738t | 79 | 18K | 12P | - | 116T | A | Rauma,FI | IM |
|---|---|---|---|---|---|---|---|---|---|---|
| 2 | BALTIC EIDER | 20865t | 89 | 19k | OP | - | 180T | A | Ulsan, SK | IM |
| 3 | BORE BRITANNICA | 15525t | 78 | 17K | OP | - | 174T | A | Ulsan, SK | FI |
| 4 | BORE GOTHICA | 14059t | 78 | 17k | OP | - | 174T | A | Ulsan, SK | SW |
| 5 | CELIA | 20172t | 79 | 16.5k | OP | - | 136T | Q | Ichihara, JA | SW |
| 6 | CORTIA | 20169t | 78 | 19k | OP | - | 136T | Q | Ichihara, JA | SW |
| 7 | TRANSBALTICA | 21224t | 90 | 19k | OP | - | 182T | A | Ulsan, SK | CY |

BALTIC EAGLE Built for *United Baltic Corporation*

BALTIC EIDER Built for *United Baltic Corporation.*

BORE BRITANNICA Built as the ATLANTIC PROJECT for *Stena Line* and chartered to ACL of Great Britain for service between Britain and Canada. In 1981 chartered to *Merzario Line* of Italy for services between Italy and Saudi Arabia and renamed the MERZARIO HISPANIA. In 1983 returned to *Stena Line* and renamed the STENA HISPANIA. In 1984 chartered to *Kotka Line* of Finland, renamed the KOTKA VIOLET and used on their services between Finland, UK and West Africa. This charter ended in 1985 and she was again named the STENA HISPANIA. In 1986 she was renamed the STENA BRITANNICA and used on *Stena Portlink* (later *Stena Tor Line*) service between Sweden and Britain. In 1988 she was chartered to *Bore Line* of Finland, renamed the BORE BRITANNICA and used on services between Finland and Britain. In 1992 chartered to *Finncarriers*.

BORE GOTHICA Built as the ATLANTIC PROSPER for *Stena Line* and chartered to *ACL* (see above). In 1981 chartered to *Merzario Line* of Italy for services between Italy and Saudi Arabia and renamed, initially, the STENA IONIA and then the MERZARIO IONIA. Later the same year she reverted to the name STENA IONIA and was chartered to *OT West Africa Line* for services between Europe and Nigeria. In 1985 she was renamed the STENA GOTHICA and used on *Stena Portlink* services. In 1988 she was chartered to *Bore Line* of Finland and renamed the BORE BRITANNICA. In 1992 chartered to *Finncarriers*.

CELIA Built as the VASALAND for *Boström AB* of Sweden and chartered to *EFFOA* of Finland for services between Scandinavia and Mediterranean ports. In 1984 chartered to *Swedish Orient Line* for similar services and renamed the HESPERUS. In 1986 sold to *Finncarriers* and renamed the CELIA.

CORTIA Built as the TIMMERLAND for *Boström AB* of Sweden and chartered to *EFFOA* of Finland for services between Scandinavia and Mediterranean ports. In 1984 chartered to *Swedish Orient Line* for similar services and renamed the HEKTOS. In 1986 sold to *Finncarriers* and renamed the CORTIA.

TRANSBALTICA Built as the AHLERS BALTIC the for *Ahlers Line* and chartered to *Finncarriers*. In 1995 renamed the TRANSBALTICA.

# FRED. OLSEN LINES

**THE COMPANY** *Fred. Olsen Lines* is a Norwegian private sector company.

**MANAGEMENT Marketing Manager:** Tor Erik Andreassen.

**ADDRESS** Fred. Olsen Gate 2, PO Box 1159, Centrum, Oslo 1, Norway.

**TELEPHONE Administration: & Reservations:** +47 22 34 10 00, **Fax:** +47 22 41 24 15, **Telex:** 412415.

**ROUTES OPERATED** Oslo/East Norway – Immingham (2 per week), Oslo/East Norway – Felixstowe (1 per week). Vessels listed below also operate from Oslo and East Norway to Rotterdam, Hamburg and Zeebrugge. Vessels used on all services.

## VESSELS

| 1 | AURORA | 20381t | 82 | 18k | 12P | - | 179T | A | Rauma, FI | NO |
|---|--------|--------|----|----|-----|---|------|---|-----------|----|
| 2 | BALDUIN | 12494t | 75 | 18k | 12P | - | 134T | A | Florø, NO | NO |
| 3 | BORAC | 20340t | 78 | 18.5k | 0P | - | 171T | A | Oskarshamn, SW | NO |
| 4 | BORACAY | 21213t | 78 | 18k | 0P | - | 171T | A | Oskarshamn, SW | NO |

AURORA Built as the ARCTURUS for *EFFOA* of Finland, chartered to *Fincarriers* and used on services from Finland to Great Britain and Germany. In 1991 she was sold to new owners and renamed the AURORA, but continued to be chartered to *Finncarriers*. In 1996 she was chartered to *Fred. Olsen Lines*.

BALDUIN Built for *Fred. Olsen Lines* for North Sea services.

BORAC Built as the EMIRATES EXPRESS for *A/S Skarhamns Oljetransport* of Norway and chartered to *Mideastcargo* for services between Europe and the Middle East. In 1981 chartered to *OT West Africa Line* for services between Europe and West Africa and renamed the ABUJA EXPRESS. In 1983 chartered to *Foss Line*, renamed the FOSSEAGLE and returned to Middle East service. In 1985 she was renamed the FINNEAGLE, chartered briefly to *Finncarriers* and then to *Fred. Olsen Lines*. In 1987 they purchased her and renamed her the BORAC.

BORACAY Built as the BANDAR ABBAS EXPRESS for *A/S Skarhamns Oljetransport* of Norway and chartered out. In 1980 renamed the SAUDI EXPRESS. During the early eighties she undertook a number of charters including *Mideastcargo* for services between Europe and the Middle East, *Atlanticargo* for services from Europe to USA and Mexico and *OT West Africa Line* (see above). In 1983 chartered to *Ignazio Messina* of Italy, renamed the JOLLY AVORIO and used on services from Italy to the Middle East. In 1986 this charter ended and she briefly reverted to the name the SAUDI EXPRESS before being chartered to *OT West Africa Line* and renamed the KARAWA. In 1987 she was sold to *Fred. Olsen Lines* who renamed her the BORACAY.

### Under Construction

| 5 | NEWBUILDING 1 | - | 97 | 24k | 0P | - | 216T | A | Ancona, IT | NO |
|---|---------------|---|----|----|-----|---|------|---|-----------|----|
| 6 | NEWBUILDING 2 | - | 98 | 24k | 0P | - | 216T | A | Ancona, IT | NO |

NEWBUILDING 1, NEWBUILDING 2 Under construction for *Fred. Olsen Lines*.

*Bore Britannica* (Michael Drewery)

*Tor Caledonia* (Michael Drewery)

# ISLE OF MAN STEAM PACKET COMPANY

**THE COMPANY, MANAGEMENT, ADDRESS AND TELEPHONE** See Section 1.

**ROUTE OPERATED** Douglas (Isle of Man) – Heysham (4 hrs 30 mins; *(2)*; daily).

**VESSELS**

| 1 | BELARD | 5801t | 79 | 15.5k | 0P | - | 54T | AS | Frederikshavn, DK | IM |
|---|--------|-------|----|-------|-----|---|-----|----|-----|-----|
| 2 | PEVERIL | 5254t | 71 | 16k | 12P | - | 40T | A | Kristiansand, NO | GB |

BELARD Built as the MERCANDIAN CARRIER II for *Mercandia* of Denmark and used on a variety of services. In 1983 she was briefly renamed ALIANZA and between 1984 and 1985 she carried the name CARRIER II. In 1985 sold to P&O, renamed the BELARD and used on *Northern Ireland Trailers* services between Ardrossan and Larne, subsequently marketed as part of *Pandoro*. In 1993 she was chartered to *IOMSP* subsidiary *Mannin Line* to inaugurate a new service between Great Yarmouth and Ijmuiden. In 1994 she was purchased by *IOMSP*; however, in 1995 the *Mannin Line* service ceased and she was chartered back to *Pandoro*. At the end of 1995 she was returned to *IOMSP* and is currently laid up, after deputising for the PEVERIL.

PEVERIL Built as the HOLMIA for *Rederi AB Silja* of Finland. She was used on *Silja Line* cargo and RO/RO services between Norrtälje (Sweden) and Turku (Finland). In 1973 she was sold and renamed the A S D METEOR. Later that year she was sold to *P&O Ferries* for their joint Heysham – Belfast service with *Sealink* and renamed the PENDA. In 1980 she was renamed the N F JAGUAR and transferred to freight services between Southampton and Le Havre. In 1981 she was chartered to *IOMSP* for a Douglas – Liverpool freight service and in 1983 she was demise chartered by *James Fisher* of Barrow and chartered to *IOMSP*. She was renamed the PEVERIL. The freight service was switched to Heysham in 1985. The charter ended in December 1992 and she was purchased by the *IOMSP*.

# MERCHANT FERRIES

**THE COMPANY** *Merchant Ferries* is a British private sector company.

**MANAGEMENT General Manager:** Richard Harrison, **Marketing Manager:** Alistair Eagles.

**ADDRESS** North Quay, Heysham Harbour, MORCAMBE, Lancs LA3 2UL.

**TELEPHONE Administration:** +44 (0)1524 855018, **Reservations:** +44 (0)1524 855018, **Fax:** +44 (0)1524 852527.

**ROUTE OPERATED** Heysham – Dublin (8 hrs; *(1,2,3)*; 3 per day).

**VESSELS**

| 1 | MERCHANT BRAVERY | 9368t | 78 | 17k | 12P | - | 106T | A | Oslo, NO | BA |
|---|------------------|-------|----|-----|-----|---|------|---|-----|-----|
| 2 | MERCHANT BRILLIANT | 9368t | 79 | 17k | 12P | - | 106T | A | Kyrksæterøra, NO | BA |
| 3 | MERCHANT VENTURE | 6056t | 79 | 17k | 12P | - | 55T | A | Castelo, PL | IM |

MERCHANT BRAVERY Launched as the STEVI for *Steineger & Wiik* of Norway and, on delivery, chartered to *Norient Line* of Norway, being renamed the NORWEGIAN CRUSADER. In 1980 chartered to *Ignazio Messina* of Italy for Mediterranean service and renamed the JOLLY GIALLO. In 1982 the charter ended and she was briefly renamed the NORWEGIAN CRUSADER before being purchased by *Ignazio Messina* and resuming the name JOLLY GIALLO. In 1993 sold to *Merchant Ferries*, renamed the MERCHANT BRAVERY and placed on the Heysham – Warrenpoint (now Dublin) service.

MERCHANT BRILLIANT Built as the NORWEGIAN CHALLENGER for *Steineger & Wiik* of Norway and chartered to *Norient Line* of Norway. In 1982, chartered to *Ignazio Messina* of Italy for Mediterranean service and renamed the JOLLY BRUNO. Later in 1982 she was purchased by *Ignazio*

*Messina*. In 1993 sold to *Merchant Ferries*, renamed the MERCHANT BRILLIANT and placed on the Heysham – Warrenpoint (now Dublin) service.

MERCHANT VENTURE Built as the FARMAN and chartered to *GNMTC* of Italy for Mediterranean services. In 1982 she was sold to *Medlines* for similar service and renamed the MED ADRIATICO. In 1985 she was sold, renamed the ARGENTEA and chartered to *SGMAT*, continuing to operate in the Mediterranean. In 1987 sold to *Cenargo* and chartered to *Merchant Ferries* who renamed her first the MERCHANT ISLE and then the MERCHANT VENTURE. Until 1993 she was used on the Fleetwood – Warrenpoint service; in 1993 the Fleetwood service was switched to Heysham and she currently operates between Heysham and Dublin.

# NORCARGO

**THE COMPANY** *NorCargo* is a Norwegian Company jointly owned by *Det Bergenske DS (Bergen Line)* and *Det Nordenfjeldske DS*.

**ADDRESS** Dokkes Kjaerskainen, PO Box 2677, Moehlenpris, 5026 BERGEN, Norway.

**TELEPHONE Administration: & Bookings:** Bergen: +47 55 32 00 00, UK +44 (0)1472 240241, **Fax:** Bergen: +47 55 32 15 88, UK: +44 (0)1472 240250.

**ROUTES OPERATED** Bergen, Grimsby-Aberdeen-Bergen(1-3 days; *(1)*; weekly).

**VESSEL**

| 1 | COMETA | | 4610t | 81 | 16k | OP | - | 28T | AS | Fevag, NO | NO |
|---|--------|---|-------|----|----|----|----|----|----|----------|----|

COMETA Built for *Nor Cargo*.

# NORFOLK LINE

**THE COMPANY** *Norfolk Line* is a Dutch private sector company owned by *A P Møller Finance* of Switzerland.

**MANAGEMENT Managing Director:** B E Hansen, **Marketing Manager:** R A Meijer, **General Manager UK:** E J Green.

**ADDRESS** Netherlands: Kranenburgweg 211, 2583 ER Scheveningen, Netherlands. UK: Norfolk House, The Dock, FELIXSTOWE, Suffolk IP11 8UY.

**TELEPHONE Administration:** Netherlands: +31 (0)70 352 74 00, UK: +44 (0)1394 673676, **Reservations:** Netherlands: +31 (0)70 352 74 71, Felixstowe: +44 (0)1394 603630, North Shields: +44 (0)191-296 1036, Immingham: +44 (0)1469 571122, **Fax:** Netherlands: +31 (0)70 354 93 30, UK: +44 (0)1394 603676, **Telex:** Netherlands: 31515, UK: 987698.

**ROUTES OPERATED** Felixstowe – Scheveningen (8 hrs; *(1,2)*; 2 per day), North Shields – Esbjerg (23 hrs; 2/3 per week), Immingham – Esbjerg (22 hrs; 4/5 per week), Harwich – Esbjerg (21 hrs; 6 per week). Danish services marketed as *Brit Line* and operated in conjunction with *DFDS*; all vessels are provided by *DFDS*.

**VESSELS**

| 1 | EUROBRIDGE | 6041t | 77 | 15k | 12P | - | 54T | A | Bremerhaven, GE | BA |
|---|------------|-------|----|----|----|----|----|----|----------------|----|
| 2 | MAERSK FLANDERS | 7199t | 78 | 15k | 12P | - | 80T | A | Tokyo, JA | NL |
| 3 | ROSEANNE | 7744t | 82 | 17k | 12P | - | 73T | AS | Vigo, SP | CY |

EUROBRIDGE Built as the MASHALA for *Mashala Shipping* of Italy and chartered to *Gilnavi* for Mediterranean services. After a long period out of service in the mid-nineteen eighties, in 1987 she was sold, renamed the HALLA and chartered for Caribbean service. In 1988 she was renamed the TIKAL. In 1989 she was sold to *Schiaffino Line* of France, renamed the SCHIAFFINO and put into service between Ramsgate and Oostende. In 1990 the company was taken over by *Sally Ferries* and in 1991 she was chartered to *Belfast Freight Ferries*. In 1993 she was renamed the SALLY EUROBRIDGE. In January 1994, she was chartered to *North Sea Ferries* to operate between Hull and Zeebrugge and renamed the EUROBRIDGE. In summer 1994 she returned to *Sally Ferries*, resumed the name SALLY EUROBRIDGE and became the second vessel on the Ramsgate – Vlissingen service; in the autumn the British terminal was switched to Dartford. In 1995 she was chartered to *Norfolk Line*, renamed the EUROBRIDGE and also sold by *Sally Ferries*.

MAERSK FLANDERS Built as the ADMIRAL ATLANTIC for *Admiral Shipping* of the USA for Caribbean service. In 1983 she was chartered to *Portlink* for North Sea services. In 1984 sold to Swedish interests and renamed the ROMIRA. In 1986 she was sold to *Norfolk Line*, renamed the DUKE OF FLANDERS and used on their *Britline* services between Great Yarmouth and Esbjerg (Denmark), Immingham and Esbjerg and Immingham and Cuxhaven. In 1990 she was renamed MAERSK FLANDERS. She now operates on the Felixstowe – Scheveningen route.

ROSEANNE Built as the REINA DEL CANTABRICO for *Labiad Andalusi*a of Spain and chartered to *Matina Line* for services between Europe and West Africa. In 1983 renamed the SALAH LABIAD but resumed her original name in 1985. In 1987 she was sold, renamed the FAROY and chartered to *Elbe-Humber Roline* for their service between Immingham and Cuxhaven. In 1989 sold again and renamed the ROSEANNE; she was chartered to *P&O European Ferries* and used on their Felixstowe – Zeebrugge service. In 1991 chartered to *Norfolk Line*.

**Under Construction**

| 4 | NEWBUILDING 1 | 12800t | 96 | 18k | 12P | - | 120T | A | Miho, JA | NL |
| 5 | NEWBUILDING 2 | 12800t | 96 | 18k | 12P | - | 120T | A | Miho, JA | NL |

NEWBUILDING 1, NEWBUILDING 2 Under construction for *Norfolk Line*.

# NORSE IRISH FERRIES

**THE COMPANY, MANAGEMENT, ADDRESS AND TELEPHONE** See Section 1.

**ROUTE OPERATED** Liverpool – Belfast (11 hrs; *(1)*; alternate days – other days passenger service – see Section 1).

**VESSELS**

| 1 | NORSE MERSEY | 13500t | 95 | 19.5k | 61P | - | 160T | A | Donanda, IT | IT |

NORSE MERSEY Built for Italian interests for charter. On delivery, chartered to *Norse Irish Ferries* and named the NORSE MERSEY (replacing another vessel with the same name).

# NORTH SEA FERRIES

**THE COMPANY, MANAGEMENT, ADDRESS AND TELEPHONE** See Section 1.

**ROUTES OPERATED** Hull – Rotterdam (Europoort) (10 hrs; *(1,2)*; daily), Middlesbrough – Rotterdam (16 hrs; *(4,)*; 3 per week), Middlesbrough – Zeebrugge (16 hrs; *(5,6)*; daily), Hull – Zeebrugge (17 hours; *(3)*; 3 per week).

**VESSELS**

| 1 | NORBANK | 17464t | 93 | 22k | 114P | - | 156T | A | Crepelle, NL | NL |
| 2 | NORBAY | 17464t | 94 | 22k | 114P | - | 156T | A | Crepelle, NL | GB |
| 3 | NORCAPE | 14086t | 79 | 18.7k | 12P | - | 138T | A | Tamano, JA | NL |
| 4 | NORCOVE | 10279t | 77 | 17.5k | 8P | - | 95T | A | Naantali, FI | SW |
| 5 | NORKING | 17884t | 80 | 19k | 12P | - | 155T | A | Rauma, FI | FI |
| 6 | NORQUEEN | 17884t | 80 | 19k | 12P | - | 155T | A | Rauma, FI | FI |

*Bruarfoss* (Michael Drewery)

*Norbay* (Miles Cowsill)

NORBANK, NORBAY Built for *North Sea Ferries* for the Hull – Rotterdam freight service.

NORCAPE Launched as the PUMA but, on completion chartered to *B&I Line* and renamed the TIPPERARY for their Dublin – Liverpool service. In 1989 sold to *North Sea Ferries*, renamed the NORCAPE and introduced onto the Ipswich – Rotterdam service. In 1995 that service ceased and she was moved to the Hull – Zeebrugge freight service.

NORCOVE Built as the ROLITA for *Merivienti* of Italy. In 1979 chartered to *Finncarriers* of Finland, renamed the FINNFOREST and used on services between Finland and North West Europe. In 1982 sold to *EFFOA* of Finland and renamed the CANOPUS. In 1992 sold to Swedish interests and chartered to *Stora Line* for services from Sweden to NW Europe. She was renamed the CUPRIA. In 1995, chartered to *North Sea Ferries* to inaugurate a new service between Middlesbrough and Rotterdam and renamed the NORCOVE.

NORKING, NORQUEEN Built as the BORE KING and the BORE QUEEN for *Bore Line* of Finland for Baltic services. In 1991 chartered to *North Sea Ferries* for their Middlesbrough – Zeebrugge service and renamed the NORKING and NORQUEEN respectively. During winter 1995/96 lengthened by 28.8 metres.

# P&O EUROPEAN FERRIES

**THE COMPANY** See Section 1.

**MANAGEMENT Freight Director (Dover):** Brian Cork, **Freight Director (Portsmouth):** Lawrence Strover.

**TELEPHONE Administration:** See Section 1, **Reservations (freight):** Dover: 0304 223344, Felixstowe: +44 (0)1394 604363/4, Portsmouth: +44 (0)1705 772277, Cairnryan: +44 (0)1581 200663/4, Larne: +44 (0)1574 272201, **Fax:** Dover: 0304 223399, Felixstowe: +44 (0)1394 604375, Portsmouth: +44 (0)1705 772075, Cairnryan: +44 (0)1581 200282, Larne: +44 (0)1574 272477, **Telex:** Dover: 96316, 965349 Felixstowe: 98236, Portsmouth: 86806, Cairnryan: 779238, Larne: 74528.

**ROUTES OPERATED** Portsmouth – Le Havre (5 hrs 30 mins; *(11)*; daily), Dover – Zeebrugge (4 hrs; *(3,4,5)*; 6 per day). Felixstowe – Rotterdam (Europoort) (7 hrs 30 mins; *(2,6,9,10)*; 4 per day), Felixstowe – Zeebrugge (6 hrs; *(7,11)*; (2 per day), Cairnryan – Larne (2 hrs 15 mins; *(1,7)*; 4-6 per day).

**VESSELS**

| 1 | EUROPEAN ENDEAVOUR | 8097t | 78 | 18.5k | 107P | - | 46L | BA2 | Bremerhaven, GE | GB |
|----|--------------------|-------|----|-------|------|------|------|-----|-----------------|-----|
| 2 | EUROPEAN FREEWAY | 21162t | 77 | 16.5k | 166P | - | 163T | A2 | Ulsan, SK | GB |
| 3 | EUROPEAN HIGHWAY | 22986t | 92 | 21k | 200P | - | 120L | BA2 | Bremerhaven, GE | GB |
| 4 | EUROPEAN PATHWAY | 22986t | 92 | 21k | 200P | - | 120L | BA2 | Bremerhaven, GE | GB |
| 5 | EUROPEAN SEAWAY | 22986t | 91 | 21k | 200P | - | 120L | BA2 | Bremerhaven, GE | GB |
| 6 | EUROPEAN TIDEWAY | 21162t | 77 | 16.5k | 166P | - | 163T | A2 | Ulsan, SK | GB |
| 7 | EUROPEAN TRADER | 8007t | 75 | 17.5k | 107P | - | 46L | BA2 | Bremerhaven, GE | GB |
| 8 | GABRIELE WEHR | 7635t | 78 | 15k | 12P | - | 80T | A | Bremerhaven, GE | GE |
| 9 | PRIDE OF FLANDERS | 18732t | 78 | 17k | 688P | 415C | 81L | A2 | Ulsan, SK | GB |
| 10 | PRIDE OF SUFFOLK | 18732t | 81 | 17k | 688P | 413C | 81L | A2 | Ulsan, SK | GB |
| 11 | THOMAS WEHR | 7628t | 77 | 16k | 12P | - | 91T | A | Bremerhaven, GE | AN |

EUROPEAN ENDEAVOUR Built as the EUROPEAN ENTERPRISE for RO/RO freight services. In 1988 she was renamed the EUROPEAN ENDEAVOUR. She was used on freight services between Dover and Calais and Dover and Zeebrugge. If space was available, a small number of passengers was sometimes conveyed on the Zeebrugge service, although the sailings were not advertised for passengers. This ceased with the withdrawal of passenger services on this route at the end of 1991.

During the summer period she provides additional freight capacity on the Dover – Calais service and has also served on other routes. In autumn 1995 she was transferred to the Cairnryan – Larne service.

EUROPEAN TRADER Built for *European Ferries* RO/RO freight services; built to a standard design rather than custom built. In late 1991 she was transferred to the Portsmouth – Le Havre route and in 1994 to the Felixstowe – Zeebrugge service to supplement the service provided by the two passenger vessels. Will operate Cairnryan-Larne as from Spring 1996.

EUROPEAN FREEWAY Built for *Stena Line* as the ALPHA ENTERPRISE and chartered to *Aghiris Navigation* of Cyprus. In 1979 she was renamed the SYRIA and chartered to *Hellas Ferries* for services between Greece and Syria. In 1981 she was lengthened by 33.6m. In 1982 she was chartered to *European Ferries* and used on freight services between *Felixstowe and Europoort*. In 1983 she was renamed the STENA TRANSPORTER and in 1986 the CERDIC FERRY. In 1992 she was renamed the EUROPEAN FREEWAY and, in 1994, purchased by *P&O European Ferries*.

EUROPEAN HIGHWAY, EUROPEAN PATHWAY, EUROPEAN SEAWAY Built for *P&O European Ferries* for the Dover – Zeebrugge freight service.

EUROPEAN TIDEWAY Launched as the STENA RUNNER by *Stena AB* of Sweden. On completion, renamed the ALPHA PROGRESS for *Aghiris Navigation* of Greece. In 1979 renamed the HELLAS and operated by *Hellas Ferries* on services between Greece and Syria. In 1982 she was lengthened by 33.6m. In 1982 she was chartered to *European Ferries* and used on freight services between Felixstowe and Rotterdam (Europoort). The following year she was returned to *Hellas Ferries*. In 1985 she returned to *European Ferries* and the Rotterdam service. In 1986 she was renamed the DORIC FERRY. In 1992 she was renamed the EUROPEAN TIDEWAY and, in 1994, purchased by *P&O European Ferries*.

GABRIELE WEHR Built for *Wehr Transport* of Germany and chartered to several operators. In 1982, chartered to *Tor Lloyd* (later *Tor Line*) for North Sea service and renamed the TOR ANGLIA. This charter terminated in 1985 when she resumed her original name and, in early 1986, she was chartered to *North Sea Ferries* for their Hull – Zeebrugge service. This charter ended in summer 1987 when the lengthened NORLAND and NORSTAR entered service. Subsequent charters included *Kent Line* and *Brittany Ferries*. In 1989 she was chartered to *P&O European Ferries* for the Portsmouth – Le Havre freight service. The charter was terminated following the transfer of the EUROPEAN TRADER to the route in late 1992 but was renewed following the transfer of the EUROPEAN CLEARWAY to *Pandoro*.

PRIDE OF FLANDERS Built as the MERZARIO ESPANIA for *Stena Line AB* of Sweden and immediately chartered to *Merzario Line* for their service between Italy and Saudi Arabia. In the same year she was renamed the MERZARIO HISPANIA. In 1979 she was chartered to *European Ferries* for their RO/RO freight service between Felixstowe and Rotterdam (Europoort) and renamed the NORDIC FERRY. In 1982 she served in the Falkland Islands Task Force. In 1986 she was modified to carry 688 passengers and, with sister vessel the BALTIC FERRY (now PRIDE OF SUFFOLK), took over the Felixstowe – Zeebrugge service. In 1992 she was renamed the PRIDE OF FLANDERS. In 1994, purchased by *P&O European Ferries*. In 1995 the Felixstowe – Zeebrugge passenger service ceased and she had her passenger accommodation removed and was transferred to the Felixstowe – Rotterdam freight service.

PRIDE OF SUFFOLK Built as the STENA TRANSPORTER, a RO/RO freight vessel for *Stena Line AB* of Sweden. In 1979 she was renamed the FINNROSE and chartered to Atlanticargo for their service between Europe and USA/Mexico. In 1980 she returned to *Stena Line* and resumed her original name. Later in 1980 she was chartered to *European Ferries* for their Felixstowe – Rotterdam (Europoort) freight only service and renamed the BALTIC FERRY. In 1982 she served in the Falkland Islands Task Force. In 1986 she was modified in the same way as the PRIDE OF FLANDERS and moved to the Felixstowe – Zeebrugge service. In 1992 she was renamed the PRIDE OF SUFFOLK. In 1994 she was purchased by *P&O European Ferries*. In 1995 the Felixstowe – Zeebrugge passenger service ceased and she had her passenger accommodation removed and was transferred to the Felixstowe – Rotterdam freight service.

THOMAS WEHR Built for *Wehr Transport* of Germany as THOMAS WEHR but on delivery chartered to *Wacro Line* and renamed the WACRO EXPRESS. In 1978 charter ended and she was renamed the THOMAS WEHR. Over the next few years she was chartered to several operators. In 1982 she was chartered to *Tor Lloyd* (later *Tor Line*) for North Sea service and renamed the TOR NEERLANDIA. In 1985 the charter was transferred to *DFDS* and she was renamed the DANA GERMANIA. This charter terminated in 1985 and she resumed her original name. In early 1986 she was chartered to *North Sea Ferries* for their Hull – Zeebrugge service. This charter ended in summer 1987. Subsequent charters included *Cobelfret* and *Elbe Humber Roline* and a twelve month period with *North Sea Ferries* again – this time on the Hull – Rotterdam and Middlesbrough – Zeebrugge routes. In 1993 she was renamed the MANA, then the SANTA MARIA and finally chartered to *TT Line* and renamed the FULDATAL. 1994 she was chartered to *Horn Line* for service between Europe and the Caribbean and renamed the HORNLINK. Later that year she was chartered to *P&O European Ferries* for the Portsmouth – Le Havre freight service following the transfer of the EUROPEAN TRADER to the Felixstowe – Zeebrugge route and resumed the name THOMAS WEHR. In late 1995 transferred to the Felixstowe – Zeebrugge freight service.

# P&O FERRYMASTERS

**THE COMPANY** *P&O Ferrymasters Ltd* is a British private sector company, part of the *P&O Group*.

**MANAGEMENT Managing Director:** J Bradshaw, **Group Tenders and Contracts Manager:** D M Brinkley.

**ADDRESS** 11-13 Lower Brook Street, IPSWICH IP4 1AQ.

**TELEPHONE Administration:** +44 (0)1642 455591, **Reservations:** +44 (0)1642 455591, **Fax:** +44 (0)1642 453439, **Telex:** 587491.

**ROUTE OPERATED** Middlesbrough – Göteborg (Sweden) – Helsingborg (Sweden)(up to 48 hrs; *(1)*; 2 per week).

**VESSEL**

| 1 | ELK | 14374t | 78 | 18k | 12P | - | 140T | A | Ulsan, SK | GB |
|---|-----|--------|----|----|-----|---|------|---|-----------|----|

ELK Built for *Stena* of Sweden and chartered to *P&O Ferrymasters*. Purchased by *P&O* in 1981. Lengthened in 1986.

# P&O SCOTTISH FERRIES

**THE COMPANY, MANAGEMENT AND ADDRESS** See Section 1.

**TELEPHONE Administration:** +44 (0)1224 589111, **Reservations:** +44 (0)1224 589111, **Fax:** +44 (0)1224 574411, **Telex:** 73344.

**ROUTES OPERATED** Aberdeen-Lerwick (14hrs; *(1)*; up to 4 per week) One southbound trip returns via Stromness or Kirkwall taking approx. 20 hours.

**VESSEL**

| 1 | ST ROGNVALD | | 5297t | 70 | 16.5k | 12P | - | 41L | A | Lübeck, GE | | GB |
|---|---|---|---|---|---|---|---|---|---|---|---|---|

ST ROGNVALD Launched as the RHONETAL but renamed the NORCAPE on delivery. She resumed the name RHONETAL in 1974. In 1975 sold to *Meridional D'Armements* of France for services to Corsica and renamed the RHONE. In 1987 sold to *Conatir* of Italy for Mediterranean services and renamed the MARINO TORRE. In 1989 taken on six months charter to *P&O Scottish Ferries*. In 1990 she was purchased by them and renamed the ST ROGNVALD. She initially operated alongside and then replaced the ST MAGNUS (1206t, 1970). Earlier calls at Leith, Hanstholm (Denmark) and Stavanger (Norway) have now been discontinued.

# PANDORO

**THE COMPANY** *Pandoro* is a British private sector company, part of the *P&O Group*.

**MANAGEMENT Managing Director:** J H Kearsley, **Sales Manager:** David Richmond.

**ADDRESS** Dock Street, FLEETWOOD, Lancashire FY7 6HR.

**TELEPHONE Administration: & Reservations:** +44 (0)1253 777111, **Fax:** +44 (0)1253 777111. **Telex:** 67166 PD FWD G.

**ROUTES OPERATED** Ardrossan – Larne (5 hrs; *(4)*; 1 per day), Fleetwood – Larne (7 hrs; *(1,8)*; 2 per day), Liverpool – Dublin (7 hrs; *(2,3,6,7)*; 4 per day), Cherbourg – Rosslare (17 hrs; *(5)*; 3 per week). Vessels are sometimes moved between routes.

**VESSELS**

| 1 | BISON | 11723t | 75 | 18.5k | 76P | - | 120T | A | Hamburg, GE | GB |
|---|---|---|---|---|---|---|---|---|---|---|
| 2 | BUFFALO | 10987t | 75 | 18.5k | 45P | - | 120T | A | Hamburg, GE | FI |
| 3 | IBEX | 14077 | 79 | 18.0k | 12P | - | 138T | A | Tamano, JA | BD |
| 4 | LION | 5897t | 78 | 16k | 12P | - | 71T | A | Bremerhaven, GE | BA |
| 5 | PANTHER | 8023t | 75 | 19k | 132P | - | 76T | BA | Bremerhaven, GE | BD |
| 6 | PUMA | 4733t | 75 | 18k | 40P | - | 100T | A | Bremerhaven, GE | GB |
| 7 | TIDERO STAR | 9690t | 78 | 17k | 12P | - | 106T | A | Crepelle, NL | NO |
| 8 | VIKING TRADER | 9085t | 77 | 18k | 48P | - | 92T | A | Korneuburg, AU | GB |

BISON Built for *P&O*. Between 1989 and 1993 operated by *B&I Line* of Ireland on a joint service with *Pandoro* between Dublin and Liverpool. Now used on the Fleetwood – Larne service. In 1995 an additional deck was added.

BUFFALO Built for *P&O*. Lengthened in 1988. Used on the Liverpool – Dublin service

IBEX Built for *P&O* for *Pandoro* Irish sea services. In 1980 chartered to *North Sea Ferries*, renamed the NORSEA and used on the Ipswich – Rotterdam service. In 1986 she was renamed the NORSKY. In 1995 she returned to *Pandoro* and was re-registered in Bermuda. She is used on the Liverpool – Dublin service. Later in 1995 she resumed her original name of IBEX.

LION Built as the SALAHALA and chartered to *Gilnavi* of Italy for Mediterranean services. In 1990 she was purchased by *Cenargo* and chartered to *Merchant Ferries* who renamed her the MERCHANT VALIANT. She was used on the Fleetwood – Warrenpoint service until 1993 when she was chartered to *Pandoro* and placed on their Ardrossan – Larne service. Purchased by *Pandoro* in 1995 and renamed the LION.

PANTHER Built as the EUROPEAN CLEARWAY for *European Ferries* RO/RO freight services. She was built to a standard design rather than custom built. She was used on freight services between Dover and Calais and Dover and Zeebrugge. In 1992 she was moved to the Portsmouth – Le Havre route. In 1993 she was sold to *Pandoro* to inaugurate a new Cherbourg – Rosslare service. In January 1996 she was renamed the PANTHER.

PUMA Built as the UNION MELBOURNE for the *Union Steamship Company* of New Zealand. In 1980 she was chartered to *P&O* and later that year purchased by them and renamed the PUMA. She is now used on the Liverpool – Dublin service.

TIDERO STAR Built as the ANZERE for *Keller Shipping* and chartered to *Nautilus Line* for services between Europe and West Africa. In 1991 she was sold to *AS Tiderø* of Norway and renamed the TIDERO STAR. She was initially chartered to *Fred. Olsen Lines* and later to *Arimure Line* for service in the Far East. In 1994 chartered to *Fred. Olsen Lines* again. In early 1996 she was briefly chartered to *North Sea Ferries* for their Hull – Rotterdam service and then chartered to *Pandoro* and placed on the Liverpool – Dublin service.

VIKING TRADER Launched as the STENA TRADER but entered service as the GOYA for *United Baltic Corporation* of Great Britain on services between Britain and Spain. In 1979 sold to *Federal Commerce* of Canada for Canadian service and renamed the FEDERAL NOVA. In 1981 briefly renamed the CARIBBEAN SKY before being sold to *Linea Manuare* of Venezuela, renamed the MANUARE VII and used on services to the USA. In 1983 she was sold the new owners chartered her to *Navigation Central* and renamed her the OYSTER BAY. Later that year she was chartered to *European Ferries*, renamed the VIKING TRADER and used on services between Portsmouth and France. In 1989 transferred to *Pandoro*. Currently used on the Fleetwood – Larne service.

# SALLY FERRIES

**THE COMPANY, MANAGEMENT AND ADDRESS** See Section 1.

**TELEPHONE Administration:** +44 (0)1843 585151 **Reservations:** +44 (0)1843 585151. **Fax:** +44 (0)1843 580894. **Telex:** 96352.

**ROUTES OPERATED** Ramsgate – Oostende (4 hrs 30 mins; *(1,2)*; 3 per day),

**VESSELS**

| 1 | SALLY EUROLINK | 9088t | 85 | 15k | 12P | - | 90T | A | Galatz, RO | BA |
| 2 | SALLY EUROROUTE | 9088t | 85 | 15k | 12P | - | 90T | A | Galatz, RO | BA |

SALLY EUROLINK Launched as the BALDER BRE. On completion sold to *Navrom* of Romania and renamed the BAZIAS 4. In 1991 chartered to *Sally Ferries* for the Ramsgate – Oostende freight service. In 1993 renamed the SALLY EUROLINK and re-registered in The Bahamas.

SALLY EUROROUTE Launched as the BALDER STEN. On completion sold to *Navrom* of Romania and renamed the BAZIAS 3. In 1991 chartered to *Sally Ferries* for the Ramsgate – Oostende freight service. In 1993 renamed the SALLY EUROROUTE and re-registered in The Bahamas.

# STENA LINE (NETHERLANDS)

**THE COMPANY, MANAGEMENT, ADDRESS AND TELEPHONE** See Section 1.

**ROUTE OPERATED** Hoek Van Holland – Harwich (7 hrs; *(1,2)*; 2 per day).

**VESSELS**

| 1 | ROSEBAY | 13700t | 76 | 17k | 63P | - | 135T | A | Hamburg, GE | CY |
| 2 | STENA SEATRADER | 17991t | 73 | 17.5k | 221P | - | 170T | A2 | Nakskov, DK | NL |

ROSEBAY Built as the TRANSGERMANIA for German interests for *Finncarriers* services between Finland and West Germany. In 1991 chartered to *Norse Irish Ferries* and used on their freight service between Liverpool and Belfast. In 1992 she was returned to *Finncarriers* and in 1993 sold to Cypriot interests for use in the Mediterranean and renamed the ROSEBAY. In 1994 chartered to *Stena Line* to inaugurate a new service between Harwich and Rotterdam (Europoort). In 1995 the service was switched to Hoek Van Holland following the construction of a new linkspan. She also, during the summer, carries cars towing caravans, motor caravans and their passengers.

STENA SEATRADER Built as the SVEALAND for *Lion Ferry AB* of Sweden and chartered to *Statens Järnvägar (Swedish State Railways)* for the train ferry service between Ystad (Sweden) and Sassnitz (East Germany). The charter ceased in 1980 and in 1982 she was sold to *Rederi AB Nordö* of Sweden. She was stretched by 33.7 metres, renamed the SVEALAND AV MALMÖ and used on their lorry/rail wagon service between Malmö and Travemünde. In 1986 she was rebuilt with a higher superstructure and in 1987 she was renamed the SVEA LINK, the service being renamed *Nordö Link*. In 1990 she was sold to *Stena Line*, renamed the STENA SEATRADER and introduced onto the Hoek van Holland – Harwich service. She also, during the summer, carries cars towing caravans, motor caravans and their passengers.

# STENA LINE (UK)

**THE COMPANY, MANAGEMENT, ADDRESS AND TELEPHONE** See Section 1.

**ROUTE OPERATED** Newhaven – Dieppe (summer only) (5 hrs; *(1)*; one per day), Holyhead – Dublin (4 hours; *(2)* 2 per day).

| 1 | MARINE EVANGELINE | <>2794t | 74 | 14.5k | 50P | - | 48T | A | Kristiansand, NO | BA |
| 2 | STENA TRAVELLER | 18332t | 92 | 18k | 120P | - | 150T | BA2 | Rima, NO | GB |

MARINE EVANGELINE Built for *A/S Larvik-Frederikshavnferjen* of Norway as DUKE OF YORKSHIRE. In 1978 she was chartered to (and later purchased by) *CN Marine* of Canada (from 1986 *Marine Atlantic*) and renamed the MARINE EVANGELINE. She was used on services between Canada, USA and Newfoundland. In 1992 she was chartered to *Opale Ferries* of France and inaugurated a new Boulogne – Folkestone freight service. In 1993 the company went into liquidation and the service and charter were taken over by *Meridian Ferries*, a British company. She was renamed the SPIRIT OF BOULOGNE. In spring 1995, *Meridian Ferries* went into liquidation and she returned to her owners, resuming the name MARINE EVANGELINE. After a period of lay up she was chartered to *Stena Sealink Line*. She spent the summer on the Newhaven – Dieppe service and was then transferred to the Stranraer – Larne (from November 1995 Stranraer – Belfast) route. She is expected to return to Newhaven in summer 1996.

STENA TRAVELLER. Built for *Stena Rederi*. Sister to the STENA CHALLENGER but with a lower passenger capacity. After a short period with *Stena Line* on the Hoek-van-Holland – Harwich service, she was chartered to *Sealink Stena Line* for their Southampton – Cherbourg route, initially for 28 weeks. At the end of the 1992 summer season she was chartered to *TT Line* to operated between Travemünde and Trelleborg and was renamed the TT TRAVELLER. In late 1995, she returned to *Stena Line*, resumed the name STENA TRAVELLER and inaugurated a new service between Holyhead and Dublin.

# TOR LINE

**THE COMPANY** *Tor Line* is one of the trading names of the freight division of *DFDS* A/S, a Danish private sector company. See also *DFDS* (Danish services).

**MANAGEMENT UK General Manager:** Brian Thompson.

**ADDRESS** Nordic House, Western Access Road, Immingham Dock, IMMINGHAM, South Humberside DN40 2LZ.

**TELEPHONE Administration: & Reservations:** +44 (0)1469 578899.

**ROUTES OPERATED** Harwich – Göteborg (24 hrs; 5 per week), Immingham – Göteborg (34 hrs; 6 per week), per week). Immingham – Rotterdam (17 hrs; 6 per week). Note: Vessels interwork on various *Tor Line* services between Sweden and Britain and other continental ports so it is not possible to assign vessels to specific services.

## VESSELS

|  |  | | | | | | | | | |
|---|------|---|---|---|---|---|---|---|---|---|
| 1 | STENA GOTHICA | 14406t | 75 | 18k | 0P | - | 150T | A | Sandefjord, NO | BA |
| 2 | TOR ANGLIA | 17492 | 77 | 15k | 12P | - | 196T | A | Kiel, GE | SW |
| 3 | TOR BELGIA | 16950t | 79 | 15k | 12P | - | 183T | A | Landskrona, SW | SW |
| 4 | TOR BRITANNIA | 21491t | 78 | 18 | 12P | - | 94T | AS | Dunkerque, FR | SW |
| 5 | TOR CALEDONIA | 14424t | 76 | 15.5 | 12P | - | 160T | A | Sandefjord, NO | DK |
| 6 | TOR DANIA | 21491t | 78 | 18 | 12P | 200C | 207T | AS | Dunkerque, FR | DK |
| 7 | TOR FLANDRIA | 16947t | 78 | 15k | 12P | - | 183T | A | Landskrona, SW | SW |
| 8 | TOR GOTHIA | 12259t | 71 | 17k | 12P | - | 120T | A | Sandefjord, NO | SW |
| 9 | TOR HOLLANDIA | 12254t | 73 | 15.5 | 12P | - | 120T | A | Sandefjord, NO | SW |
| 10 | TOR SCANDIA | 16950t | 79 | 15k | 12P | - | 183T | A | Landskrona, SW | SW |

STENA GOTHICA Built as the MELBOURNE TRADER for *Australian National Line* for services in Australia. In 1987 sold to *Forest Shipping* and then in 1988 sold to *Cotunav* and renamed the MONAWAR L. In 1990 she was sold to *Stena Line*, renamed the STENA GOTHICA, 'stretched' and chartered to *Tor Line*.

TOR ANGLIA Built as the MERZARIO GALLIA and chartered to *Merzario Line* of Italy for services between Italy and Saudi Arabia. In 1981 she was chartered to *Wilhelmsen*, renamed the TANA and used between USA and West Africa. In 1983 she was chartered to *Salenia AB* of Sweden and renamed the NORDIC WASA. In 1987 she had a brief period on charter to *Atlantic Marine* as the AFRICAN GATEWAY and later that year she was chartered to *Tor Line* and renamed the TOR ANGLIA.

TOR BELGIA Built as the EVA ODEN for *AB Norsjöfrakt* of Sweden and chartered to *Oden Line* of Sweden for North Sea services, in particular associated with the export of Volvo cars and trucks from Göteborg. In 1980 *Oden Line* was taken over by *Tor Lloyd AB*, a joint venture between *Tor Line* and *Broströms AB* and the charter transferred to them, moving to *Tor Line* in 1981 when *DFDS* took over. In 1987 she was lengthened and on re-entry into service in early 1988 was renamed the TOR BELGIA and became regular vessel on the Göteborg – Ghent (Belgium) service, largely operated for Volvo. However, she does sometimes operate on UK routes.

TOR BRITANNIA Built as the VILLE DU HAVRE for *Société Française de Transports Maritimes* of France. Between 1979 and 1981 she was renamed the FOSS HAVRE. In 1987 she was renamed the KAMINA. In 1990 she was chartered to *Maersk Line* of Denmark, renamed the MAERSK KENT and used on *Kent Line* services between Dartford and Zeebrugge. In 1992 she was chartered to and later purchased by *Tor Line* and renamed the TOR BRITANNIA.

TOR CALEDONIA Built for charter to *Tor Line* for freight service between Sweden and UK/Netherlands. In 1984 she was chartered to *Grimaldi Lines* of Italy, renamed the GOTHIC WASA. Later that year she was renamed the GALLOWAY but in 1985 she was returned to *Tor Line* and renamed the TOR CALEDONIA. In 1988 she was purchased.

TOR DANIA Built as the VILLE DE DUNKERQUE for *Société Française de Transports Maritimes* of France. Between 1979 and 1981 she was renamed the FOSS DUNKERQUE. In 1986 she was chartered to *Grimaldi Line* of Italy and renamed the G AND C EXPRESS. In 1988 she was briefly was briefly renamed the RAILO and then she was chartered to *DFDS* where she was renamed the DANIA HAFNIA. The following year she was chartered to *Maersk Line* of Denmark, renamed the MAERSK ESSEX and used on *Kent Line* services between Dartford and Zeebrugge. In 1992 she was chartered to and later purchased by *DFDS* and renamed the TOR DANIA. In 1993 she was renamed the BRIT DANIA but later in the year reverted to her original name. She was generally used on the Harwich – Esbjerg service, working in consort with the passenger ferry DANIA ANGLIA (see *Scandinavian Seaways*). In spring 1995 she was lengthened to increase trailer capacity and transferred to *Tor Line*.

TOR FLANDRIA Built as the ANNA ODEN and in 1988 renamed the TOR FLANDRIA. Otherwise as the TOR BELGIA.

*Borac* (Mike Louagie)

*Loverval* (Mike Louagie)

TOR GOTHIA Built for *Tor Line*.

TOR HOLLANDIA Built for charter to *Tor Line*. In 1975 she was chartered to *Salenrederierna* for service in the Middle East and renamed the BANDAR ABBAS EXPRESS. In 1978 she was lengthened and returned to *Tor Line* and resumed the name TOR DANIA. Purchased by *Tor Line* in 1986. In 1992 she was renamed the TOR DAN and in 1993 the TOR HOLLANDIA.

TOR SKANDIA Built as the BRITTA ODEN and in 1988 renamed the TOR SCANDIA. Otherwise as the TOR BELGIA.

# TRANSFENNICA

**THE COMPANY** *Transfennica* is a Finnish private sector company.

**ADDRESS** Eteläranta 12, FIN-00101, Finland.

**TELEPHONE Administration: & Reservations:** +358 (9)0 13262, **Fax:** +358 (9)0 652377.

**ROUTES OPERATED** Harwich (Navy Yard) – Turku – Rauma – Oulu.

**VESSELS**

| 1 | BORDEN | 10100t | 77 | 17.5k | 12P | - | 105T | A | Fredrikstad, NO | FI |
|---|--------|--------|----|----|-----|---|------|---|------------------|----|

BORDEN Built as the BORE SKY for Bore Line of Finland and used on services between Finland, Northern Europe and Britain; subsequently sold and chartered back. In 1991 Bore Line began to pull out of regular shipping services, the charter ceased and she was renamed the BLUE SKY. In 1992 she was chartered to Transfennica and renamed the BORDEN.

# TRUCKLINE FERRIES

**THE COMPANY** *Truckline Ferries* is *Brittany Ferries'* freight division.

**MANAGEMENT Managing Director:** Ian Carruthers, **Freight Director:** Gordon Day.

**ADDRESS** Truckline Ferries, New Harbour Road, POOLE, Dorset BH15 4AJ.

**TELEPHONE Administration: & Reservations:** +44 (0)1202 675048. **Fax:** +44 (0)1202 679828. **Telex:** 41744, 41745.

**ROUTES OPERATED** Cherbourg – Poole (4 hrs 30 mins; *(1)*; 2 per day), Caen – Portsmouth (6 hrs; *(2)*; 1 per day).

**VESSELS**

| 1 | COUTANCES | 3046t | 78 | 17k | 58P | - | 64T | BA | Le Havre, FR | FR |
|---|-----------|-------|----|----|-----|---|-----|----|--------------|----|
| 2 | NORMANDIE SHIPPER | <>4078t | 73 | 17k | 36P | - | 86T | BA | Crepelle, NL | CI |

COUTANCES Built for *Truckline Ferries* for their Cherbourg – Poole service. In 1986 stretched to increase vehicle capacity by 34%.

NORMANDIE SHIPPER Built as the UNION WELLINGTON. In 1977 chartered to *Aghiris Navigation* of Greece and renamed the ALPHA EXPRESS. Later that year sold to *Stena Line*, renamed the STENA SHIPPER and used on a variety of services. In 1980 chartered to *Sealink*; rail tracks were fitted and she was operated on the Harwich – Zeebrugge train ferry service, being renamed the SPEEDLINK VANGUARD. In 1987 the charter was terminated, rail tracks were removed and, after a brief period as the CARIBE EXPRESS, she was renamed the STENA SHIPPER. In 1988 she was chartered to *Kirk Line* of the USA for service in the Caribbean and renamed the KIRK SHIPPER. In 1989 she was chartered to *Truckline Ferries*, renamed the NORMANDIE SHIPPER and inaugurated a Caen – Portsmouth freight service.

# SECTION 4 - CHAIN, CABLE ETC. FERRIES

In addition to the ferries listed above, there are a number of short chain ferries, cable ferries and ferries operated by unpowered floats:

## Bournemouth-Swanage Motor Road and Ferry Company

**Address and Telephone Number** Floating Bridge, Ferry Way, Sandbanks, POOLE, Dorset BH13 7QN. +44 (0)1929 450203.

**Route:** Sandbanks – Studland (Dorset).

| 1 | BRAMBLE BUSH BAY | 93 | 400P | 48C | BA | Hessle, | GB |
|---|---|---|---|---|---|---|---|

BRAMBLE BUSH BAY chain ferry, built for the *Bournemouth-Swanage Motor Road and Ferry Company.*

## C Toms & Son

**Address and Telephone Number** East Street, Polruan, FOWEY, Cornwall PL23 1PB. +44 (0)1872 580309.

**Route:** Fowey – Bodinnick (Cornwall).

| 1 | NO 3 | 63 | 47P | 6C | BA | Fowey, | GB |
|---|---|---|---|---|---|---|---|
| 2 | NO 4 | 75 | 48P | 8C | BA | Fowey, | GB |

NO 3, NO 4 (Floats propelled by motor launches) built for *C Toms & Son.*

## Cumbria County Council

**Address and Telephone Number** Economy & Environment Department, Citadel Chambers, CARLISLE CA3 8SG. +44 (0)1228 812633.

**Route:** Across Windermere (near Bowness-on-Windermere).

| 1 | MALLARD | 90 | 100P | 18C | BA | Borth, Dyfed, | GB |
|---|---|---|---|---|---|---|---|

MALLARD Chain Ferry built for *Cumbria County Council.*

## Isle of Wight Council (Cowes Floating Bridge)

**Address and Telephone Number** Ferry Office, Medina Road, COWES, Isle of Wight PO31 7BX. +44 (0)1983 293041.

**Route:** Cowes – East Cowes.

| 1 | NO 5 | 76 | - | 18C | BA | East Cowes, | GB |
|---|---|---|---|---|---|---|---|

NO 5 Chain ferry built for *Isle of Wight County Council,* now *Isle of Wight Council.*

## King Harry Steam Ferry Company

**Address and Telephone Number** Feock, TRURO, Cornwall TR3 6QJ. +44 (0)1872 862312.

**Route:** Across River Fal, King Harry Ferry (Cornwall).

| 1 | KING HARRY FERRY | 74 | 100P | 28C | BA | Falmouth, | GB |
|---|---|---|---|---|---|---|---|

KING HARRY FERRY Chain ferry built for *King Harry Steam Ferry Company.*

## Philip Ltd

**Address and Telephone Number** Noss Works, DARTMOUTH, Devon TQ6 0EA. +44 (0)1803 833351.

**Route:** Dartmouth – Kingswear (Devon) across River Dart (higher route) (forms part of A379).

| 1 | PHILIP | 60 | 200P | 18C | BA | Dartmouth, | GB |
|---|--------|----|------|-----|----|-----------|----|

PHILIP Diesel electric paddle propelled vessel guided by cross-river cable. Built by *Philip Ltd.*

## Reedham Ferry

**Address & Telephone Number** Reedham Ferry, Ferry Inn, Reedham, NORWICH NR13 3HA. +44 (0)1493 700429.

**Telephone:** +44 (0)1493 700429, **Fax:** +44 (0)1493 700999.

**Route:** Reedham – Norton (across River Yare, Norfolk).

| 1 | REEDHAM FERRY | 84 | 12P | 3C | BA | Oulton Broad, | GB |
|---|---------------|----|-----|----|----|--------------|----|

REEDHAM FERRY Chain ferry built for *Reedham Ferry.*

## South Hams District Council

**Address & Telephone Number** Lower Ferry Office, The Square, Kingswear, DARTMOUTH, Devon TQ6 0AA. +44 (0)1803 752342.

**Route:** Dartmouth – Kingswear (Devon) across River Dart (lower route).

| 1 | THE TOM AVIS | 94 | 50P | 8C | BA | Fowey, | GB |
|---|--------------|----|-----|----|----|--------|----|
| 2 | THE TOM CASEY | 89 | 50P | 8C | BA | Portland, | GB |

THE TOM AVIS, THE TOM CASEY Floats propelled by tugs built for *South Hams District Council.*

## Torpoint Ferry

**Address & Telephone Number** 2 Ferry Street, TORPOINT, Cornwall PL11 2AX. +44(0)1752 812233.

**Route:** Devonport (Devon) – Torpoint (Cornwall) across the Tamar. Pre-booking is not possible and the above number cannot be used for that purpose.

| 1 | LYNHER | 61 | 350P | 48C | BA | Southampton, | GB |
|---|--------|----|------|-----|----|--------------|----|
| 2 | PLYM | 68 | 350P | 54C | BA | Bristol, | GB |
| 3 | TAMAR | 60 | 350P | 48C | BA | Southampton, | GB |

LYNHER, PLYM, TAMAR Cable ferries built for the *Torpoint Ferry.* The three ferries operate in parallel on their own 'track'.

## Waterford Castle Hotel

**Address & Telephone Number** The Island, WATERFORD, Irish Republic. +353 (0)51 78203.

**Route:** Grantstown – Little Island (in River Suir, County Waterford).

| 1 | LITTLE ISLAND FERRY | 68 | 24P | 6C | BA | Cork, | IR |
|---|---------------------|----|-----|----|----|-------|----|

LITTLE ISLAND FERRY Chain ferry built for *Waterford Castle Hotel.*

# SECTION 5– MAJOR PASSENGER FERRIES

There are a surprisingly large number of passenger only ferries operating in the British Isles, mainly operated by launches and small motor boats. There are, however, a few 'major' operators who operate only passenger vessels (of rather larger dimensions) and have not therefore been mentioned previously.

**Clyde Marine Motoring** FENCER (18t, 1976, 51 passengers), KENILWORTH (44t, 1936, 150 passengers), ROVER (48t, 1964, 120 passengers), THE SECOND SNARK (45t, 1938, 120 passengers). **Route Operated:** Gourock – Kilcreggan – Helensburgh.

**Dart Pleasure Craft** KINGSWEAR BELLE (43t, 1972, 257 passengers). **Route operated:** Dartmouth – Kingswear. Note: Pleasure craft owned by this operator are also used for the ferry service on some occasions.

**Gosport Ferry** GOSPORT QUEEN (159t, 1966, 550 passengers), PORTSMOUTH QUEEN (159t, 1966, 500 passengers), SOLENT ENTERPRISE (274t, 1971, 500 passengers) (ex GAY ENTERPRISE) (mainly used on excursion work)). **Route operated:** Gosport – Portsmouth.

**Lundy Company** OLDENBURG (288t, 1958, 267 passengers). **Routes Operated:** Bideford – Lundy Island, Ilfracombe – Lundy Island.

**Mersey Ferries** MOUNTWOOD (646t, 1960, 1118 passengers), OVERCHURCH (468t, 1962, 1200 passengers), WOODCHURCH (464t, 1960, 1102 passengers). **Routes operated:** Liverpool – Birkenhead (Woodside), Liverpool – Wallasey (Seacombe).

**Tyne & Wear PTE** PRIDE OF THE TYNE (222t, 1993, 350 passengers), SHIELDSMAN (93t, 1976, 350 passengers). **Route operated:** North Shields – South Shields.

**Waverley Excursions** BALMORAL (735t, 1949, 800 passengers), WAVERLEY (693t, 1947, 950 passengers). **Routes operated:** Excursions all round British Isles. However, regular cruises in the Clyde and Bristol Channel provide a service which can be used for transport rather than an excursion and therefore both vessels are, in a sense, ferries.

**White Horse Ferries** GREAT EXPECTATIONS (66t, 1992, 95 passengers)(catamaran). **Route operated:** Gravesend (Kent) – Tilbury (Essex). HOTSPUR IV (50t, 1946, 243 passengers), NEW FORESTER (49t, 1982, 97 passengers). **Route operated:** Southampton – Hythe (Hants).

# SECTION 6 – NORTHERN EUROPE

# BALTIC SHIPPING

*Baltic Shipping* is a Russian company, recently privatised. All services are currently suspended and the marketing company in Scandinavia, *Baltic Line* recently went into liquidation. The future of the vessels is unknown at the time of going to print; two are laid up and the third is believed to still be operating – although it is unclear for whom.

## CONVENTIONAL FERRIES

| 1 | ANNA KARENINA | 14623t | 80 | 21.3k | 2000P | 500C | 78T | BA | Helsinki, FI | RU |
|---|---|---|---|---|---|---|---|---|---|---|
| 2 | ILLICH | 12281t | 73 | 19k | 360P | 344C | 44T | BA | Turku, FI | RU |
| 3 | KONSTNATIN SIMONOV | 9885t | 82 | 20k | 496P | 150C | - | A | Szczecin, PO | RU |

ANNA KARENINA Built as the VIKING SONG for *Rederi AB Sally* of Finland and used on the *Viking Line* service between Stockholm and Helsinki. In 1985 replaced by the MARIELLA (36400t, 85) of *SF Line* and sold to *Fred. Olsen Lines*. She was named BRAEMAR and used on services between Norway and Britain as well as Norway and Denmark. Services to Britain ceased in June 1990 and she continued to operate between Norway and Denmark. She was withdrawn in 1991 and sold to *Rigorous Shipping* of Cyprus (a subsidiary of *Fred. Olsen Lines*). She was chartered to the *Baltic Shipping Company* of Russia and inaugurated a service between Kiel and St Petersburg. In 1992 a Nynäshamn call was introduced. Believed still to be operating.

ILLICH Built as the BORE 1 for *Ångfartygs AB Bore* of Finland for *Silja Line* services between Turku and Stockholm. In 1980, *Bore Line* left the *Silja Line* consortium and disposed of its passenger ships. She was acquired by *EFFOA* of Finland and continued to operate on *Silja Line* service, being renamed the SKANDIA. In 1983 she was sold to *Stena Line* and renamed the STENA BALTICA. She was then resold to *Latvia Shipping* of the USSR, substantially rebuilt, renamed the ILLICH and introduced onto a Stockholm – Leningrad (now St Petersburg) service trading as *ScanSov Line*. In 1986 ownership

CRUISE OF THE FINEST FLEET IN THE BALTIC

# SILJA LINE OFFERS MORE

The majestic ships of Silja Line

*Silja Serenade & Silja Symphony*

*Helsinki-Stockholm route* . . . . .

*Silja Scandinavia & Silja Europa*

*Turku-Stockholm route* . . . . . .

*Silja Festival*

*Helsinki-Tallinn route* . . . . . . .

*Gts Finnjet*

*Helsinki-Travemünde route* . . . .

*Wasa Queen & Fennia*

*The Gulf of Bothnia route* . . . . .

**SILJA LINE**

To learn more about Silja Line's cruises, please contact your travel agency.
In Finland call directly Silja **9800-74 552** (SILJA) every day at 8 am. to 8 pm.

was transferred to *Baltic Shipping Company*. In 1992 she inaugurated a new service between Stockholm and Riga but continues to also serve St Petersburg. In 1995 the Swedish terminal was changed to Nynäshamn. In 1995 arrested and laid up in Stockholm.

KONSTANTIN SIMONOV Built for *Baltic Shipping Company* of the USSR. In 1988 rebuilt in Bremerhaven. She operates between St Petersburg and Helsinki. In 1995 arrested and laid up in Helsinki.

# BORNHOLMSTRAFIKKEN

*Bornholmstrafikken* is a Danish state owned company.

**MANAGEMENT Managing Director:** N V Rask, **Marketing Manager:** S T Jensen.

**ADDRESS** Havnen, DK-3700 Rønne, Bornholm, Denmark.

**TELEPHONE Administration:** +45 56 95 18 66, **Reservations:** +45 56 95 18 66, **Fax:** +45 56 91 07 66.

**ROUTES OPERATED** København – Rønne (Bornholm) (7 hrs; *(1,3)*; 1/2 per day), Ystad (Sweden) – Rønne (Bornholm) (2 hrs 30 mins; *(1,3)*; 2-4 per day), Neu Mukran (Germany) – Rønne (3 hrs 30 mins; *(2)*; up to 6 per week).

## CONVENTIONAL FERRIES

| 1 | JENS KOFOED | 12131t | 79 | 19.5k | 1500P | 300C | 44T | BA | Aalborg, DK | DK |
|---|---|---|---|---|---|---|---|---|---|---|
| 2 | PEDER OLSEN | 8586t | 74 | 19.0k | 1150P | 230C | 33T | BA | Bremerhaven, GE | DK |
| 3 | POVL ANKER | 12131t | 78 | 19.5k | 1500P | 300C | 44T | BA | Aalborg, DK | DK |

JENS KOFOED, POVL ANKER Built for *Bornholmstrafikken*. Used on the København – Rønne service.

PEDER OLSEN Launched as KATTEGAT II for *Jydsk Faergefart* of Denmark. Before delivery, she was renamed the KALLE III and used on their service between Juelsminde (Jutland) and Kalundborg (Sealand). In 1981 the other service of this company – between Grenaa (Jutland) and Hundested (Sealand) – was taken over by *DFDS* and operations transferred to a *DFDS* subsidiary called *Grenaa – Hundested Line*. The Juelsminde – Kalundborg service was not taken over by *DFDS* and operations were transferred to a new company called *Juelsminde-Kalundborg Line*, the ownership of KALLE III passing to *Dansk Investeringsfond*, a financial institution. In 1983 she was chartered to *Rederi AB Sally*, modified in Bremerhaven to make her suitable for Channel operations (eg stabilisers, large duty free supermarket), renamed THE VIKING and, in July, introduced onto the Ramsgate-Dunkerque service. She was subsequently re-registered in Finland. In 1989 she was transferred to associated company *Vaasanlaivat* of Finland for their service between Vaasa (Finland) and Umeå (Sweden) and renamed the WASA PRINCE. In 1991 the charter ended and she was renamed the PRINCE. She was then chartered by *Bornholmstrafikken*, renamed the PEDER OLSEN and is used on summer services between Rønne and Neu Mukran.

# CAT-LINK

**THE COMPANY** *Cat-Link* is a Danish private sector company, 75% owned by the *Holyman Group* of Australia.

**MANAGEMENT Managing Director:** Peter Schrøder Jeppersen.

**ADDRESS** Hallandsgade, Pier 3, DK-8000 Aarhus, Denmark.

**TELEPHONE Administration:** +45 98 41 20 00, **Reservations:** +45 98 41 20 20, **Fax:** +45 89 41 20 40.

**ROUTE OPERATED** Aarhus – Kalundborg. (1 hr 20 mins; *(1)*; 8 per day).

## FAST FERRIES

| 1 | CAT LINK 1 | 3989t | 95 | 35k | 600P | 139C | - | BA | Hobart, AL | DK |
|---|---|---|---|---|---|---|---|---|---|---|
| 2 | CAT LINK 2 | 3989t | 95 | 35k | 600P | 139C | - | BA | Hobart, AL | DK |

CAT LINK 1 Built for the *Holyman Group* and chartered to *Cat-Link*.

CAT LINK 2 Built for the *Holyman Group* as the CONDOR 11 and in summer 1995 used on *Condor Ferries* services between Weymouth and the Channel Islands. In late 1995, transferred to *Cat-Link* and renamed the CAT LINK 2.

# COLOR LINE

**THE COMPANY** *Color Line AS* is a Norwegian private sector stocklisted limited company.

**MANAGEMENT Managing Director:** Jon Erik Nygaard, **Marketing Manager:** Elisabeth Anspach.

**ADDRESS** *Commercial:* Postboks 1422 Vika, 0115 Oslo, Norway. *Technical Management:* Color Line Marine AS, PO Box 2090, 3210 Sandefjord, Norway.

**TELEPHONE Administration:** +47 22 94 44 00, **Reservations:** +47 22 94 44 44, **Fax:** +47 22 83 07 76.

**ROUTES OPERATED** Oslo – Kiel (Germany) (19 hrs 30 mins; *(3,4)*; daily), Oslo – Hirtshals (Denmark) (8 hrs 30 mins; *(2)*; 1 per day), Kristiansand (Norway) – Hirtshals (Denmark) (4 hrs 30 mins; *(1,5)*; 4 daily). Also UK Route – see section 1.

## CONVENTIONAL FERRIES

| 1 | CHRISTIAN IV | 21669t | 82 | 21k | 2000P | 530C | 64T | BA2 | Bremerhaven, GE | NO |
|---|---|---|---|---|---|---|---|---|---|---|
| 2 | COLOR FESTIVAL | 34417t | 85 | 22k | 2000P | 440C | 88T | BA2 | Helsinki, FI | FI |
| 3 | KRONPRINS HARALD | 31914t | 87 | 21.5k | 1432P | 700C | 100T | BA | Turku, FI | NO |
| 4 | PRINSESSE RAGNHILD | 38438t | 81 | 19.5k | 1875P | 770C | 78T | BA | Kiel, GE | NO |
| 5 | SKAGEN | 12333t | 75 | 19.5k | 1238P | 400C | 22T | BA | Aalborg, DK | NO |

CHRISTIAN IV Built as the OLAU HOLLANDIA for *Olau Line* of Germany for their service between Vlissingen (Netherlands) and Sheerness (England). In 1989 sold to *Nordström and Thulin* of Sweden for delivery in spring 1990. She was subsequently resold to *Fred. Olsen Lines* of Norway and, on delivery, renamed the BAYARD and used on their service between Kristiansand and Hirtshals. In 1991 she was acquired by *Color Line* and renamed the CHRISTIAN IV.

COLOR FESTIVAL Built as the SVEA for *Johnson Line* for the *Silja Line* Stockholm – Mariehamn – Turku service. During winter 1991/92 she was extensively rebuilt and in 1991 renamed the SILJA KARNEVAL; ownership was transferred to *Silja Line*. In 1993 she was sold to *Color Line* and renamed the COLOR FESTIVAL. She is used on the Oslo – Hirtshals service.

KRONPRINS HARALD Built for *Jahre Line* of Norway for the Oslo – Kiel service. In 1991 ownership transferred to *Color Line*

PRINSESSE RAGNHILD Built for *Jahre Line* of Norway for the Oslo – Kiel service. In 1991 ownership transferred to *Color Line*. In 1992 rebuilt in Spain with an additional midships section and additional decks.

SKAGEN Built as the BORGEN for *Fred. Olsen Lines* of Norway for Norway – Denmark services. In 1990 acquired by *Color Line* and renamed the SKAGEN.

# COLORSEACAT

**THE COMPANY** *ColorSeaCat* is operated in a joint venture by *Sea Containers* and *Color Line*, under the name *ColorSeaCat KS*.

**MANAGEMENT Acting General Manager:** Jan Walle.

**ADDRESS** Fishamgatan 2, Box 4040, S400-440 Göteborg, Sweden.

**TELEPHONE Administration:** +46 (0)31-775 42 00, **Reservations:** +46 (0)31-775 08 00, **Fax:** +46 (0)31-42 00 15.

**ROUTES OPERATED** Göteborg (Sweden) – Frederikshavn (Denmark) (1 hr 45 mins; *(1)*; up to four per day), Langesund (Norway) – Frederikshavn (3hrs 15 mins; *(2)*; 2 per day).

**FAST FERRY**

| 1 | SEACAT DANMARK | 3003t | 91 | 37k | 432P | 80C |  | BA | Hobart, AL | BA |
|---|----------------|-------|----|-----|------|-----|---|----|-----------|-----|
| 2 | SEACAT NORGE | 3003t | 91 | 37k | 540P | 80C | - | BA | Hobart, AL | BA |

SEACAT DANMARK InCat 74m model. Christened in 1991 as HOVERSPEED BELGIUM and renamed HOVERSPEED BOULOGNE before entering service. Third SeaCat introduced in 1992 to enable a three vessel service to be operated across The Channel, including a new SeaCat route between Folkestone and Boulogne (replacing the *Sealink Stena Line* ferry service which ceased at the end of 1991). With the HOVERSPEED FRANCE and the HOVERSPEED GREAT BRITAIN she operated on all three Channel routes. In 1993 she was transferred to *SeaCat AB (Sweden)* (trading as *SeaCat Danmark*), renamed the SEACATAMARAN DANMARK and inaugurated a service between Göteborg (Sweden) (for legal reasons it was not possible to call her the SEACAT DANMARK as intended). In 1995 these problems were resolved and she was renamed the SEACAT DANMARK. She has also relieved on UK routes. From January 1996 transferred to the new joint venture company *ColorSeaCat KS*.

SEACAT NORGE InCat 74m model. Built as the HOVERSPEED FRANCE, the second SeaCat. She inaugurated Dover – Calais/Boulogne service in 1991. In 1992 she was chartered to *Sardinia Express* of Italy and renamed the SARDEGNA EXPRESS; she did not operate on the Channel that year. This charter was terminated at the end of 1992 and in 1993 she was renamed the SEACAT BOULOGNE and operated on the Dover – Calais and Folkestone – Boulogne services. In 1994 she was chartered to *Isle of Man Steam Packet*, renamed the SEACAT ISLE OF MAN and replaced the LADY OF MANN on services between Douglas (Isle of Man) and Britain and Ireland. During winter 1994/5 operated for *SeaCat Scotland* between Stranraer and Belfast. She returned to *Isle of Man Steam Packet* in June 1995. During spring 1995 she was chartered to *Condor*; she then was chartered again to *Isle of Man Steam Packet Company* and returned to *Sea Containers* in the autumn. In 1996 she will be chartered to *ColorSeaCat KS*, renamed the SEACAT NORGE and will inaugurate a new service between Langesund (Norway) and Frederikshavn (Denmark).

# DFO

**THE COMPANY** *DFO (Deutsche Fährgesellschaft Ostsee)* is a German state owned corporation formed in 1993 by the merging of the ferry interests of *Deutsche Bundesbahn (German Federal Railways)* (which operated in the former West Germany) and *Deutsche Reichsbahn (German State Railways)* (which operated in the former East Germany).

**MANAGEMENT Managing Directors:** O Van Dyk, B Blumenthal, D May, **Marketing Manager:** M Ehrhardt, J Kock.

**ADDRESS** Hochhaus am Fährhafen, D-18119 Rostock-Warnemünde, Germany.

**TELEPHONE Administration:** +49 (0)381 5435113, **Reservations:** +49 (0)180 5343441, +49

(0)180 5343443, **Fax:** +49 (0)180 5343442, +49 (0)180 5343444.

**ROUTES OPERATED** Puttgarden – Rødby (Denmark) (55 mins; *(1,2,6)*; half hourly) (joint with *DSB* under the name *Vogelfluglinie*), Rostock (Germany) – Gedser (Denmark) (2 hrs 15 mins; 7 per day), Rostock (Germany) – Trelleborg (Sweden)(4 hrs; *(5)*; 4 per day), Sassnitz (Germany) – Trelleborg (Sweden) (3 hrs 30 mins; *(3)*; 5 per day) (both Trelleborg services are joint with *SweFerry* under the name *Hansaferry*), Sassnitz – Rønne (Bornholm, Denmark) (3 hrs 15 mins; *(4)*; irregular).

**CONVENTIONAL FERRIES**

| 1 | DEUTSCHLAND | 11110t | 72 | 18k | 1500P | 348C | 327r | BA2 | Rendsburg, GE | GE |
|---|---|---|---|---|---|---|---|---|---|---|
| 2 | KARL CARSTENS | 12830t | 86 | 18.1k | 1500P | 333C | 405r | BA | Kiel, GE | GE |
| 3 | ROSTOCK | 13788t | 77 | 18k | 110P | 100C | 598r | A | Bergen, NO | GE |
| 4 | RÜGEN | 12289t | 72 | 20.5k | 1468P | 220C | 480r | A2 | Rostock, GE | GE |
| 5 | SASSNITZ | 20276t | 89 | 17k | 800P | 100C | 59T | A2 | Frederikshavn, DK | GE |
| 6 | THEODOR HEUSS | 8505t | 57 | 17k | 1500P | 220C | 300r | BA | Kiel, GE | GE |

DEUTSCHLAND, KARL CARSTENS Built for *DB* and used on the Puttgarden – Rødby service.

ROSTOCK Built for *Deutsche Reichsbahn* of the former East Germany for freight services between Trelleborg and Rostock. In 1992 modified to increase passenger capacity in order to run in passenger service. In 1993 ownership transferred to *DFO*.

RÜGEN Built for *Deutsche Reichsbahn* of the former East Germany. In 1993 ownership transferred to *DFO*. Used on the Sassnitz – Rønne service.

SASSNITZ Built for *Deutsche Reichsbahn*. In 1993 ownership transferred to *DFO*. Used on the Sassnitz – Trelleborg service.

THEODOR HEUSS Built for *DB*. She now generally used in a freight only role on the Puttgarden – Rødby service.

**Under Construction**

| 7 | NEWBUILDING | c35000t | 96 | 20k | 1000P | 100C | 178T | BA | Bremerhaven, GE | GE |
|---|---|---|---|---|---|---|---|---|---|---|

NEWBUILDING Under construction for the Rostock – Trelleborg service.

# DSB

**THE COMPANY** *DSB Rederi A/S* is joint stock company 100% owned by *DSB (Danske Statsbaner – Danish State Railways)*, a Danish state corporation.

**MANAGEMENT Managing Director:** Jens Stephensen, **Deputy Managing Director:** Geir Jansen.

**ADDRESS** Dampfærgevej 10, DK-2100 København Ø, Denmark.

**TELEPHONE Administration:** +45 35 29 02 00, **Reservations:** +45 33 15 15 15, **Fax:** +45 33 15 15 15.

**ROUTES OPERATED** Helsingør (Sealand) – Helsingborg (Sweden) (25 mins; *(15,16,19)*; every 20 mins) (joint with *Sweferry* of Sweden under the *Scandlines* name), Aarhus (Jutland) – Kalundborg (Sealand) (3 hrs; *(2,20)*; 6 per day), Kalundborg (Jutland) – Samsø (2 hrs; *(7)*; 2/3 per day), Knudshoved (Jutland) – Halsskov (Sealand) (1 hr; *(1,10,17,18)*; half hourly), Nyborg (Fynn) – Korsør (Sealand) (1 hr; *(4,11,14)*; hourly) (train ferry (no cars)), Rødby (Sealand) – Puttgarden (Germany) (1 hrs; *(3,5,12,13)*; half hourly) (train ferry) (joint with *DFO* of Germany).

*Prinsesse Anne-Marie (Anders Ahlerup)*

*SeaCat Norge*

## CONVENTIONAL FERRIES

|  |  | | | | | | | | | | |
|---|------|------|----|-------|-------|------|------|-----|------------------|----|
| 1 | ARVEPRINS KNUD | 8548t | 63 | 17k | 1500P | 341C | 30T | BA | Helsingør, DK | DK |
| 2 | ASK | 11160t | 82 | 18k | 610P | 291C | 76T | AS | Venezia, IT | DK |
| 3 | DANMARK | 10350t | 68 | 17.5k | 1325P | 211C | 342r | BA2 | Helsingør, DK | DK |
| 4 | DRONNING INGRID | 16071t | 80 | 19.5k | 2280P | - | 494r | BA | Helsingør, DK | DK |
| 5 | DRONNING MARGRETHE II | 10850t | 73 | 16.5k | 1500P | 211C | 344r | BA | Nakskov, DK | DK |
| 6 | HEIMDAL | 9975t | 83 | 15k | 540P | 275C | 74T | BAQ | Frederikshavn, DK | DK |
| 7 | HOLGER DANSKE | 2779t | 76 | 14.5k | 600P | 55C | 14T | BA | Aalborg, DK | DK |
| 8 | KONG FREDERIK IX | 6592t | 54 | 17K | 1000P | 82C | 22T | BA | Helsingør, DK | DK |
| 9 | KNUDSHOVED | 6811t | 61 | 17k | 1200P | 169C | 245r | BA | Helsingør, DK | DK |
| 10 | KRAKA | 9986t | 82 | 15k | 540P | 275C | 74T | BA | Frederikshavn, DK | DK |
| 11 | KRONPRINS FREDERIK | 16071t | 81 | 19.5k | 2280P | - | 494r | BA | Nakskov, DK | DK |
| 12 | LODBROG | 10404t | 82 | 15k | 600P | 273C | 74T | BAQ | Frederikshavn, DK | DK |
| 13 | PRINS HENRIK | 10850t | 74 | 17k | 1500P | 211C | 344r | BA | Nakskov, DK | DK |
| 14 | PRINS JOACHIM | 16071t | 80 | 18k | 2280P | - | 494r | BA | Nakskov, DK | DK |
| 15 | PRINSESSE ELISABETH | 5148t | 64 | 16k | 1125P | 124C | 23T | BA | Aalborg, DK | DK |
| 16 | PRINSESSEE ANNE-MARIE | 5293t | 60 | 17k | 800P | 157C | 23T | BA | Aalborg, DK | DK |
| 17 | ROMSØ | 9401t | 73 | 18k | 1500P | 338C | 26T | BA | Helsingør, DK | DK |
| 18 | SPROGØ | 6590t | 62 | 17k | 1200P | 172C | 252r | BA | Helsingør, DK | DK |
| 19 | TYCHO BRAHE | 10845t | 91 | 13.5k | 1250P | 240C | 259r | BA | Tomrefjord, NO | DK |
| 20 | URD | 11030t | 81 | 17k | 610P | 291C | 76T | AS | Venezia, IT | DK |

ARVEPRINS KNUD Built for *DSB*. Used on the Knudshoved – Halsskov service.

ASK Built as the LUCKY RIDER for *Delpa Maritime* of Greece. In 1985 she was acquired by *Stena Line* and renamed the STENA DRIVER. Later that year she was acquired by *Sealink British Ferries* and renamed the SEAFREIGHT FREEWAY to operate freight only services between Dover and Dunkerque. In 1988 she was sold to *SOMAT* of Romania for use on *Medlink* services in the Mediterranean and renamed the SERDICA. In 1990 she was sold and renamed the NORTHERN HUNTER. In 1991 she was sold to *Blaesbjerg* of Denmark, renamed the ARKA MARINE and chartered to *DSB*. She was the converted into a passenger/vehicle ferry, renamed the ASK and introduced onto the Aarhus – Kalundborg service.

DANMARK Built for *DSB* for the Rødby – Puttgarden service.

DRONNING MARGRETHE II Built for *DSB* for the Nyborg – Korsør service. In 1981 transferred to the Rødby – Puttgarden service.

DRONNING INGRID Built for *DSB* for the Nyborg – Korsør service.

HEIMDAL Built as the MERCANDIAN ADMIRAL II, a freight ferry, for *Mercandia* of Denmark. Used on various freight services. In 1988 she was chartered to *Comanav* of Algeria for service between Algeria and France and renamed the FERRYMAR I. In 1990 acquired by *DSB*, converted into a passenger/vehicle ferry, renamed the HEIMDAL and introduced onto the Knudshoved – Halsskov service.

HOLGER DANSKE Built for *DSB* for the Helsingør – Helsingborg service. In 1991 transferred to the Kalundburg – Samsø route.

KONG FREDERIK IX Built for *DSB* and has served on a variety of routes. In recent years she has operated a summer service from Korsør to Kiel (Germany) but this has now ceased. She is now a reserve vessel.

KNUDSHOVED Built for *DSB* for the Nyborg – Korsør service. Since the delivery of new tonnage in the early seventies she has also served on the Knudshoved – Halsskov and Rødby – Puttgarden services. Now a reserve vessel.

KRAKA Built as the MERCANDIAN PRESIDENT, a freight ferry, for *Mercandia* of Denmark. Used on various freight services. In 1988 acquired by *DSB*, converted into a passenger/vehicle ferry, renamed the KRAKA and introduced onto the Knudshoved – Halsskov service.

KRONPRINS FREDERIK Built for *DSB* for the Nyborg – Korsør service.

LODBROG Built as the MERCANDIAN GOVERNOR for *Mercandia* of Denmark. Between 1984 and 1985 she was renamed the GOVERNOR. She was used on various freight services. In 1988 chartered to *DSB*, converted into a passenger/car ferry, renamed the LODBROG and introduced onto the Rødby – Puttgarden service to provide additional road vehicle capacity.

PRINS HENRIK Built for *DSB* for the Nyborg – Korsør service. In 1981 transferred to the Rødby – Puttgarden service.

PRINS JOACHIM Built for *DSB* for the Nyborg – Korsør service.

PRINSESSE ANNE MARIE Built for *DSB* for the Aarhus – Kalundborg service. In 1986 transferred to the Helsingør – Helsingborg service. A relief vessel.

PRINSESSE ELISABETH Built for *DSB* for the Aarhus – Kalundborg service. In 1986 transferred to the Helsingør – Helsingborg service.

ROMSØ Built for *DSB* for the Knudshoved – Halsskov service.

SPROGØ Built for *DSB* for the Nyborg – Korsør service. Now generally used on the Knudshoved – Halsskov service.

TYCHO BRAHE Train ferry built for *DSB* for the *ScandLines* service between Helsingør and Helsingborg.

URD Built as the EASY RIDER for *Delpa Maritime* of Greece and used on Mediterranean services. In 1985 she was acquired by *Sealink British Ferries* and renamed the SEAFREIGHT HIGHWAY to operate freight only service between Dover and Dunkerque. In 1988 she was sold to *SOMAT* of Romania for use on *Medlink* services in the Mediterranean and renamed the BOYANA. In 1990 she was resold to *Blaesbjerg* of Denmark, renamed the AKTIV MARINE and chartered to *DSB*. In 1991 she was converted into a passenger/vehicle ferry, renamed the URD and introduced onto the Aarhus – Kalundborg service.

Under construction

| 21 | NEWBUILDING 1 | - | 97 | 18.5K | 900P | 286C | 36L | BA | Frederikshavn, | DK, | DK |
| 22 | NEWBUILDING 2 | - | 97 | 18.5K | 900P | 286C | 36L | BA | Frederikshavn, | DK, | DK |

NEWBUILDING 1, NEWBUILDING 2 Under construction for DSB Rederi for the Rødby-Puttgarden service.

# ECKERÖ LINJEN

**THE COMPANY** *Eckerö Linjen* is an Åland Islands company.

**MANAGEMENT Managing Director:** Jarl Danielsson, **Marketing Director:** Christer Lindman.

**ADDRESS** Torggatan 2, Box 158, FIN-22100 Mariehamn, Åland.

**TELEPHONE Administration:** +358 (9)28 28000, **Reservations:** +358 (9)28 28000, **Fax:** +358 (9)28 12011.

**ROUTE OPERATED** Eckerö (Åland) – Grisslehamn (Sweden) (2 hrs; *(1,2)*; 5 per day).

**CONVENTIONAL FERRIES**

| 1 | ALANDIA | | 6754t | 72 | 17k | 1200P | 225C | 34T | BA | Papenburg, GE | FI |
|---|---------|---|-------|----|-----|-------|------|-----|----|----------------|----|
| 2 | ROSLAGEN | | 6652t | 72 | 18.7k | 1200P | 225C | 34T | BA | Papenburg, GE | FI |

ALANDIA Built as the DIANA for *Rederi AB Slite* of Sweden for *Viking Line* services. In 1979 she was sold to *Wasa Line* of Finland and renamed the BOTNIA EXPRESS. In 1982 she was sold to *Sally Line* of Finland; later that year she was sold to *Suomen Yritysraheitis Oy* and chartered back. In 1992 she was sold to *Eckerö Linjen* and renamed the ALANDIA. She is also used by associated company *Eestin-Linjat.*

ROSLAGEN Built as the VIKING 3 for *Rederi AB Sally* and used on *Viking Line* Baltic services. In 1976 she was sold to *Vaasanlaivat* of Finland for their service between Vaasa (Finland) and Umeå/Sundsvall (Sweden) and renamed the WASA EXPRESS. In 1982 *Vaasanlaivat* was taken over by *Rederi AB Sally* and in April 1983 she resumed her original name, was transferred to *Sally Line* and used on the Ramsgate-Dunkerque service. She remained in the Channel during winter 1983/4 on freight only services. However, in early 1984 she returned to *Vaasanlaivat* and resumed the name WASA EXPRESS. In 1988 she was sold to *Eckerö Linjen* and renamed the ROSLAGEN. During winter 1992/3 she operated between Helsinki and Tallinn for *Estonia New Line* and returned to *Eckerö Linjen* in the spring.

# ESTLINE

**THE COMPANY** *EstLine* is jointly owned subsidiary of *Nordström & Thulin*, a Swedish private sector company and the *Estonian Shipping Company* of Estonia, a state owned company

**MANAGEMENT Managing Director:** Mats Björud, **Marketing Manager:** Michel Collas.

**ADDRESS** Frihamnen Magasin 2, Box 27304, SE-10254 Stockholm, Sweden.

**TELEPHONE Administration:** +46 (0)8-666 60 00, **Reservations:** +46 (0)8-667 00 01, **Fax:** +46 (0)8-666 60 52.

**ROUTE OPERATED** Stockholm – Tallinn (Estonia) (14 hrs; *(1)*; alternate days).

**CONVENTIONAL FERRY**

| 1 | MARE BALTICUM | 17955t | 79 | 21k | 1340P | 480C | 58T | BA2 | Papenburg, GE | ES |
|---|---------------|--------|----|-----|-------|------|-----|-----|----------------|----|

MARE BALTICUM Built as DIANA II for *Rederi AB Slite* for *Viking Line* services between Stockholm and Turku, Mariehamn, Kapellskär and Naantali. In 1992 sold to a *Nordbanken* and chartered to *TR Line* for service between Trelleborg and Rostock. In 1994 sold and chartered to *EstLine* and renamed the MARE BALTICUM. During winter 1994/95 she was completely renovated.

# EESTIN-LINJAT

**THE COMPANY** *Eestin-Linjat* is a joint Finnish-Estonian company, associated with *Eckerö Linjen* of Åland, Finland.

**MANAGEMENT Managing Director:** Jarl Danielsson, **Marketing Manager:** Håkan Nordström.

**ADDRESS** Fabiankatu 9, FIN-00130 Helsinki, Finland.

**TELEPHONE Administration:** +358 (9)0 669 971, **Reservations:** +358 (9)0 669 944, **Fax:** +358 (9)0 669 990.

**ROUTE OPERATED** Helsinki – Tallinn (Estonia) (3 hrs 30 mins; *(1)*; 2 per day).

## CONVENTIONAL FERRIES

| 1 | APOLLO | 6840t | 70 | 17.5k | 870P | 250C | 34T | BA | Papenburg, GE | ES |
|---|--------|-------|----|-------|------|------|-----|----|----------------|-----|

APOLLO Built as the APOLLO for *Rederi AB Slite* of Sweden, a partner in the *Viking Line* consortium (see *Sally Ferries*). In 1975 sold to *Olau Line* and renamed the OLAU KENT. In 1978, when the company was sold to *TT Line*, she remained in the ownership of Ole Lauritzen although remaining in service with *Olau Line*. In late 1980, she was 'arrested' in Vlissingen in respect of non-payment of debts relating to her owner's unsuccessful *Dunkerque-Ramsgate Ferries* venture. In 1981 she was sold to *Nordisk Faergefart* of Denmark, renamed the GELTING NORD and used on their service between Faarborg (Denmark) and Gelting (Germany). In 1982 she inaugurated a new service between Hundested (Denmark) and Sandefjord (Norway). In 1984 this service ceased and she was taken by *Brittany Ferries* on long term charter, renamed the BENODET and used on the Plymouth-Roscoff service. In 1985 transferred to *Channel Island Ferries*, renamed the CORBIERE and used on their Portsmouth – Channel Islands service. In 1989 she was transferred to *Brittany Ferries'* subsidiary *Truckline Ferries* for their service between Poole and Cherbourg. At the end of the 1991 season the charter was terminated and she was sold to *Eckerö Linjen* of Åland. She inaugurated services for *Estonia New Line* between Helsinki and Tallinn. Initially she operated as LINDA I, although she was never formally renamed (she continued to carry the CORBIERE on her bows), but this name was subsequently abandoned. In 1994 she operated with *Tallink* but in 1995 the service became separately operated again – this time with *Eestin-Linjat*. In 1995 she resumed her original name of APOLLO.

*Eestin-Linjat* also utilise the ALANDIA of associated company *Eckerö Linjen*.

# EUROPA LINIEN

**THE COMPANY** *Europa Linien* is a Danish private sector company, a subsidiary of *Emea Shipping AB*.

**MANAGEMENT Managing Director:** John Steen-Mikkelsen, **Marketing Manager:** Jes Svare.

**ADDRESS** Moltzaugade 5, DK-4874 Gedser, Denmark.

**TELEPHONE Administration:** +45 53 87 92 33, **Reservations:** +45 53 87 00 55, **Fax:** +45 53 87 00 75.

**ROUTE OPERATED** Gedser (Denmark) – Rostock (Germany) (2 hrs; *(1,2)*; 4 per day) (joint with *DSB*).

## CONVENTIONAL FERRIES

| 1 | FALSTER LINK | 8319t | 69 | 21k | 1300P | 210C | 32T | BA | Schiedam, NL | BA |
|---|--------------|-------|----|-----|-------|------|-----|-----|---------------|-----|
| 2 | ROSTOCK LINK | 13788t | 75 | 18k | 1000P | 350C | 78T | BA2 | Bremerhaven, GE | BA |

FALSTER LINK Built as the FREE ENTERPRISE IV for *Townsend Thoresen* and used on Dover-Calais and Dover-Zeebrugge services. In 1976 she was transferred to the Cairnryan-Larne service and in 1986 she was transferred to the Dover-Boulogne service. In 1987 she was replaced on the Dover-Boulogne service by FREE ENTERPRISE VIII and withdrawn. In 1988 she was sold to *GT Link* and renamed the FALSTER LINK. Used initially on the Gedser – Travemünde service, she now operates between Gedser and Rostock.

ROSTOCK LINK Launched as the EUROPEAN EXPRESS but entered services as the EUROPEAN GATEWAY for *Townsend Thoresen* of Britain for freight services between Dover and Zeebrugge and Felixstowe and Rotterdam. In 1981 she was stretched by 15.7m to enable her to operate on passenger services on the Cairnryan – Larne route. She also continued to operate on a relief basis on the Felixstowe – Rotterdam service and on 19th December 1982, whilst leaving Felixstowe, she was in collision with the SPEEDLINK VANGUARD of *Sealink* (now the NORMANDIE SHIPPER of

*Truckline*) and sank. She was raised and sold to *Clorinda Navigation* of Cyprus, renamed the FLAVIA and used on freight services between Cyprus and Greece. In 1984 she was rebuilt to accommodate up to 1000 passengers, chartered to *ANCO Ferries* of Greece and used on services between Patras (Greece) and Brindisi (Italy). In 1988 she was sold to *Sea Link AB* of Sweden and renamed the TRAVEMÜNDE LINK I. The following year she was renamed the TRAVEMÜNDE LINK. She was used on *GT Link* services between Gedser and Travemünde. In 1992 she was renamed the ROSTOCK LINK and switched to operating between Gedser and Rostock.

# FAABORG-GELTING LINIEN

**THE COMPANY** *Faaborg-Gelting Linien* is the trading name of *Nordisk Faergefart*, a Danish private sector company.

**MANAGEMENT Managing Director:** Esben Jensen, **Marketing Manager:** Axel Jörgensen.

**ADDRESS** Odensevej 95, DK-5600, Faaborg, Denmark.

**TELEPHONE Administration:** +45 62 61 93 76, **Reservations:** +45 62 61 15 00, **Fax:** +45 62 61 15 42.

**ROUTE OPERATED** Faaborg (Fyn, Denmark) – Gelting (Germany) (2 hrs; *(1)*; 2-3 per day).

**CONVENTIONAL FERRY**

| 1 | GELTING SYD | 6672t | 74 | 19.5k | 800P | 145C | 34T | BA | Papenburg, GE | DK |
|---|---|---|---|---|---|---|---|---|---|---|

GELTING SYD Built as the STELLA SCARLETT for *Stockholms Rederi AB Svea* of Sweden and used on the *SL (Skandinavisk Linjetrafik)* (later *Scandinavian Ferry Lines*) service between Landskrona (Sweden) and København (Tuborg Havn). In 1980 the Swedish terminal became Malmö. The service ceased in 1981 and she was sold to *Nordisk Faergefart*, renamed the GELTING SYD and took over the Fåborg – Gelting service.

# FJORD LINE

**THE COMPANY** *Fjord Line* is 100% owned by *Bergen-Nordhordland Rutelag AS(BNR)*, a Norwegian company.

**MANAGEMENT Managing Director:** Geir Synnevåg **Marketing Manager:**.Linda F. Vikenes

**ADDRESS** Slottsgatan 1, Postboks 4088, 5023 Bergen, Norway.

**TELEPHONE Administration:** +47 55 54 88 00, **Reservations:** +47 55 32 37 70, **Fax:** +47 55 32 38 15.

**ROUTE OPERATED** Bergen – Egersund – Hanstholm (Denmark) (15 hrs 30 mins; *(1)*; 3 per week), Egersund – Hanstholm (6 hrs 45 mins; *(1)*; 7 per week).

**CONVENTIONAL FERRIES**

| 1 | BERGEN | 16000t | 93 | 20k | 900P | 530C | 58T | BA | Fosen, NO | NO |
|---|---|---|---|---|---|---|---|---|---|---|

BERGEN Built for *Rutelaget Askøy-Bergen* and used on *Fjord Line* service.

# GOTLANDSLINJEN

**THE COMPANY** *Gotlandslinjen* is a Swedish private sector company, a subsidiary of *Nordström & Thulin*.

**MANAGEMENT Managing Director:** Hans Laidwa, **Marketing Manager:** Vacant.

**ADDRESS** Box 27304, S-102 54 Stockholm, Sweden.

**TELEPHONE Administration:** +46 (0)8-666 60 70, **Reservations:** +46 (0)8-520 640 00, +46 (0)498-29 30 00, +46 (0)491-190 19, **Fax (Admin):** +46 (0)8-520 158 04, **Fax (Reservations):** +46 (0)491-108 24.

**ROUTE OPERATED** Visby (Gotland) – Nynäshamn (Swedish mainland) (5 hrs 30 mins; *(1,2)*; 1/2 per day), Visby – Oskarshamn (Swedish mainland) (4 hrs 30 mins; *(1,2)*; 1/2 per day).

### CONVENTIONAL FERRIES

| 1 | GRAIP | 19779t | 77 | 17k | 1600P | 500C | 88T | BA | Hyundai, SK | SW |
|---|---|---|---|---|---|---|---|---|---|---|
| 2 | NORD GOTLANDIA | 21473t | 81 | 21k | 2048P | 530C | 64T | BA | Bremerhaven, GE | SW |
| 3 | NORD NEPTUNUS | 8547t | 77 | 17k | 412P | - | 62T | BA | Korneuburg, AU | SW |

GRAIP Built *Stena Line* of Sweden as the NORSKY and chartered to *North Sea Ferries* of Great Britain/Netherlands for freight services between Ipswich and Rotterdam. This charter terminated in late 1980 and she was briefly renamed the STENA SHIPPER before being chartered to *Merzario* as MERZARIO IONIA for services in the Mediterranean and to Saudi Arabia. In 1981 she was chartered to *Constellation Line* of the USA, renamed the CONSTELLATION EXPRESS and served between the USA and the Middle East. When this charter ended in 1987 she was again renamed the STENA SHIPPER. After sale to *Nordström and Thulin* she was converted to a passenger ferry and she entered service later that year with *Gotlandslinjen* as the GRAIP.

NORD GOTLANDIA Built as the OLAU HOLLANDIA for *Olau Line* of Germany for the service between Vlissingen (Netherlands) and Sheerness (England). In 1989 she was replaced by a new vessel of the same name and she was sold to *Nordström & Thulin*. She was renamed the NORD GOTLANDIA and introduced onto *Gotlandslinjen* services between Gotland and the Swedish mainland.

NORD NEPTUNUS Built as the STENA TOPPER, a RO/RO freight vessel for *Stena Line AB* of Sweden. Purchased by *James Fisher of Barrow* in 1978 and renamed the DARNIA. Chartered to *Sealink UK* for use on the Stranraer – Larne route. In 1982 passenger capacity was increased from 92 to 412 in order to replace AILSA PRINCESS on passenger/car ferry services. In 1991 she was sold to *Nordström & Thulin*, renamed the NORD NEPTUNUS and used generally on a freight only role. She also has also operated for associated company *EstLine* and has been chartered to *TT Line*.

# GRENAA – HUNDESTED LINIEN

**THE COMPANY** Grenaa – Hundested Linien is the trading name of *Driftsselskabet Grenaa Hundested AS*, a Danish private sector company.

**MANAGEMENT Managing Director:** J Vestergaard, **Marketing Manager:** H K Rasmussen.

**ADDRESS** Faregeved 4, 3390 Hundested, Denmark.

**TELEPHONE Administration:** +45 42 33 96 48, **Reservations:** +45 42 33 96 88, **Fax:** +45 42 33 70 80.

**ROUTE OPERATED** Grenaa (Jutland) – Hundested (Sealand) (1 hr 30 mins; *(1,2)*; 8 per day).

### FAST FERRIES

| 1 | DJURSLAND | 4675t | 96 | 35k | 600P | 160C | 12T | BA | Bergen, NO | DK |
|---|---|---|---|---|---|---|---|---|---|---|
| 2 | KATTEGAT | 4675t | 95 | 35k | 600P | 160C | 12T | BA | Bergen, NO | DK |

DJURSLAND, KATTEGAT Built for *Grenaa – Hundested Linien*. See **Stop Press**

# KATTEGATBROEN

**THE COMPANY** Kattegatbroen is a Danish private sector company, a subsidiary of *Mercandia Rederierne* of Denmark.

**MANAGEMENT Managing Director:** Per Henriksen, **Marketing Manager:** John Christiensen.

*Sandefjord (Dirk Jankowsky)*

*Lion King (Frank Lose)*

**ADDRESS** Amaliegade 27, DK-1256 København K, Denmark.

**TELEPHONE Administration:** +45 33 12 01 55, **Reservations:** +45 75 69 48 00, **Fax:** +45 75 69 44 65.

**ROUTE OPERATED** Juelsminde (Jutland) – Kalundborg (Sealand) (3 hrs; *(1,2)*; 8 per day).

**CONVENTIONAL FERRIES**

| 1 | MERCANDIA I | 4101t | 88 | 13k | 253P | 170C | 24T | BA | Sunderland, GB | DK |
|---|-------------|-------|----|-----|------|------|-----|-----|----------------|-----|
| 2 | MERCANDIA IV | 4296t | 88 | 13k | 253P | 170C | 24T | BA | Sunderland, GB | DK |

MERCANDIA I, MERCANDIA IV Built as the SUPERFLEX KILO and SUPERFLEX NOVEMBER respectively for *Vognmandsruten* of Denmark. In 1989 sold to *Mercandia* and renamed but remained unused. Vessels began operating on the Juelsminde – Kalundborg service in 1990.

# LANGELAND-KIEL LINJEN

**THE COMPANY** *Langeland-Kiel Linjen* is a Danish private sector company.

**MANAGEMENT Managing Director:** Erik Lund-Nielsen, **Marketing Manager:** Jytte Holmøe.

**ADDRESS** Fahrhafen, DK-5935, Bagenkop, Denmark.

**TELEPHONE Administration & Reservations:** +45 62 56 14 00, **Fax:** +45 62 56 19 59.

**ROUTES OPERATED** Bagenkop (Langeland, Denmark) – Kiel (Germany) (2 hrs 30 mins; *(1)*; 3 per day).

**CONVENTIONAL FERRY**

| 1 | LANGELAND III | 6721t | 89 | 15.7k | 1100P | 140C | 26T | BA | Svendborg, DK | DK |
|---|---------------|-------|----|-------|-------|------|-----|-----|---------------|-----|

LANGELAND III Built for *Langeland-Kiel Linjen*.

# LARVIK LINE

*Larvik Line* is a Norwegian private sector company.

**MANAGEMENT Managing Director:** Knut C Hals, **Marketing Manager:** Nina Roer.

**ADDRESS** Hoffsveien 15, Postboks 265, Skøyen, 0212 Oslo, Norway.

**TELEPHONE Administration:** +47 22 52 45 00, **Reservations:** +47 22 52 55 00, **Fax:** +47 22 52 15 40.

**ROUTE OPERATED** *Conventional Ferry:* Larvik (Norway) – Frederikshavn (Denmark)(6 hrs 15 mins; *(1)*; 1 or 2 per day), *Fast Ferry:* Larvik – Skagen (Denmark)(3 hrs; *(2)*; up to 3 per day).

**CONVENTIONAL FERRY**

| 1 | PETER WESSEL | 29706t | 81 | 21k | 2200P | 650C | 80T | BA2 | Landskrona, SW | NO |
|---|--------------|--------|----|-----|-------|------|-----|------|----------------|-----|

PETER WESSEL Built for *Gotlandsbolaget* of Sweden. A sister vessel of the VISBY (14939t, 1980), now the STENA FELICITY of *Stena Line*, it was intended that she should be named the GOTLAND. However, she was delivered as the WASA STAR and chartered to *Vaasanlaivat* of Finland and used on their Vaasa – Sundsvall service. In 1982 she was chartered to *Karageorgis Line* of Greece for service between Patras (Greece) and Ancona (Italy). This charter was abruptly terminated in 1983 following a dispute over payment of charter dues. She returned the Baltic and was laid up until February 1984 when she was sold to *Larvik Line*. She was renamed the PETER WESSEL. In 1988 she was 'stretched' in Hamburg to increase capacity.

## FAST FERRY

| 2 | ALBAYZIN | | 3265t | 94 | 35k | 450P | 76C | - | BA | Cadiz, SP | | UY |
|---|----------|---|-------|----|----|------|-----|---|----|----------|---|----|

ALBAYZIN Built for *Bunquebus* of Argentina. After service between North and South Island of New Zealand, during summer 1995 she was chartered to *Transmediterranea* of Spain for services from Palma (Majorca) to the mainland. In summer 1996 to be chartered to *Larvik Line*.

# LION FERRY

**THE COMPANY** *Lion Ferry* is a Swedish private sector company, a subsidiary of *Stena Line AB* of Sweden.

**MANAGEMENT Managing Director:** Björn Johansson, **Marketing Manager:** Anita A'son-Strandahl.

**ADDRESS** Box 94, S-432 22 Varberg, Sweden.

**TELEPHONE Administration:** +46 (0)340-180 30, **Reservations:** +46 (0)340-190 10, **Fax:** +46 (0)340-851 25.

**ROUTES OPERATED** Halmstad (Sweden) – Grenaa (Denmark) (4 hrs 30 mins; *(1,2)*; 2 per day), Varberg (Sweden) – Grenaa (Denmark) (4 hrs; *(1,2)*; 2 per day), Karlskrona (Sweden) – Gdynia (Poland) (10 hrs 30 mins; *(3)*; daily).

## CONVENTIONAL FERRIES

| 1 | LION PRINCE | *9809t | 69 | 19.5 | 1400P | 250C | 40T | BA | Ålborg, DK | SW |
|---|-------------|--------|----|------|-------|------|-----|----|-----------|----|
| 2 | LION KING II | 16630t | 79 | 21.3k | 1700P | 549C | 140T | BA2 | Turku, FI | SW |
| 3 | LION QUEEN | 12764t | 67 | 18k | 1200P | 2725C | 32T | A | Göteborg, SW | SW |

LION PRINCE Built as the PRINSESSAN CHRISTINA for *Göteborg-Frederikshavn Linjen* of Sweden (trading as *Sessan Linjen*) for their service between Göteborg and Frederikshavn. In 1979 she was purchased by *JCE Safe Rederi* (a subsidiary of *Consafe Offshore* (an oil industry supply company)) and chartered back to *Sessan Linjen*. In 1981 she was delivered to *JCE Safe Rederi* and renamed the SAFE CHRISTINA. She was intended to be used as an accommodation vessel but in August 1981 she was chartered to *Sally Line* for service between Ramsgate (England) and Dunkerque (France) and continued to operate until October when the service was suspended for the winter. In 1982 *JCS Safe Rederi* formed *Vinga Line* and operated the vessel on the Göteborg-Frederikshavn route in competition with *Stena Line*. However, after ten days they agreed to sell the vessel back to *Stena Line* and the service ended. She was re-introduced onto *Stena's* Göteborg-Frederikshavn service and reverted to the name PRINSESSAN CHRISTINA. In 1983 she inaugurated a new service between Frederikshavn and Moss (Norway) and was renamed the STENA NORDICA. In 1985 she was transferred to the Grenaa-Helsingborg (Sweden) service, following *Stena Line's* acquisition of the service, replacing EUROPAFÄRJAN IV (4391t, 1967) and renamed the EUROPAFÄRJAN I. In 1986, following a reorganisation within the *Stena* group, ownership was transferred to subsidiary company *Lion Ferry AB* and she was renamed the LION PRINCE. The Helsingborg route having been closed in 1989.

LION KING II Built as the TURELLA for *SF Line* of Finland for the *Viking Line* Stockholm – Mariehamn – Turku service and later moved to the Kapellskär – Mariehamn – Naantali service. In 1988 she was sold to *Stena Line*, renamed the STENA NORDICA and introduced onto the Frederikshavn – Moss (night) and Frederikshavn – Göteborg (day) service. In 1996 the Frederikshavn – Moss service ceased and she was transferred to *Lion Ferry* and renamed the LION KING II.

LION QUEEN Built as the PATRICIA for *Swenska Lloyd* of Sweden for their service between Southampton and Bilbao (Spain). In 1977 the service ceased and she was laid up. In 1978 she was purchased by *Stena Line*, and renamed the STENA OCEANICA and rebuilt in order to accommodate commercial vehicles. Following the rebuilding she was, in 1979, renamed the STENA SAGA and inaugurated an Oslo – Frederikshavn service. Replaced by a new STENA SAGA in 1988 (now the STENA EUROPE) she was renamed the LION QUEEN and transferred to *Lion Ferry*. She initially operated between Halmstad and Grenaa and was then moved to the Helsingborg – Grenaa route until this ceased in 1989. In 1990 she was renamed the CROWN PRINCESS VICTORIA and transferred to *BC Stena Line* of Canada to operate between Victoria (Canada) and Seattle (USA). This venture did not last very long and she was withdrawn later the same year and laid up. In 1991 she was chartered to *Starlite Cruises* of Greece for cruises between USA and Mexico and renamed the PACIFIC STAR. In 1993 she was renamed the SUN FIESTA. In 1994 she returned to *Lion Ferry* in the name LION QUEEN. After initially operating on Sweden – Denmark services, in 1995 she inaugurated a service between Karlskrona and Gdynia.

# MOLS-LINIEN

**THE COMPANY** *Mols-Linien A/S* is a Danish private sector company; previously a subsidiary of *J Lauritzen A/S*, it became an independent company in 1994.

**MANAGEMENT Managing Director:** William Jørgensen, **Marketing Manager:** Christian Hingelberg.

**ADDRESS** Faergehavnen, 8400 Ebeltoft, Denmark.

**TELEPHONE Administration:** +45 89 52 52 00, **Reservations:** +45 89 52 52 52, **Fax (Admin):** +45 89 52 52 90, **Fax (Reservations):** +45 89 52 52 92.

**ROUTES OPERATED** Ebeltoft (Jutland) – Sjaellands Odde (Sealand) (1 hr 40 mins; *(1,2,3)*; 2 hourly).

**CONVENTIONAL FERRIES**

| 1 | MAREN MOLS | 11668t | 75 | 20k | 1750P | 420C | 40T | BA2 | Helsingør, DK | DK |
|---|------------|--------|----|-----|-------|------|-----|-----|----------------|----|
| 2 | METTE MOLS | 11668t | 75 | 20k | 1750P | 420C | 40T | BA2 | Helsingør, DK | DK |
| 3 | MIE MOLS   | 7201t  | 73 | 18k | 400P  | -    | 64T | BA  | Florø, NO      | DK |

MAREN MOLS, METTE MOLS Built for *Mols-Linien*.

MIE MOLS Built as the LALLI for *Alander Frachtschiff KG* of Germany for general charter work. In 1979 sold to *Wingham Ltd* of Singapore and renamed the STAR EXPRESS. The following year she sold to *Parang Shipping* of The Channel Islands and was chartered to *Nopal Line* of the USA, renamed the LADY LUCIENNE and used on services between the USA and Venezuela and later for *Medlines* between Italy and Libya. In 1982 she was briefly chartered to *Townsend Thoresen* of Britain before being acquired by *Grenaa Faergefart* of Denmark and renamed LUCIE. She was modified to carry 400 passengers and the following year was renamed the JULLE and replaced KALLE II (now the PEDER OLSEN of *Bornholmstrafikken*) on the Juelsminde – Kalundborg service of *Juelsminde – Kalundborg Line*. In 1985 this company went into liquidation and the service was taken over by *Vognmandsruten*, who continued the charter. In 1989 she was chartered to *Mols Linien* to provide additional freight capacity on the Ebeltoft – Sjaellands Odde route.

**Under Construction – Conventional ferries**

| 4 | MAREN MOLS | - | 96 | 19k | 600P | 343C | 100T | BA2 | Ørskov, DK | DK |
|---|------------|---|----|-----|------|------|------|-----|------------|----|
| 5 | METTE MOLS | - | 96 | 19k | 600P | 343C | 100T | BA2 | Ørskov, DK | DK |

MAREN MOLS, METTE MOLS 'ROPax' vessel under construction for *Mols-Linien*.

**Under Construction – Fast ferries**

| 6 | MAI MOLS | - | 96 | 38k | 450P | 120C | - | BA | Aalborg, DK | DK |
|---|----------|---|----|-----|------|------|---|----|--------------|----|
| 7 | MIE MOLS | - | 96 | 38k | 450P | 120C | - | BA | Aalborg, DK | DK |

MAI MOLS, MIE MOLS High speed vessels under construction for *Mols-Linien*.

# NORDÖ-LINK

**THE COMPANY** *Nordö-Link* is a Swedish private sector company, a subsidiary of *Sea-Link AB*.

**MANAGEMENT Managing Director:** Wilhelm Axkull **Marketing Manager:** Rudiger Meyer.

**ADDRESS** PO Box 201, S-201 21, Malmö, Sweden.

**TELEPHONE Administration:** +46 (0)40-72416, **Reservations:** +46 (0)40-611 16 70, **Fax:** +46 (0)40-97 36 85.

**ROUTES OPERATED** Malmö – Travemünde (9 hrs; *(1,2)*; 2 per day).

**CONVENTIONAL FERRIES**

| 1 | LÜBECK LINK | 33163t | 80 | 19k | 240P | - | 250T | BS | Oskarshamn, SW | SW |
|---|---|---|---|---|---|---|---|---|---|---|
| 2 | MALMÖ LINK | 33163t | 80 | 19k | 240P | - | 250T | BS | Oskarshamn, SW | SW |

LÜBECK LINK Built as the FINNROSE for *Finncarriers* of Finland and used on deep sea services. In 1990 sold to *Sea Link AB*, converted to 'Ro-Pax' format with passenger accommodation and rail tracks, and placed on the Malmö – Travemünde service.

MALMÖ LINK Built as the FINNHAWK; otherwise as the LÜBECK LINK.

# POLFERRIES

**THE COMPANY** *Polferries* is the trading name of *Polska Zegluga Baltycka* (*Polish Baltic Shipping Company*), a Polish state owned corporation.

**MANAGEMENT Managing Director:** Andrezej Grotowski, **Marketing Manager:** Urszula Marchlewicz.

**ADDRESS** ul Portowa 41, PL 78 100 Kolobrzeg, Poland.

**TELEPHONE Administration:** +48 (0)965 25211, **Reservations:** +48 (0)58 431887, **Fax (Admin):** +48 (0)965 26612, **Fax: (Reservations):** +48 (0)58 436574, **Telex:** 532502.

**ROUTES OPERATED** Świnoujście – Malmö (9 hrs 30 mins; *(1,4)*; 2 per day), Świnoujście – København (9hrs 45 mins; *(5)*; 5 per week), Świnoujście – Rønne (6 hrs; *(5)*; 1 per week), Gdańsk – Oxelösund (Sweden) (18 hrs 30 mins; *(3)*; alternate days).

**CONVENTIONAL FERRIES**

| 1 | NIEBOROW | 8697t | 73 | 22k | 920P | 225C | 36T | BA | Rendsburg, GE | PO |
|---|---|---|---|---|---|---|---|---|---|---|
| 2 | POMERANIA | 10550t | 78 | 18k | 984P | 277C | 38T | BA | Szczecin, PO | PO |
| 3 | ROGALIN | 10241t | 72 | 21k | 984P | 146C | 22T | BA | Nantes, FR | PO |
| 4 | SILESIA | <>7414t | 79 | 19k | 984P | 277C | 38T | BA | Szczecin,PO | PO |
| 5 | WILANOW | <>6474t | 65 | 20k | 750P | 150C | 32T | BA | Rendsburg, GE | PO |

NIEBOROW Built for *Prinzenlinien* of Germany as PRINZ HAMLET for the Harwich-Hamburg service. In 1981 *Prinzenlinien* was acquired by *DFDS*. In 1987 she was renamed the PRINS HAMLET, re-registered in Denmark and transferred to the seasonal Newcastle – Esbjerg and Newcastle – Göteborg summer services. During winter 1987/88 she operated for *B&I Line* of Ireland between Rosslare and Pembroke Dock. At the end of the 1988 summer season she was acquired by a *Stena Line* subsidiary, chartered to *Polferries* and renamed the NIEBOROW. Used on the Świnoujście – Malmö service.

POMERANIA Built for *Polferries*. She used to operate on the Gdańsk – Helsinki service. This service is suspended and she now operates on other routes as required.

ROGALIN Built as the AALLOTAR for the *EFFOA* of Finland. Used on overnight *Silja Line* services (joint with *Svea Line* of Sweden and *Bore Line* of Finland) between Stockholm and Helsinki. Later used on the Stockholm – Mariehamn – Turku service. In 1978 she was sold to *Polferries*. She was renamed the ROGALIN and operated on various services between Poland, West Germany and Scandinavia. In 1983 she was chartered to *Farskip* of Iceland from the end of May until September, renamed the EDDA and inaugurated a service between Reykjavik (Iceland), Newcastle and Bremerhaven (Germany). In September of that year she returned to *Polferries* and resumed the name ROGALIN. This service was not repeated in 1984 and she continued to operate for *Polferries* until chartered (with crew) by *Swansea Cork Ferries* in 1987. She was renamed the CELTIC PRIDE and inaugurated a new Swansea – Cork service. This service also operated during summer 1988 but during winter 1987/88 and after the 1988 summer season she was returned to *Polferries* and resumed the name ROGALIN, operating on Baltic services. She did not serve with *Swansea Cork Ferries* in 1989 or 1990 but in 1991 she was taken on charter (again with crew) and was again renamed the CELTIC PRIDE. This charter terminated at the end of 1992 and she returned to the Baltic and resumed the name ROGALIN. Now used mainly on the Gdank – Oxclösund service.

SILESIA Built for *Polferries*. Operated between Świnoujście and Ystad; now operates to Malmö.

WILANOW Built as KRONPRINS CARL GUSTAF for *Lion Ferry AB* of Sweden and chartered to *Statens Järnvägar (Swedish State Railways)* for the Malmö – Travemünde service. In 1975 sold to *Polferries* and renamed WILANOV. Used mainly on the Świnoujście -København service.

# SCANDI LINE

**THE COMPANY** *Scandi Line* is a Norwegian private sector company.

**MANAGEMENT Managing Director:** Trygve Sigerset, **Marketing Manager:** Ingebjørg Tollnes.

**ADDRESS** Tollbugata 5, Postboks 404, 3201 Sandefjord, Norway.

**TELEPHONE Administration:** +47 33 46 13 00, **Reservations:** +47 33 46 08 00 **Fax:** +47 33 46 03 56.

**ROUTE OPERATED** Sandefjord (Norway) – Strömstad (Sweden) (2 hrs 30 mins; *(1,2)*; 6 per day).

**CONVENTIONAL FERRIES**

| 1 | BOHUS | 8772t | 71 | 19.5 | 1480P | 280C | 40T | BA | Aalborg, DK | SW |
| 2 | SANDEFJORD | 5678t | 65 | 17.8k | 1100P | 165C | 30T | BA | Lübeck, GE | NO |

BOHUS Built as the PRINSESSEN DESIREE for *Rederi AB Göteborg-Frederikshavn Linjen* of Sweden (trading as *Sessan Linjen*) for their service between Göteborg and Frederikshavn. In 1981 the company was taken over by *Stena Line* and she became surplus to requirements. During 1981 she had a number of charters including *B&I Line* of Ireland and *Sealink UK*. In 1982 she was chartered to *Sally Line* to operate as second vessel on the Ramsgate-Dunkerque service between June and September. She bore the name VIKING 2 in large letters on her hull although she was never officially renamed and continued to bear the name PRINSESSAN DESIREE on her bow and stern. In September 1982 she returned to *Stena Line* and in 1983 she was transferred to subsidiary company *Varberg-Grenaa Line* for their service between Varberg (Sweden) and Grenaa (Denmark) and renamed the EUROPAFÄRJAN. In 1985 she was renamed the EUROPAFÄRJAN II. In 1986, following a reorganisation within the *Stena Line* group, ownership was transferred to subsidiary company *Lion Ferry AB* and she was named the LION PRINCESS. In 1993 she was sold to *Scandi Line* and renamed the BOHUS.

SANDEFJORD Built as the VIKING III for *Otto Thoresen* of Norway for the *Thoresen Car Ferries* Southampton (England) – Cherbourg and Southampton – Le Havre services. During the winter, until 1970/71, she was chartered to *Lion Ferry* of Sweden for their Harwich – Bremerhaven service. In

*SeaWind (Nick Widdows)*

*Silja Europa (Anders Ahlerup)*

1967 the service was acquired by *European Ferries* of Great Britain, trading as *Townsend Thoresen*. She was chartered to this organisation and retained Norwegian registry. During winter 1971/72 and 1972/73 she was chartered to *Larvik Line*. She became surplus to requirements following the delivery of the 'Super Vikings' in 1975 and was the subject of a number of short term charters until 1982 when she was sold to *Da-No Linjen* of Norway, renamed the TERJE VIGEN and used on their Frederikstad (Norway) – Frederikshavn (Denmark) service. In 1986 she was sold to *KG Line* to operate between Kaskinen (Finland) and Gävle (Sweden) and renamed the SCANDINAVIA. In 1990 she was sold *Johnson Line* and used on *Jakob Line* service, being renamed the FENNO STAR. During winter 1990/91 she was chartered to *TT Line*. In 1991 she served briefly on the *Corona Line* service between Karlskrona and Gdynia. She was sold to *Scandi Line*, renamed the SANDEFJORD and introduced onto the Sandefjord – Strömstad service in 1992.

# SCANDINAVIAN SEAWAYS

**THE COMPANY** *Scandinavian Seaways* is the trading name of the passenger division of *DFDS (Det Forenede Dampskibs Selskab – The United Steamship Company)*, a Danish private sector company.

**MANAGEMENT Managing Director:** Niels Bach.

**ADDRESS** Sankt Annæ Plads 30, DK-1295 København K, Denmark.

**TELEPHONE Administration:** +45 33 42 33 42, **Reservations:** +45 33 42 30 00, **Fax:** +45 33 42 33 41, **Telex:** 19435.

**ROUTES OPERATED** All year: København – Helsingborg (Sweden) – Oslo (Norway) (16 hrs; *(1,2)*; daily), Kristiansand (Norway) – Ijmuiden (Netherlands) (20 hrs 30 mins; *(3)*; alternate days). See Section 1 for services operating to Britain.

**CONVENTIONAL FERRIES**

| 1 | CROWN OF SCANDINAVIA | 35498t | 94 | 19.5k | 2136P | 450C | 80T | BA2 | Split, CR | DK |
|---|---|---|---|---|---|---|---|---|---|---|
| 2 | QUEEN OF SCANDINAVIA | 33575t | 81 | 21k | 1624P | 430C | 86T | BA | Turku, FI | DK |
| 3 | WINSTON CHURCHILL | 10513t | 67 | 20k | 840P | 180C | 22T | BA | Genova, IT | DK |

CROWN OF SCANDINAVIA Launched as the THOMAS MANN for *Euroway* for their Lübeck – Travemünde service. However, political problems led to serious delays and, before delivery, the service had ceased. She was purchased by *DFDS*, renamed the CROWN OF SCANDINAVIA and introduced onto the København – Oslo service.

QUEEN OF SCANDINAVIA Built as the FINLANDIA for *EFFOA* of Sweden for *Silja Line* services between Helsinki and Stockholm. In 1990 she was sold to *DFDS*, renamed the QUEEN OF SCANDINAVIA and introduced onto the København – Helsingborg – Oslo service.

WINSTON CHURCHILL Built for the Harwich – Esbjerg service. When DANA ANGLIA was introduced in 1978 she inaugurated a new twice weekly service from Newcastle to Göteborg, jointly with *Tor Line* until *Tor Line* was taken over by *DFDS* in 1981. In 1981 she took over the seasonal Newcastle – Esbjerg – Tórshavn service from the ENGLAND (8117t, 1964). In summer 1984 she operated a service between København and Tórshavn and did not visit Britain but in 1985 she resumed her previous role. Since 1987 she also operated cruises in the spring and autumn periods (Baltic and North Cape). During winter 1989/90 she was used as an accommodation ship for refugees in Malmö. In 1993 she inaugurated a new Newcastle – Hamburg service, alternating with her Newcastle – Esbjerg service. The Esbjerg – Tórshavn service ceased at the end of the 1992 summer season. In 1995 she inaugurated a new Newcastle – Ijmuiden (Netherlands) service. In 1996 she will operate between Ijmuiden and Kristiansand (Norway).

# SEAWIND LINE

**CONVENTIONAL FERRY**

**THE COMPANY** *SeaWind Line* is a Swedish private sector company owned by *Silja Oy Ab*.

**MANAGEMENT Managing Director:** Sören Lindman, **Marketing Manager:** Ole Engblom.

**ADDRESS** Linnankatu 84, FIN-20100 Turku, Finland.

**TELEPHONE Administration:** +358 (9)21-210 28 00, **Reservations:** +358 (9)21-210 28 00, **Fax:** +358 (9)21-210 28 10.

**ROUTE OPERATED** Stockholm (Sweden) – Turku (Finland) (10 hrs 45 mins; *(1)*; daily).

| 1 | SEA WIND | 15879t | 71 | 18k | 260P | 60C | 600r | BAS | Helsingør, DK | SW |
|---|----------|--------|----|-----|------|-----|------|-----|---------------|-----|

SEA WIND Built as the SVEALAND for *Stockholms Rederi AB Svea* and used on the *Trave Line* Helsingborg (Sweden) – København (Tuborg Havn) – Travemünde freight service. Later she operated between Travemünde and Malmö, first for *Saga Line* and then for *TT Saga Line*. In 1984 she was rebuilt to increase capacity and renamed the SAGA WIND. In 1989 she was acquired by *SeaWind Line*, renamed the SEA WIND and inaugurated a combined rail freight, trailer and lower priced passenger service between Stockholm and Turku.

# SILJA LINE

**THE COMPANY** *Silja Line* is a subsidiary of *Silja Oy Ab*, an international (Finnish/Swedish) company. In 1993 the services of *Jakob Line* and *Wasa Line* were integrated into *Silja Line*.

**MANAGEMENT Managing Director (Finland):** Lars Wendelin, **Managing Director (Sweden):** Gunnar Östin.

**Marketing Manager (Finland):** Ritva Tiivola, **Marketing Manager (Sweden):** Camilla Laaksonen.

**ADDRESS** Finland: POB 880, Mannerheimintie 2, FIN-00101 Helsinki, Finland, Sweden: Positionen 8, S-115 74 Stockholm, Sweden.

**TELEPHONE Administration:** Finland: +358 (9)0 18041, Sweden: +46 (0)8-666 33 30, **Reservations:** Finland +358 (9)0 1804 422, Sweden: +46 (0)8-222 140, **Fax:** Finland: +358 (9)0 1804 279, Sweden: +46 (0)8-667 86 81.

**ROUTES OPERATED** Stockholm (Sweden) – Helsinki (Finland) (14/16hrs; *(3,7)*; daily), Stockholm (Sweden) – Mariehamn (Åland) – Turku (Finland) (11 hrs; *(5,6)*; 2 per daily), Helsinki (Finland) – Travemünde (Germany) (23 hrs; *(2)*; 3 per week), Vaasa – Umeå (Sweden) (4 hrs; *(1,8)*; 1/2 per day), Helsinki – Tallinn (Estonia) (3hrs 30 mins (4hrs 30 mins in ice period); *(4,8)*; 2 per day), Summer Only: Pietarsaari (Finland) – Skellefteå (Sweden) (5 hrs; *(1)*; daily).

**CONVENTIONAL FERRIES**

| 1 | FENNIA | 10515t | 66 | 18k | 1200P | 265C | 36T | BA | Landskrona, SW | FI |
|---|--------|--------|----|-----|-------|------|-----|-----|----------------|-----|
| 2 | FINNJET | 34940t | 77 | 31k | 1790P | 374C | 50T | BA | Helsinki, FI | FI |
| 3 | SILJA EUROPA | 55000t | 93 | 21.5k | 3000P | 400C | 78T | BA | Papenburg, GE | SW |
| 4 | SILJA FESTIVAL | 33830t | 85 | 22k | 2000P | 400C | 88T | BA2 | Helsinki, FI | FI |
| 5 | SILJA SCANDINAVIA | 34384t | 92 | 21.5k | 2200P | 480C | 80T | BA2 | Split, CR | SW |
| 6 | SILJA SERENADE | 58376t | 90 | 21k | 2641P | 450C | 78T | BA | Turku, FI | FI |
| 7 | SILJA SYMPHONY | 58376t | 91 | 21k | 2641P | 450C | 78T | BA | Turku, FI | FI |
| 8 | WASA QUEEN | 16546t | 75 | 22k | 1200P | 240C | - | B | Nantes, FR | FI |

FENNIA Built for *Silja Line* of Finland to operate services between Sweden and Finland. In 1970 she was transferred to *Stockholms Rederi AB Svea*, following *Silja Line's* become a marketing organisation. In 1983 she was withdrawn and operated for a short period with *B&I Line* of Ireland between Rosslare and Pembroke Dock. In 1984 she was sold to *Jakob Line*. In 1985 she was sold to *Vaasanlaivat*. In 1992 she was returned to *Jakob Line*. During winter 1992/3 she operated for *Baltic Link* between Norrköping (Sweden) and Riga (Latvia), but returned to *Silja Line* in summer 1993 and is used on the Vaasa – Umeå and Pietarsaari – Skellefteå services.

FINNJET Built for *Finnlines* to operate between Helsinki and Travemünde, replacing several more conventional ferries with intermediate calls. Her exceptionally fast speed was achieved by the use of jet turbine engines. During winter 1981/82 she was equipped with diesel engines for use during periods when traffic did not justify so many crossings per week. Later the trading name was changed to *Finnjet Line*. In 1986 the company was acquired by *EFFOA* and the trading name changed to *Finnjet Silja Line*.

SILJA EUROPA Ordered by *Rederi AB Slite* of Sweden for *Viking Line* service between Stockholm and Helsinki and due to be called EUROPA. In 1993, shortly before delivery was due, the order was cancelled. A charter agreement with her builders was then signed by *Silja Line* and she was introduced onto the Stockholm – Helsinki route as SILJA EUROPA. In early 1995 she was transferred to the Stockholm – Turku service.

SILJA FESTIVAL Built as the WELLAMO for *EFFOA* for the *Silja Line* Stockholm – Mariehamn – Turku service. In 1990, following the sale of FINLANDIA to *DFDS*, she was transferred to the Stockholm – Helsinki service until the SILJA SERENADE was delivered later in the year. During winter 1991/92 she was extensively rebuilt and in 1991 renamed the SILJA FESTIVAL; ownership was transferred to *Silja Line*. In 1993 she was transferred to the Malmö – Travemünde service of *Euroway*, which was at this time managed by *Silja Line*. This service ceased in 1993 and she was transferred to the Vaasa – Sundsvall service. In 1994 and 1995 she has operated on this route during the peak summer period and on the Helsinki – Tallinn route during the rest of the year. Initially she operated 20 hour cruises but from August 1995 she has operated a conventional ferry service. The Vaasa – Sundsvall service has now ceased and she now operates between Helsinki and Tallinn all year.

SILJA SCANDINAVIA Built as the FRANS SUELL for *Euroway*, who established a service between Lübeck – Travemünde and Malmö. In 1994 this service ceased and she was chartered to *Silja Line* and transferred to the Stockholm – Turku service.

SILJA SERENADE, SILJA SYMPHONY Built for *Silja Line* for the Stockholm – Helsinki service. In 1993, SILJA SERENADE was transferred to the Stockholm – Turku service but in early 1995 she was transferred back to the Helsinki route.

WASA QUEEN Built as the BORE STAR for *Bore Line* of Finland for *Silja Line* services between Finland and Sweden (Helsinki-Stockholm, Turku-Stockholm). She also performed a number of cruises. In 1981 *Bore Line* left the *Silja Line* consortium and she was sold to the *Finland Steamship Company (EFFOA)* and renamed the SILJA STAR. In January 1986 she was sold to *British Ferries* to inaugurate, in May 1986, a new service between Venice and Istanbul connecting with the Orient Express rail service, also operated by a subsidiary of *Sea Containers*. She was renamed the ORIENT EXPRESS. During winter 1986/7 she was chartered to *Club Sea Inc* of the USA to operate Caribbean cruises and renamed the CLUB SEA but this charter was terminated prematurely and she was laid up for a time. In 1989 she was renamed the EUROSUN and chartered to *Europe Cruise Lines* for Mediterranean and Canary Island Cruises. In 1991 she was chartered to *Damens Service Far East*, renamed the ORIENT SUN and operated cruises from Singapore. In 1992 she 'returned home' as WASA QUEEN for *Effjohn* subsidiary *Wasa Line* and received Finnish registration. She is used on the Vaasa – Umeå service during the summer period when the FENNIA moves to the Pietarsaari – Skellefteå route. At other times, she operates mainly on the Helsinki – Tallinn service with the SILJA FESTIVAL.

# SMYRIL LINE

**THE COMPANY** *Smyril Line* is a Faroe Islands registered company.

**ADDRESS** Jonas Bronksgöta 37, 100 Tórshavn, Faroe Islands.

**TELEPHONE Administration:** +298-15900, **Reservations:** Faroe Islands: +298-15900, UK: +44 (0)1224 572615 (*P&O Scottish Ferries*), **Fax:** +298-15707, **Telex:** 81296.

**Routes operated:** Tórshavn (Faroes) – Esbjerg(Denmark)(34 hrs 30 mins; *(1)*; 1 per week), Tórshavn – Bergen (Norway) (20 hrs; *(1)*; 1 per week), Tórshavn – Seydisfjordur (Iceland)(15 hrs; *(1)*; 1 per week) (summer only).

**VESSEL**

| 1 | NORRÖNA | 12000t | 73 | 19k | 1050P | 300C | 44L | BA2 | Rendsburg, GE | FA |

NORRÖNA Built as the GUSTAV VASA for *Lion Ferry AB* of Sweden, a sister vessel of the NILS DACKE (see the QUIBERON, *Brittany Ferries*). In 1982 the Travemünde – Malmö service ceased and in 1983 she was sold to *Smyril Line* and renamed the NORRÖNA. She was rebuilt in Flensburg, Germany, to increase passenger capacity and in the summer took over services from the SMYRIL of *Strandfaraskip Landsins*. In 1993 Esbjerg replaced Hanstholm as the Danish port and calls to Lerwick (Shetland) ceased. Because the service only operates in the summer period, she has, since purchase, undertaken a number of charters and cruises during the winter months. During autumn 1994 she initially served on the short-lived service between Wismar (Germany) and Newcastle for *North Sea Baltic Ferries* under the name WISMAR II. During the early part of 1996 she was chartered to *Stena Line* to operate between Stranraer and Belfast.

# STENA LINE

**THE COMPANY** *Stena Line* is a Swedish private sector company.

**MANAGEMENT Managing Director:** Bo Levenius.

**ADDRESS** Första Linggatan 26, S-405 19 Göteborg, Sweden.

**TELEPHONE Administration:** +46 (0)31-85 80 00, **Reservations:** +46 (0)31 775 00 00, **Fax:** +46 (0)31-24 10 38, **Telex:** 21914 StenaL S.

**ROUTES OPERATED** *Conventional Ferries:* Göteborg (Sweden) – Frederikshavn (Denmark) (3 hrs 15 mins; *(1,2,4,5)*; 7 per day), Göteborg – Kiel (Germany) (14 hrs; *(2,4)*; daily), Frederikshavn – Oslo (Norway) (8 hrs 45 mins; *(3)*; daily). *Fast Ferries:* Göteborg – Frederikshavn (2 hrs; *(6)*; 4 per day (from June)).

**CONVENTIONAL FERRIES**

| 1 | STENA DANICA | 28727t | 83 | 20k | 2300P | 630C | 136T | BA2 | Dunkerque, FR | SW |
| 2 | STENA GERMANICA | 38772t | 87 | 21.5k | 2500P | 700C | 140T | BA2 | Gdynia, PO | SW |
| 3 | STENA SAGA | 33750t | 81 | 22k | 2000P | 450C | 55L | BA | Turku, FI | SW |
| 4 | STENA SCANDINAVICA | 38756t | 88 | 21.5k | 2500P | 700C | 140T | BA2 | Gdynia, PO | SW |

STENA DANICA Built for *Stena Line* for the Göteborg – Frederikshavn service. Sister vessel STENA JUTLANDICA is to be transferred to the Dover – Calais service in July 1996 and renamed the STENA EMPEREUR. She is listed in section 1.

STENA GERMANICA, STENA SCANDINAVICA Built for *Stena Line* for the Göteborg – Kiel service. There were originally intended to be four vessels. Only two were delivered to *Stena Line*. The third was sold by the builders as an unfinished hull to *Fred. Olsen Lines* of Norway and then resold to ANEK of Greece who had her completed at Perama and delivered as EL VENIZELOS for service between Greece and Italy. The fourth hull was never completed. During the summer period, the vessel arriving in Göteborg overnight from Kiel operates a round trip to Frederikshavn before departing for Kiel the following evening.

STENA SAGA Built as the SILVIA REGINA for Stockholms Rederi AB Svea of Sweden. She was registered with subsidiary company Svea Line of Turku, Finland and was used on Silja Line services between Stockholm and Helsinki. In 1981 she was sold to Johnson Line and in 1984 sold to a Finnish Bank and chartered back. In 1990 she was purchased by Stena Line of Sweden for delivery in 1991. In 1991 she was replaced by the 58800 ton vessel SILJA SYMPHONY and took up service on the Hoek van Holland – Harwich service for Dutch subsidiary Stena Line bv. She operated with a British crew. In 1994 she was transferred to the Oslo – Frederikshavn route and renamed the STENA SAGA.

### Under Construction – Conventional Ferry

| 5 | STENA JUTLANDICA | - | 96 | 22k | 1500P | 550C | 166T | BA | Krimpen, NL | SW |
|---|---|---|---|---|---|---|---|---|---|---|

STENA JUTLANDICA Under construction for Stena Line to operate between Göteborg and Frederikshavn, carrying both road and rail freight and passengers in June1996.

### Under Construction – Fast Ferries

| 6 | NEWBUILDING 2 | - | 96 | 40k | 900P | 210C | - | A | Kristiansand, NO | SW |
|---|---|---|---|---|---|---|---|---|---|---|
| 7 | NEWBUILDING 3 | - | 96 | 40k | 900P | 210C | - | A | Kristiansandl, NO | SW |

NEWBUILDING 2 and NEWBUILDING 3 HSS 900 craft under construction for Stena Line for Göteborg – Ferderikshavn service. NEWBUILDING 2 enters service in June; NEWBUILDING 3 will enter service later in the year.

### Awaiting Allocation

| 8 | LION KING | 19763t | 86 | 19.4k | 2000P | 330C | 48T | BA | Nakskov, DK | BD |
|---|---|---|---|---|---|---|---|---|---|---|

LION KING Built as the NIELS KLIM for DSB (Danish State Railways) for their service between Aarhus (Jutland) and Kalundborg (Sealand). In 1990 she was purchased by Stena Line of Sweden and renamed the STENA NAUTICA. In 1992 she was chartered to B&I Line, renamed the ISLE OF INNISFREE and introduced onto the Rosslare – Pembroke Dock service, replacing the MUNSTER (8093t, 1970). In 1993 she was transferred to the Dublin – Holyhead service. In early 1995 returned to Stena Line and transferred to Lion Ferry. She was renamed the LION KING. In 1996 replaced by LION KING II (ex STENA NAUTICA) and returned to Stena Line. She may be used elsewhere within Stena Line or she may be chartered out.

# SWEFERRY

**THE COMPANY** SweFerry AB is a Swedish state owned company.

**MANAGEMENT Managing Director:** Bo Severed.

**ADDRESS** Knutpunkten 43, S-252 78 Helsingborg, Sweden.

**TELEPHONE Administration:** +46 (0)42-18 62 00, **Reservations:** Helsingborg: +46 (0)42-18 61 00, Limhamn: +46 (0)40-36 20 20, Trelleborg: +46(0)410-621 00, **Fax (Admin):** +46 (0)42-18 60 49, **Fax (Reservations):** Helsingborg: +46 (0)42-18 74 10, Limhamn: +46 (0)40-16 13 87, Trelleborg: +46 (0)410-620 29, **Telex:** 725 02 ferry s.

**ROUTES OPERATED** Helsingborg (Sweden) – Helsingør (Denmark) (25 mins; (1,5,9); every 20 mins) (joint with DSB Rederi of Denmark under the Scandlines name, Limhamn (Sweden) – Dragør (Denmark) (55 mins; (3,4,6); approx hourly) (joint with Dampskibsselskabet Øresund A/S (DSØ) of Denmark under the Limhamn-Dragör name. DSØ no longer operates vehicle ferries – all are provided by SweFerry), Trelleborg (Sweden) – Rostock (Germany) (4 hrs; (2); 4 per day), Trelleborg (Sweden) – Sassnitz (Germany) (3 hrs 30 mins; (7); 5 per day) (Trelleborg services are joint with DFO of Germany under the HansaFerry name).

*Isabella (Anders Ahlerup)*

*Stena Jutlandica (Mike Louagie)*

## CONVENTIONAL FERRIES

| 1 | AURORA AF HELSINGBORG | 10918t | 92 | 14.9k | 1250P | 240C | 260r | BA | Tomrefjord, NO | SW |
|---|---|---|---|---|---|---|---|---|---|---|
| 2 | GÖTALAND | 18060t | 73 | 18.5k | 400P | 118C | 811r | A2S | Nakskov, DK | SW |
| 3 | HAMLET | 3638t | 68 | 14k | 800P | 95C | 16T | BA | Bremen, GE | SW |
| 4 | OFELIA | 3639t | 72 | 14k | 800P | 95C | 16T | BA | Rendsburg, GE | SW |
| 5 | REGULA | 3774t | 71 | 14.5k | 800P | 105C | 16T | BA | Papenburg, GE | SW |
| 6 | SCANIA | 3474t | 72 | 14k | 800P | 70C | 16T | BA | Aalborg, DK | SW |
| 7 | TRELLEBORG | 20028t | 82 | 21k | 900P | 108C | 755r | A2 | Landskrona, SW | SW |
| 8 | URSULA | 3774t | 73 | 16k | 900P | 105C | 18T | BA | Papenburg, GE | SW |

AURORA AF HELSINGBORG Train ferry built for *SweFerry* for *ScandLines* service between Helsingborg and Helsingør.

GÖTALAND Train ferry built for *Statens Järnvägar (Swedish State Railways)* for freight services between Trelleborg and Sassnitz. In 1990 transferred to *SweFerry*. In 1992 modified to increase passenger capacity in order to run in passenger service. She is used on the Trelleborg – Rostock service.

HAMLET, OFELIA, SCANIA Built for *Svenska Rederi-AB Öresund* of Sweden and used on the Limhamn – Dragør service. In 1980 sold to *Scandinavian Ferry Lines*. In 1990 transferred to *SweFerry*.

REGULA, URSULA Built for *Stockholms Rederi AB Svea* of Sweden for the service between Helsingborg and Helsingør operated by *Linjebuss International AB* (a subsidiary company). In 1980 she was sold to *Scandinavian Ferry Lines*. During winter 1984/85 she was rebuilt to increase vehicle and passenger capacity. In 1991 ownership was transferred to *SweFerry*. Used on the Helsingborg – Helsingør service.

TRELLEBORG Built for *Svelast* of Sweden (an *SJ* subsidiary). In 1990 ownership transferred to *SweFerry*. She is a train ferry and is used on the Trelleborg – Sassnitz service.

**Under Construction**

| 9 | NEWBUILDING 1 | - | 97 | 21k | 600P | - | 100r | AS2 | Cadiz, SP | SW |
|---|---|---|---|---|---|---|---|---|---|---|
| 10 | NEWBUILDING 2 | | 96 | | 600P | 100C | - | BA | Hamilton,AL | SW |

NEWBUILDING 1 Under construction for the Trelleborg – Rostock service. NEWBUILDING 2 Fast Ferry under construction for *SweFerry* for the Limhamn-Drager service

# TALLINK

**THE COMPANY** *Tallink* is the trading name of *Hansatee Ltd*, an Estonian company owned by the *Estonian Shipping Company* (45%), *Inreko Laevad Ltd* (45%), *Union Bank of Estonia* (10%). Services are marketed by *Tallink Finland Oy*, a Finnish company owned by the *Estonian Shipping Company*.

**MANAGEMENT Director, Tallink Finland Oy** Keijo Mehtonen.

**ADDRESS** PO Box 195, 00181 Helsinki, Finland.

**TELEPHONE Administration:** +358 (9)0 228211 **Reservations:** +358 (9)0 22821211,
**Fax:** +358 (9)0 228 21242.

**ROUTE OPERATED** Helsinki – Tallinn (Estonia) (3 hrs 30 mins; *(1,2,3)*; 4 per day).

## CONVENTIONAL FERRIES

| 1 | GEORG OTS | 12549t | 80 | 20k | 1200P | 110C | 26T | BA | Gdan´sk, PO | ES |
|---|-----------|--------|----|-----|-------|------|-----|-----|-------------|-----|
| 2 | TALLINK | 10341t | 72 | 21k | 1090P | 146C | 22L | BA | Nantes, FR | ES |
| 3 | VANA TALLINN | 10002t | 74 | 18k | 1500P | 300C | 48L | BAS | Helsingsør, DK | ES |

GEORG OTS Built for *Estonian Shipping Company*. Chartered to *Tallink*.

TALLINK Built at SVEA REGINA for *Stockholms Rederi AB Svea* of Sweden for *Silja Line* service between Stockholm and Helsinki. In 1978 she was sold to *Karageorgis Line* of Greece and renamed the REGINA. After modifications to make her suitable for Mediterranean service, she was, in 1979, renamed the MEDITERRANEAN SUN and used on their service between Patras (Greece) and Ancona (Italy). In 1982 she was sold to *Lesvos Maritime* of Greece, renamed the ODYSSEAS ELYTIS and used on their Ancona (Italy) – Corfu (Greece) – Patras or Pireus (Greece) – Heraklion (Crete) – Alexandria (Egypt) service. In 1985 she was sold to *Sea Escape* of the Bahamas, renamed the SCANDINAVIAN SKY and used on their service between Port Canaveral (USA) and Freeport (Bahamas) and cruises. In 1989 she was sold to the *Estonian Shipping Company*, chartered to *Tallink*, renamed the TALLINK and inaugurated a new car/passenger ferry service between Helsinki and Tallinn.

VANA TALLINN Built as the DANA GLORIA for *DFDS* and used on the Esbjerg – Harwich service until 1983 when she was moved to the København – Oslo service. In 1990 she was sold to *Nordström and Thulin* of Sweden, renamed the NORD ESTONIA and used on the *EstLine* Stockholm – Tallinn service. In 1992 she was chartered to *Larvik Line* to operate as a second vessel between Larvik and Frederikshavn and renamed the THOR HEYERDAHL. This did not prove successful and in 1994 she was sold to *Inreko Ships Ltd*, chartered to *Tallink* and renamed the VANA TALLINN.

# TT LINE

**THE COMPANY** *TT Line* is a German private sector company.

**MANAGEMENT Managing Director:** Haus Heinrich Couzeu, **Marketing Manager:** Mr Büsold.

**ADDRESS** Mattenwiete 8, 20457 Hamburg, Germany.

**TELEPHONE Administration:** Hamburg: +49 (0)40 3601 3725, Rostock: +49 (0)381 6707911, **Reservations:** Hamburg: +49 (0)40 3601 442 – +49 (0)40 3601 446, Rostock: +49 (0)381 670790, **Fax:** Hamburg: +49 (0)40 3601 407, Rostock: +49 (0)381 6707980, **Telex:** Hamburg: 215185.

**ROUTES OPERATED** Travemünde (Germany) – Trelleborg (Sweden) (7 hrs 30 mins; *(2,3,4,5)*; 5 per day), Rostock (Germany) – Trelleborg (Sweden) (6 hrs; *(1,6)*; 3 daily) (marketed as *TR Line*).

## CONVENTIONAL FERRIES

| 1 | KAHLEBERG | 10271t | 83 | 15.5k | 50P | - | 50T | AS | Wismar, GE | GE |
|---|-----------|--------|----|-------|------|------|------|-----|---------------|-----|
| 2 | NILS DACKE | 26500t | 95 | 21k | 308P | - | 200T | BA | Rauma, FI | GE |
| 3 | NILS HOLGERSSON | 30740t | 89 | 20k | 1040P | 280C | 110T | AS | Bremerhaven, GE | BA |
| 4 | PETER PAN | 30740t | 88 | 18k | 1040P | 280C | 110T | AS | Bremerhaven, GE | BA |
| 5 | ROBIN HOOD | 26500t | 95 | 21k | 308P | - | 200T | BA | Rauma, FI | GE |
| 6 | SAGA STAR | 17672t | 81 | 19k | 180P | - | 116T | BA | Göteborg, SW | BA |

KAHLEBERG Built for *DSR Line* of the former East Germany. In 1991 chartered to *TT Line* for *TR Line* service between Rostock and Trelleborg. Primarily a freight vessel.

NILS DACKE, ROBIN HOOD Built for *TT Line*. Primarily a freight vessel but accompanied cars – especially camper vans and cars towing caravans – are conveyed.

NILS HOLGERSSON Built as the ROBIN HOOD, a 'combi' vessel. During winter 1992/93 rebuilt to transform her into a passenger/car ferry and renamed the NILS HOLGERSSON, replacing a similarly named vessel (31,395t, 1987) which had been sold to *Brittany Ferries* and renamed the VAL DE LOIRE.

PETER PAN Built as the NILS DACKE, a 'combi' vessel. During summer 1993 rebuilt to transform her into a passenger/car ferry and renamed the PETER PAN, replacing a similarly named vessel (31,356t, 1986) which had been sold to *Tasmanian Transport Commission (TT Line)* of Australia and renamed ABEL TASMAN.

SAGA STAR Built as the SAGA STAR for *TT Saga Line* and used on freight services between Travemünde and Trelleborg/Malmö. In 1989 sold to *Cie Meridonalc* of France, renamed the GIROLATA and used on *SNCM* (later *CMR* services in the Mediterranean. In 1993 she was chartered back to *TT Line*, resumed her original name and has been used on both Travemunde and Rostock services. Following delivery of the ROBIN HOOD and the NILS DACKE she now operates mainly between Rostock and Trelleborg.

### Under Construction

| 7 | DELPHIN | | - | 96 | 38k | 600P | 175C | - | BA | Hamilton, AL | | SW |
|---|---------|---|---|----|-----|------|------|---|----|--------------|---|----|

DELPHIN Fast ferry under construction for *TT Line*. She will operate between Rostock and Trelleborg.

# UNITY LINE

**THE COMPANY** *Unity Line* is a Polish Company, jointly owned by *Polish Steamship Company* and *Euroafrica Shipping*.

**MANAGEMENT Managing Director:** Pawel Porzycki, **Marketing Manager:** Mariusz Odkata

**ADDRESS** Plac Rodtas 8, 70-419 Szczecin, Poland.

**TELEPHONE Administration:** +48 (0)91 595 795, **Reservations:** +48 (0)91 595 673, **Fax:** +48 (0)91 595 885.

**ROUTE OPERATED** Świnoujście (Poland) – Ystad (Sweden) (7 hrs; *(1)*; 1 per day).

**VESSEL**

| 1 | POLONIA | 29875t | 95 | 17k | 250P | - | 180T | BA | Tomrefjord, NO | BA |
|---|---------|--------|----|-----|------|---|------|----|----------------|----|

POLONIA Built for *Unity Line*. She also conveys rail wagons and has 1060 metres of track.

# VIKING LINE

**THE COMPANY** *Viking Line Ab* is a Åland (Finland) company (previously *SF Line*, trading as *Viking Line*). Services are marketed by subsidiary company *Viking Line Marketing Ab Oy* of Finland and Sweden; this dates from the time that *Viking Line* was a consortium of three operators.

**MANAGEMENT Managing Director (Viking Line AB):** Nils-Erik Eklund, **Managing Director (Viking Line Marketing Ab Oy):** Boris Ekman.

**ADDRESS Viking Line AB:** Norragatan 4, FIN-22100 Mariehamn, Åland, **Viking Line Marketing Ab Oy:** PO Box 35, FIN-22101 Mariehamn, Åland.

**TELEPHONE Administration:** +358 (9)28 26011, **Reservations:** +358 (9)0 12351, **Fax:** +358 (9)0 1235292.

**ROUTES OPERATED** *Conventional Ferries:* Stockholm (Sweden) – Helsinki (Finland) (14 hrs; *(4,5)*; daily), Stockholm (Sweden) – Mariehamn (Åland) – Turku (Finland) (9 hrs 10 mins; *(2, 3 (summer peak), 6(off-peak)*; 2 per day), Kapellskär (Sweden) – Naantali (Finland) (5 hrs; *(6)*; daily)(summer peak only) ,

Kapellskär (Sweden) – Mariehamn (Åland) (2 hrs 15 mins; *(1)*; 3 per day)(summer only). *Fast Ferries:* Helsinki – Tallinn (Estonia) (1 hr 45 mins; 3 per day) (April-December).

## CONVENTIONAL FERRIES

| | | | | | | | | | |
|---|---|---|---|---|---|---|---|---|---|
| 1 | ÅLANDSFÄRJAN | 6172t | 72 | 17k | 1004P | 200C | 18T | BA | Helsingør, DK | SW |
| 2 | AMORELLA | 34384t | 88 | 21.5k | 2420P | 550C | 53T | BA2 | Split, CR | FI |
| 3 | CINDERELLA | 46398t | 89 | 21.5k | 2700P | 480C | 60T | BA | Turku, FI | FI |
| 4 | ISABELLA | 34937t | 89 | 21.5k | 2200P | 410C | 30T | BA2 | Split, CR | FI |
| 5 | MARIELLA | 37799t | 85 | 22k | 2700P | 480C | 60T | BA | Turku, FI | FI |
| 6 | ROSELLA | 16850t | 80 | 21.3k | 1700P | 350C | 43T | BA2 | Turku, FI | FI |

ÅLANDSFÄRJAN Built as the KATTEGAT for *Jydsk Faergefart* on Denmark for the Grenaa – Hundested service. She was used on this route until 1978 when the service became a single ship operation. She was then sold to *P&O Ferries*, renamed the N F TIGER and introduced as the second vessel on the Dover – Boulogne service. Sold to *European Ferries* in 1985 and withdrawn in June 1986. In 1986 sold to *Finlandshammern AB, Sweden*, renamed the ÅLANDSFÄRJAN and used on *Viking Line* summer service between Kapellskär and Mariehamn.

AMORELLA Built for *SF Line* for the Stockholm – Mariehamn – Turku service.

CINDERELLA Built for *SF Line*. Until 1993 provided additional capacity between Stockholm and Helsinki and undertook weekend cruises from Helsinki. In 1993 replaced the OLYMPIA (37583t, 1985) (sister vessel of the MARIELLA) as main Stockholm – Helsinki vessel after she had been chartered to *P&O European Ferries* and renamed the PRIDE OF BILBAO. In 1995 switched to operating 20 hour cruises from Helsinki in the off peak and the Stockholm – Mariehamn – Turku service during the peak summer period (end of May to end of August).

ISABELLA Built for *SF Line*. Used on the Stockholm – Naantali service until 1992 until she was switched to operating 24 cruises from Helsinki. In 1995 transferred to the Stockholm – Helsinki route.

MARIELLA Built for *SF Line*. Used on the Stockholm – Helsinki service.

ROSELLA Built for *SF Line*. During the summer peak period, operates on the Kapellskär – Mariehamn – Naantali service. At other times operates on the Stockholm – Mariehamn – Turku route.

**FAST FERRIES**:- A fast vehicle ferry is to be chartered for the Helsinki – Tallinn service. At the time of going to press it is uncertain which vessel this will be. A passenger only vessel will also operate.

# VOGNMANDSRUTEN

**THE COMPANY** *Vognmandsruten* is a Danish private sector company now owned by *DIFKO (Dansk Investeringsfond)*.

**MANAGEMENT Managing Director:** F Wesenberg-Luno.

**ADDRESS** Yderhavnsvej 2, DK-4220 Korsør, Denmark.

**TELEPHONE Administration:** +45 53 57 12 33, **Reservations:** +45 53 57 02 04, **Fax:** +45 53 57 07 05.

**ROUTE OPERATED** Nyborg (Fyn) – Korsør (Sealand) (1 hr 15 mins; *(1,2,3,4)*; hourly).

## CONVENTIONAL FERRIES

| | | | | | | | | | |
|---|---|---|---|---|---|---|---|---|---|
| 1 | DIFKO FYN | 4104t | 87 | 12.7k | 253P | 170C | 48T | BA | Sunderland, GB | DK |
| 2 | DIFKO KORSØR | 4104t | 87 | 12.7k | 253P | 170C | 48T | BA | Sunderland, GB | DK |
| 3 | DIFKO NYBORG | 4104t | 87 | 12.7k | 253P | 170C | 48T | BA | Sunderland, GB | DK |
| 4 | DIFKO STOREBAELT | 4296t | 87 | 12.7k | 300P | 170C | 24T | BA | Sunderland, GB | DK |

DIFKO FYN Built as the SUPERFLEX ECHO for *Vognmandsruten*. She was unused until 1995, when she was renamed the DIFKO FYN and placed on the Nyborg – Korsør service.

DIFKO KORSØR, DIFKO NYBORG, DIFKO STOREBAELT Built as the SUPERFLEX CHARLIE, SUPERFLEX ALPHA and SUPERFLEX DELTA respectively for *Vognmandsruten* to establish a new service between Korsør (Fyn) and Nyborg (Sealand), competing with *DSB*. In 1990 this company was taken over by *DIFKO* and the vessels renamed the DIFKO KORSØR, DIFKO NYBORG, DIFKO STOREBAELT.

# DISPOSALS

The following vessels, listed in 'Ferries of the British Isles 1995' have been disposed of – either to other companies listed in this book or others. Company names are as used in that publication.

ATLANTIC FREIGHTER *(Pandoro)* Charter terminated in 1995.

BELARD *(Mannin Line)* Service ceased in 1995. Chartered to *Pandoro* but charter terminated. Laid up.

CONDOR 11 *(Condor Ferries)* Transferred to associated company *Cat-Link* of Denmark in 1995 and renamed the CAT-LINK 2.

DANA CORONA *(DFDS)* In 1995 transferred to *Dan-Liet Line* (71% owned by *DFDS*)to operate between Fredericia (Denmark) and Klaipeda (Lithuania).

DANA HAFNIA *(Tor Line)* Transferred to *DFDS* in 1995.

Q SHIP EXPRESS *(Sea Containers)* Returned to *Sea Containers* in 1995 and resumed the name SEACAT SCOTLAND.

MORVERN *(Caledonian MacBrayne)* Sold to *Arranmore Island Ferries* of the Irish Republic in 1995. Not renamed.

NORMAN COMMODORE *(Commodore Ferries)* Sold to *Lilgård* of Finland in 1995 to operate between Åland and Finland.

NORSKY *(North Sea Ferries)* Charter terminated in 1995 and returned to *Pandoro* and later renamed the IBEX (her original name).

PURBECK *(Commodore Ferries)* Sub-chartered to *Sally Ferries* for their Dartford – Vlissingen service. In 1996 charter terminated and new sub charter sought.

SALLY EUROBRIDGE *(Sally Ferries)* Chartered to *Norfolk Line* in 1995 and renamed the EUROBRIDGE.

SALLY EUROWAY *(Sally Ferries)* Charter terminated following the take over of the Dartford – Vlissingen service by *Dart Line* in 1996.

SEACAT ISLE OF MAN *(Isle of Man Steam Packet)* Not to be chartered in 1996. Instead charted to *ColorSeaCat a/s* and renamed the SEACAT NORGE.

SPIRIT OF BOULOGNE *(Meridian Ferries)* Service ceased in 1995. After being laid up for a period, chartered to *Stena Sealink Line*. Renamed MARINRE EVANGELINE

SPIRIT OF INDEPENDENCE *(Meridian Ferries)* Service ceased in 1995. Returned to *Corsica Ferries*.

STENA LONDONER *(Stena Sealink Line)* Charter terminated in March 1996; returned to *SeaFrance*.

SUILVEN *(Caledonian MacBrayne)* Sold to *Straits Shipping* of New Zealand in 1995 to operate freight services between Wellington (North Island) and Picton (South Island). Not renamed.

TIDERO STAR *(Fred. Olsen Lines)* Charter terminated in early 1996. Chartered to *Pandoro*.

# RENAMINGS

The following vessels have been renamed without change of operator:

AHLERS BALTIC *(Finanglia Ferries)* In 1995 renamed the TRANSBALTICA.

COTE D'AZUR *(Sealink SNAT)* In 1996 renamed the SEAFRANCE RENOIR.

CUPRIA *(North Sea Ferries)* In 1995 renamed the NORCOVE.

EUROPEAN CLEARWAY *(Pandoro)* In 1996 renamed the PANTHER.

FIESTA *(Sealink SNAT)* In 1996 renamed the SEAFRANCE CEZANNE.

MERCHANT VALIANT *(Pandoro)* In 1995 purchased and renamed the LION

NORD PAS-DE-CALAIS *(Sealink SNAT)* In 1996 renamed the SEAFRANCE NORD PAS-DE-CALAIS.

STENA HIBERNIA *(Stena Sealink Line)* In 1996 renamed the STENA ADVENTURER

STENA SEA LYNX I *(Stena Sealink Line)* In 1996 renamed the STENA LYNX I.

STENA SEA LYNX II *(Stena Sealink Line)* In 1996 renamed the STENA LYNX II.

# STOP PRESS

P&O European Ferries announced in March that they would operate a fast ferry service between Cairnryan and Larne as from June. The *Djursland* which was due to operate for the Grenaa-Hundested Line will operate the service for P&O European Ferries. The *Pride of Ailsa* will be withdrawn from service on the commencement of the new fast ferry service.

On 29th March 1996, Sea Containers took control of the Isle of Man Steam Packet Company. At the time of going to press, it was understood that the *King Orry, Peveril* and *Lady of Mann* will be withdrawn from service and replaced by a fast ferry and freight/passenger ferry.

# FERRY PUBLICATIONS

Ferry Publications was formed in 1987 by Miles Cowsill and John Hendy who had joined together to write and publish their highly successful 'Townsend Thoresen Years'. Since then they have produced a continuous stream of titles which have covered most areas of the North Sea, English Channel and Irish Sea.

Disenchantment with writing for other magazines led the partners to launch their own quarterly journal *British Ferry Scene* in the Summer of 1989. Now a firmly established as Europe's leading magazine, and renamed in 1996 as *European Ferry Scene,* it has gained praise from both the enthusiast fraternity and the ferry industry alike.

For further information on the tiltles produced by the company and *European Ferry Scene* contact:

**Ferry Publications, 12 Millfields Close, Kilgetty, Pembrokeshire, SA68 0SA, UK.**
**Tel: +44 (0) 1834 813991 Fax: 44 (0) 1834 814484**

# INDEX

*Georg Ots* (Anders Ahlerup)